MONITORING
GOVERNMENT

P A U L C. L I G H T

MONITORING GOVERNMENT

Inspectors General and the Search for Accountability

The Brookings Institution | Washington, D.C.

The Governance Institute | Washington, D.C.

Copyright © 1993

THE BROOKINGS INSTITUTION

1775 Massachusetts Avenue, N.W., Washington, D.C. 20036

Library of Congress Cataloging-in-Publication data:

Light, Paul Charles.
    Monitoring government: inspectors general and the search for
accountability/Paul C. Light.
        p.   cm.
    Includes bibliographical references and index.
    ISBN 0-8157-5256-3—ISBN 0-8157-5255-5
    1. Finance, Public—United States—Auditing.   2. Administrative
agencies—United States—Auditing.   3. Governmental
investigations—
–United States.   I. Title.
HJ9801.L54   1992
353.0072'32—dc20   92-32451
                                                                            CIP

9 8 7 6 5 4 3 2 1

The paper used in this publication meets the minimum
requirements of the American National Standard for
Information Sciences—Permanence of Paper for Printed
Library Materials, ANSI Z39.48-1984

The Brookings Institution

The Brookings Institution is an independent, nonprofit organization devoted to nonpartisan research, education, and publication in economics, government, foreign policy, and the social sciences generally. Its principal purposes are to aid in the development of sound public policies and to promote public understanding of issues of national importance. The Institution was founded on December 8, 1927, to merge the activities of the Institute for Government Research, founded in 1916, the Institute of Economics, founded in 1922, and the Robert Brookings Graduate School of Economics, founded in 1924.

The Institution maintains a position of neutrality on issues of public policy to safeguard the intellectual freedom of the staff. Interpretations or conclusions in Brookings publications should be understood to be solely those of the authors.

The Governance Institute

The Governance Institute, a nonprofit organization incorporated in 1986, is concerned with exploring, explaining, and easing problems associated with both the separation and division of powers in the American federal system. It is interested in how the levels and branches of government can best work with one another. It is attentive to problems within an organization or between institutions that frustrate the functioning of government. The Governance Institute is concerned as well with those professions and mediating groups that significantly affect the delivery and quality of public services.

The Institute's focus is on institutional process, a nexus linking law, institutions, and policy. The Institute believes that problem solving should integrate research and discussion. This is why the Institute endeavors to work with those decisionmakers who play a role in making changes in process and policy. The Institute currently has three program areas: problems of the judiciary; problems of the administrative state; and challenges to the legal profession.

Foreword

FEW elected officials come to Washington without first promising the voters that they will clean up government, make it work better, and return it to the people. However, once in office, they soon discover that reforming government management is not an easy task. The federal government is a far-flung enterprise, composed of hundreds of departments and agencies. It is difficult to understand and even more difficult to manage.

Nevertheless, since the early 1970s, rising budget deficits and highly visible scandals—from Watergate to the savings and loan debacle—have made the war on fraud, waste, and abuse a national priority. Enlisted in the fight were the new Offices of Inspector General (OIGs), situated throughout the federal government and created as part of the Inspectors General Act of 1978. The OIGs worked to improve government management through increasingly detailed rules and procedures—compliance monitoring—instead of performance incentives or basic investments in the way government pursues its mission.

During the 1980s, the OIGs became one of the fastest growing elements of the federal government. Even as personnel freezes limited growth in many agencies, OIGs expanded, gaining new staff and additional dollars. In this book Paul C. Light traces the evolution of the OIGs and their growing focus on investigations. Light also reviews the organization and institutionalization of the OIGs, examines what the government-wide investment in the OIG concept reveals about the prevailing philosophy of governance, and addresses how the OIG concept can be made more pertinent to the improvement of government management.

This book is a joint publication of the Brookings Institution and the Governance Institute. Paul Light is professor of public affairs at the Hubert H. Humphrey Institute of Public Affairs at the University of Minnesota and a senior fellow of the Governance Institute. He gratefully acknowledges the support of the Institute and its president, Robert Katzmann. In addition, the author would like to thank his colleagues who provided input at various stages of this project, including Babak Armajani, John Brandl, Mort Cohen, Terry Cooper, George Frederickson, James Jernberg, Fred Kaiser, Judy Leahy, Jeffrey Lubbers, Thomas E. Mann, Mark H. Moore, Carole Neves, and G. Edward Schuh, as well as the many inspectors general and other government officials who gave generously of their time, especially Charles Dempsey, Sherman Funk, Richard Kusserow, Tom Morris, and James Naughton. He also acknowledges Patricia Ingraham, Don Kettl, Lorraine Lewis, Gilbert Steiner, and an anonymous reviewer, who read the manuscript in detail and offered important suggestions for refinement. Leslie Bruvold, John Mingus, and Gayle Zoffer provided research assistance; Colleen McGuiness and Patricia Dewey edited the manuscript; Allison Rimsky verified its factual content; Helen Hall, Susan Thompson, and Elizabeth Toy provided administrative support; and Max Franke prepared the index. The author would like to make special mention of Steven Kelman's work, which proved particularly useful in shaping his understanding of the accountability question. Finally, the author thanks his wife, Sharon Pamepinto-Light, and his daughter, Kate, for their patience and support.

The Governance Institute is grateful to the Charles E. Culpeper Foundation for its critical support for this project. The Institute also acknowledges that it was a request for assistance from the Administrative Conference of the United States that led to the decision to sponsor research on the offices of inspector general. Although this book is separate from the Administrative Conference's own on-going examination, the Institute hopes that this volume will contribute to their work.

The views expressed in this book are those of the author and should not be ascribed to the persons and organizations acknowledged above, to the trustees, officers, or staff members of the Brookings Institution, or to the directors, officers, or other staff members of the Governance Institute.

BRUCE K. MACLAURY
President, the Brookings Institution

November 1992
Washington, D.C.

Contents

Introduction / 1

    Why Study IGs? / 2
    Methods of Inquiry / 4
    Plan of the Book / 5

PART I
Frameworks

1. The Newest Monitors / 11

    Paths to Accountability / 12
    Monitoring toward Accountability / 16
    Conclusion: An Era of Limits / 21

2. The Rise of the IG Concept / 23

    An Introduction to the IG Act / 23
    A Brief History / 25
    A Statutory Prototype / 28
    A Nonstatutory Alternative / 31
    Conclusion: A Barbed Wire Fence / 35

PART 2
Designing the Concept

3. Why Congress Acted / 39

    The Three Horsemen of the IG Concept / 39

The Politics of Fraud Busting / 43
The Information Imperative / 48
Conclusion: The Choice of Compliance / 57

4. Creating a Strong Right Arm / 58

What Might Have Been / 59
The IG Job Description / 61
Institutionalized Ambivalence / 68

PART 3
Implementing the Act

5. The Class of 1979 / 81

Carter's Choices / 82
An Abbreviated Term / 90
Conclusion: Too Much to Do, Too Little Time / 100

6. Glory Days / 102

Fear of Firing / 103
Getting Started . . . Again / 104
The Seeds of Alliance / 111
Conclusion: A Match Made in Heaven? / 118

7. Backlash / 121

The Class of 1985 / 121
Fine-Tuning / 128
Into the Bush Years / 131
Conclusion: Uncertain Futures / 145

PART 4

Organizing for Accountability

8. A Drift toward Investigation / 149

   Auditors and Investigators / 150
   The Investigatory Impulse / 160
   Conclusion: Protecting IGs / 169

9. The Organizational IGs / 175

   An Organizational History of the OIGs / 177
   The Organizational Future / 189
   The IGs as Institutional Memory / 200

PART 5

Questions of Effectiveness

10. Measuring the Impact of IGs / 203

    Measures of Effectiveness / 204
    Conclusion: Questions of Performance / 220

11. The Future of the IG Concept / 224

    The IG Act Innovations / 225
    A Reprise on Reform / 229
    A Safe Harbor for Analysis / 234

Appendix: Interview Contacts / 236

Notes / 241
Index /265

TABLES

1-1. Aspects of Accountability / 14

1-2. Aspects of Monitoring / 18

2-1. Expansion of the IG Concept, 1976–89 / 26

3-1. Trends in Committee and Subcommittee Activity, 1955–83 / 52

3-2. IG Congressional Appearances, 1977–88 / 54

4-1. HUD Semiannual Executive Summaries, 1981–85 / 72

5-1. The IG Demographic Profile, Carter versus Reagan / 83

5-2. Backgrounds and Opinions of IGs, Carter versus Reagan / 85

5-3. The IG Nomination Process, Carter versus Reagan / 88

5-4. Audiences and Operations of IGs, Carter versus Reagan / 93

5-5. The Nature of the IG Job, Carter versus Reagan / 96

5-6. Presidential Appointee Goals, 1964–84 / 98

6-1. IG, Civilian, and Political Appointee Growth, 1980–86 / 109

6-2. Career and Noncareer Appointee Growth, 1980–90 / 110

6-3. Status of Reform '88 Proposals, 1987–89 / 114

6-4. Location of Job Held before Becoming IG, First and Second Reagan Administration Appointees / 117

7-1. The IG Educational Profile, by Class / 122

7-2. Backgrounds and Opinions of IGs, by Class / 123

7-3. Audiences and Operations of IGs, by Class / 125

7-4. The Nature of the IG Job, by Class / 126

8-1. The IG Demographic Profile, by Career Focus / 151

8-2. Backgrounds and Opinions of IGs, by Career Focus / 152

8-3. Audiences and Operations of IGs, by Career Focus / 154

8-4. The Nature of the IG Job, by Career Focus / 156

8-5. Support for IG Reform, by Career Focus / 159

8-6. IG Staffing Decisions, by Career Focus / 160

8-7. Audit versus Investigation Staff, 1983 and 1990 / 162

8-8. Change in Total Staff Devoted to Investigation versus Audit, 1983–90 / 164

9-1. Measures of Organizational Expansion, 1980–89 / 176

9-2. Measures of Organizational Independence, 1983, 1989 / 180

9-3. Organizational Gains and Losses, 1983–89 / 182

9-4. OIG Evaluation and Inspection Units, 1989 / 198

10-1. Ratios of OIG Coverage, 1989 / 206

10-2. Relative OIG Savings, April 1–September 30, 1989 / 208

10-3. IG Policing Rates, 1989 / 211

10-4. Characteristics of Successful Investigations / 214

10-5. Rankings of OIG Activity, 1978–89 / 215

10-6. Determinants of OIG Visibility / 218

11-1. Support for IG Reform, by Class / 232

Introduction

NO story did more to put the federal inspectors general (IGs) on the map than the 1989 Department of Housing and Urban Development (HUD) scandal. The HUD IG, Paul Adams, was quoted in almost every newspaper story about the scandal, whether revealing new details about "Robin HUD," as one of the players was nicknamed; testifying before Congress about $300,000 consultants, such as former interior secretary James Watt, who had used their influence to win housing projects for high-priced clients; or reporting on the investigation of the apparent political slush fund that operated out of the HUD secretary's office. Suddenly, the IG was front-page news.

Despite this visibility, and the fact that the HUD story broke after an IG investigation, some in Washington believed that the IG had missed the story. Seeking answers to a scandal that went to the top of the department, Congress and the press also asked about the IG. *Time* magazine, in its story on "The Housing Hustle," said this: "How could such a scandal remain uncovered for so long? The answer lies partly in the fact that no one was looking."[1] By implication, that "no one" included the HUD IG, a point argued by Representative Christopher Shays (R-Conn.) in an exchange with Adams before the House investigating committee:

> Mr. SHAYS. My impression of the IG's office was you looked at wrongdoing, you found it out, and then you made sure something was done about it. . . .
>
> Mr. ADAMS. First of all, Mr. Shays, the investigation was ongoing, so we didn't have the final report nor did we have the final audit. We did report it to Congress in our September 30, 1988, report, semiannual report to Congress, that we had problems and it was an ongoing effort.
>
> Mr. SHAYS. You are missing my point here. I am talking in general. See, I have a lot of faith, historically have had a lot of

I

faith in the concept of an IG's office. My understanding is we have an IG's office so we wouldn't have the kind of problems we are uncovering, and I, frankly, think this is—you know, I am not going to be shocked any more, I am simply not going to be because nothing is going to shock me. . . .

My point, though, is it is your job to make sure this doesn't happen, isn't it? That is the whole reason why we have the IG's office. And once you uncover it, to make sure it doesn't happen again.[2]

Whatever one thinks of Shay's comment, it sets the stage for asking about the IG's role in ensuring accountability in government.

WHY STUDY IGs?

An IG existed at HUD because of the Inspector General Act of 1978. Passed against nearly uniform executive branch opposition, the bill created Offices of Inspector General (OIGs) in twelve departments and agencies, adding to the two statutory OIGs that already existed—one in the Department of Health, Education, and Welfare (HEW), which in 1980 was divided into the departments of Health and Human Services (HHS) and Education, and the other in the Department of Energy. By 1989 the IG concept had been expanded to include the rest of the federal government, including thirty-four small agencies.

The basic thrust of the IG Act was organizational: first, consolidate the government's scattered audit and investigation units into single department and agency-wide OIGs; second, put quasi-independent presidential appointees in charge of each OIG; third, give the IGs wide latitude in setting their operational agendas and structuring their offices; last, provide greater resources for the war on fraud, waste, and abuse. Not surprisingly, as the number of OIGs continued to increase, so did their staff and funding. Despite staff cuts across much of government during the 1980s, OIGs actually grew by almost a quarter.

Beyond the draw of occasional scandals such as HUD or a fascination with the impact of government reorganization, at least two other reasons exist for examining IGs. First, IGs are interesting in their own right. Created under the same basic statute, during the same period of time, IGs and their offices provide an opportunity to examine the consequences of eight specific "innovations" in the search for accountability:

1. The IGs are among the few presidential officers in government who report to both Congress and the president, an innovation that the Department of Justice vehemently opposed in 1978.

2. The IGs also are among the few presidential appointees to be selected "without regard to political affiliation and solely on the basis of integrity and demonstrated ability."

3. The IGs are fully removable by the president requiring only a notification to Congress.

4. The OIGs combine two different professions—auditing and investigating—into a single operating unit.

5. The OIGs are allowed wide latitude in the hiring and structuring of their offices, latitude guaranteed under their basic operating statute.

6. Although the IGs are far from the only officers in government required to submit semiannual reports to Congress, they are among the few who are governed by highly detailed formats.

7. The IGs have enormous authority to blow the whistle on their departments and agencies through issuance of a warning letter that the secretary or administrator can hold for seven days but cannot edit or kill.

8. The IGs are the strong right arms of their departments and agencies, yet also provide indirect access to information for any member, committee, or subcommittee of Congress.

Second, beyond the insights that might be gained from considering questions about the implementation and impact of the 1978 act, studying the law also provides a rare glimpse into the tensions among three basic approaches to accountability in government. The first approach, *compliance accountability*, rests on efforts to assure conformity with carefully drawn rules and regulations. Using negative sanctions targeted primarily at individuals inside or outside (for example, contractors and beneficiaries) of government, compliance accountability places its faith in correcting problems after they occur and in the deterrence value of visible punishment. The second approach, *performance accountability*, centers on the establishment of incentives and rewards for desired outcomes. Using positive sanctions, again targeted primarily at individuals, performance accountability puts its emphasis on moving individuals toward the preferred result from the beginning. The third approach, *capacity-based accountability*, involves the creation of organizational competence through technologies (that is, people, systems, and structures), and the maintenance of the conditions of success through initial investment. With the availability of adequate resources, capacity building focuses on building organizations that are staffed, trained, structured, and equipped to be effective.

Although all three approaches exist in government, compliance accountability was the preferred method throughout the 1980s, relying heavily on the IGs' role as monitors. As a metaphor for a broad philosophy of governance that rests more on fear than inducement, the government's investment in compliance monitoring offers important lessons about the general reluctance of Congress and the president to invest in performance and capacity. Compliance monitoring not only generates a much greater volume of findings of failure, and therefore higher visibility, and thus more opportunities for credit claiming by Congress and the administration, but also produces recommendations for actions that are less expensive, more politically palatable, cleaner jurisdictionally, and faster to implement. The unanswered question, however, is whether those recommendations lead to more effective government.

METHODS OF INQUIRY

Three research methods were used to compile data for this book: (1) a structured questionnaire mailed to the IGs that served under Jimmy Carter and Ronald Reagan, (2) ninety-one semistructured face-to-face and telephone interviews, and (3) analysis of primary documents. This triangular approach allowed each method to correct and confirm the findings of the other two.

The mail survey was designed to elicit information from the thirty-eight individuals who served as presidentially appointed IGs from 1979 to 1989.[3] Partially based on questionnaire items developed for the National Academy of Public Administration's survey of more than five hundred appointees from Kennedy through Reagan, this questionnaire was pretested on a small group of IGs before being launched to the full sample.[4] As with most data sets, not every variable proved useful.

Of the thirty-eight IGs targeted for the survey, thirty-four returned completed questionnaires, yielding a response rate of 90 percent. Because several of the IGs served in more than one post during the ten-year period, the sample actually represents forty appointees from a period that totaled forty-four. Therefore, the survey produced two different samples: one of the thirty-four individuals who served between 1979 and 1989; and one of the forty appointees who were nominated and confirmed by the Senate. Both samples are used.

The sample of thirty-four IGs provided an understanding of individual differences between auditors and investigators (chapters 8 and 9) and attitudes toward IG reform (chapter 11). The sample of forty appointees yielded data for analyzing why and how the Carter and Reagan administrations selected their IGs (chapters 5, 6, and 7). When Reagan fired all of the Carter IGs on inauguration day, no guarantee was made that any would be rehired. Thus comparing the Carter and Reagan appointments requires that some IGs be asked the same questions for each post they occupied.

The face-to-face and telephone interviews, some short, some detailed, were designed to broaden the IG survey, while providing alternative points of view. The list of participants was drawn from a range of positions and backgrounds—IGs, congressional staff, General Accounting Office (GAO) employees, White House advisers, presidential appointees, cabinet secretaries, and even a former U.S. vice president. Unless otherwise noted, all interviewees were promised that their responses would be treated on a not-for-attribution basis; that is, no quotes would be identified by name without prior clearance. When face-to-face interviews could not be scheduled, telephone interviews were substituted.[5]

Finally, the search for primary materials was designed to provide historical and analytic context. Among the more easily accessible primary materials were IG semiannual reports, federal phone books, organizational charts, congressional hearings, records, and reports. Among the more esoteric sources were private memos to key legislators, personal diaries of a former secretary of agriculture, meeting logs of a former White House domestic policy adviser, detailed interview notes collected by the House Government Operations Committee for a 1988 ten-year review, surveys by the Senate Governmental Affairs Committee, internal departmental and agency memoranda on the IGs (particularly relating to the 1989 Office of Legal Counsel opinion discussed in chapter 7), uncorrected hearing transcripts, internal IG audit and investigatory plans, and semipublic studies on or by the IGs. In addition, an office-by-office phone survey was conducted in early 1990 to ascertain staffing numbers and organizational structure. However, because departments and agencies sometimes vary in how they count staff, these numbers should be considered rough approximations of relative OIG size.

PLAN OF THE BOOK

The three research methods yielded a rich portrait of the pressures that faced the IGs as they established their offices and set operational priorities. Before reporting on the findings, however, part 1, Frameworks, offers two introductory chapters.

Chapter 1 begins by focusing on the three types of accountability: compliance, performance, and capacity building. After comparing the different approaches, the discussion turns to the nature of monitoring, which is the only tool IGs have in the search for accountability; the political incentives surrounding the findings and recommendations that IGs make; and the dominance of a bureaucratic paradigm in government that supports compliance monitoring as the front line of defense against fraud, waste, and abuse.

Chapter 2 follows with a brief history of the IG concept. Congress had two models to choose from as it began drafting the HEW IG bill in 1975, which laid the foundation for the 1978 act that followed: one leading to a highly independent lone wolf investigator, the other to a more accommodating strong right arm. By going with the second, Congress gave future IGs the option to pursue performance and capacity-based accountability—albeit under more influence from the president.

The rest of the book follows the IG Act in rough chronology. Part 2, Designing the Concept, recounts the legislative debate surrounding its enactment. Chapter 3 asks why Congress was so attracted to the IG concept, particularly when the departments and agencies about to be covered were so adamantly opposed. More was at work than a simple concern for fraud, waste, and abuse or a lurid fascination with headlines about scandal. The legislation also reflected a need for information among increasingly entrepreneurial members of Congress and their staffs; not just any kind of information, but small bits that could be spread among more members and hearings, the kind that more easily would emerge from compliance monitoring.

Chapter 4 examines the legislative choices made en route to final passage of the bill. Congress was never sure what it wanted from the IGs. On the one hand, the IGs were to be the strong right arms of their department or agency heads, thereby pushing the performance and capacity-building visions of accountability. On the other hand, they were to serve as a source of inside information, a "mole" as one executive branch opponent put it. Institutionalized ambivalence was the result, as illustrated by the HUD case and the problem of reporting to two bosses—the president and Congress.

Part 3, Implementing the Act, focuses on the first decade under the IG Act, while examining differences among the Carter and first- and second-term Reagan appointees. Chapter 5 begins by detailing the difficulties facing the new IGs as they struggled to establish their offices during Carter's troubled third and fourth years. Chapter 6 reports on the expansion of the IG concept under Reagan. Arriving in departments and agencies that had opposed their creation, the IGs quickly learned that they would have to fight for every staff position and every dollar. Thus, when the Reagan Office of Management and Budget (OMB) offered its hand in a new alliance, the IGs quickly accepted. Not only did the IGs earn staff and funding in return for ever-growing statistical accomplishments in the war on waste, they also won a substantial role in selecting their successors. The message was clear: A high volume of compliance findings meant institutional protection, even independence.

However, as discussed in chapter 7, these deals were easily broken when a new administration took office with much less interest in fraud busting. Once celebrated for their war on waste, the IGs were relegated to the back seat as the George Bush administration looked abroad for its policy agenda. The war on waste was no longer a top priority. Moreover, the sharp attack on the IGs held an important lesson on accountability. The IGs were safest when they stuck to the most traditional concept of compliance-based monitoring and most vulnerable when they branched into bigger questions of performance or capacity building.

Part 4, Organizing for Accountability, asks a set of questions about what IGs do and how their organizations work. Chapter 8, for example, chronicles the drift toward investigation in the staffing of the IG offices, while comparing differences between the auditors and investigators who have been appointed IGs in the 1980s. Chapter 9 then examines the overall growth in the Offices of Inspector General, including efforts to insulate those units from the day-to-day constraints others in their departments and agencies must endure. Both chapters conclude with suggested reforms for the IG concept: chapter 8 offers new ways of recruiting IGs and raises questions regarding IG bonuses, while chapter 9 poses the trade-off between expanded OIG law enforcement powers and a greater presence in evaluation.

Part 5, Questions of Effectiveness, asks the central questions of the book: Are the IGs effective? How might the IG concept be strengthened to include more support for performance and capacity-based accountability? As chapter 10 demonstrates, the issue is exceedingly difficult to address and requires answers to a series of specific queries: (1) How professional are the offices? (2) How deep is the coverage? (3) How great are the savings? (4) How good are the cases? (5) How visible are the results? Passing muster on these five indicators is not enough for an IG. Effectiveness also must involve some element of performance. Is the public more trusting? Is government less vulnerable to fraud, waste, and abuse? Is government producing greater value—that is, a higher quality of life, better schools, a cleaner environment, less crime, and so forth? The answers are mixed.

Chapter 11 envisions a somewhat broader role for the IGs than the founders may have intended. After taking stock of the IG innovations, the chapter asks three more questions about the impact of IGs: (1) What is the best way to improve government accountability? (2) What kinds of monitoring are most useful in improving accountability? (3) What is the best way to assure objectivity whatever the chosen IG role? The book concludes by arguing that the IGs would be most helpful in the search for accountability by strengthening their evaluation capacity, thereby acting as a source of long-term institutional memory in government.

Frameworks

The Newest Monitors

THE fall of 1978 was a busy season in the search for government accountability. During the final month of the legislative session, Congress passed the Civil Service Reform Act, the Ethics in Government Act, and a government-wide Inspector General Act, which together were arguably the most important package of administrative reforms in fifty years.[1]

The statutes, however, were not part of a unified reform strategy. The bills came from different committees, involved different advocates, and never crossed paths in the legislative process. Nor were they the only efforts to strengthen accountability. First came the congressional reforms of the 1960s and early 1970s—an expanded committee system, a stronger General Accounting Office, a new Office of Technology Assessment, a new Congressional Budget Office, the War Powers Resolution, and the Budget and Impoundment Control Act.[2] Then came the "sunshine" laws and other limits on bureaucratic discretion of the early to mid-1970s: the Federal Advisory Committee Act, the Freedom of Information Act Amendments, the Privacy Act, the Federal Election Campaign Act, the Government in the Sunshine Act, as well as assorted legislative vetoes, appropriations riders, personnel floors and ceilings, deadlines, and triggers.[3]

Then, late in this reform history came the two IG acts—the first at HEW, the second covering the whole of government. Each made up a small portion of what was a wide swath of reform measures, the most important of which was the dramatic increase in the number of reviewers of and in government—from congressional staff to the media, GAO investigators to interest groups. The IGs merely were the newest monitors of the era.

The 1978 IG Act was the only reform statute to combine all three contemporary strategies of accountability—rule-based compliance, performance incentives, and improvements in basic governmental capacity. While the Civil Service Reform Act, for example, operated primarily through performance incentives and capacity building, and the Ethics in Government Act through compliance, the IG Act invited questions of design, implementation, organization, and effectiveness. The IGs' eventual reliance almost exclusively on compliance in their search for accountability reveals a great deal about the politics of administrative reform.

PATHS TO ACCOUNTABILITY

Despite experiments with performance incentives, such as merit pay, and occasional investments in civil service reform, the definition of accountability in government has remained relatively constant over the past fifty years: limit bureaucratic discretion through compliance with tightly drawn rules and regulations. Public administration scholar Francis Rourke wrote in the late 1970s that,

> The reformers of the 1960s and the 1970s seem bent not on extending but on curtailing the independence of bureaucratic organizations. They argue that bureaucracies represent formidable concentrations of power in contemporary society, and that executive agencies should be brought back within the political system and made more accountable. If traditional efforts at reform could be described as an attempt to depoliticize the administrative process in the United States, the reform movement in our day seems rather aimed at repoliticizing administration—at least in the sense of restoring public control over previously independent agencies.[4]

This definition is well supported to this day in public administration scholarship. Even a cursory review of contemporary public administration textbooks suggests that the dominant definition is one of command-and-control. Accordingly, accountability is seen as the product of limits on bureaucratic discretion—limits that flow from clear rules (commands), and the formal procedures, monitoring, and enforcement that make them stick (controls). Public administration scholars Dennis Palumbo and Steven Maynard-Moody, for example, summarized the two methods of bureaucratic accountability as follows:

> One is *external*; this involves controls by legislatures through such mechanisms as legislative oversight, by the courts through review of decisions and administrative law, or by citizen participation. The second method is through *internal* controls; this

includes development of professional standards and ethics, the use of rules, whistle-blowers, representative bureaucracy, and opening up administrative proceedings.[5]

The problem with the control definition, however, is that it creates an artificial trade-off between accountability and values such as creativity and innovation. Addressing the potential cost of accountability, for example, Frederick Mosher wrote:

> I begin with the premise that accountability, anymore than any other single value, is not an absolute. If everyone were held accountable for everything he did or tried or thought or imagined, this would be a pretty sterile, dull, and static world. Accountability is not commonly associated with invention or novelty or serendipity, but rather with carrying out assignments, which are more or less specifically defined, honestly, efficiently, effectively, and at minimal cost. Thus, at the very outset, there is a conflict between the value associated with accountability and the values of originality, experimentation, inventiveness, and risk-taking.[6]

Defined in such command-and-control terms, accountability breeds just such conflicts. However, other definitions exist in the field. Public administration scholars James Fesler and Donald Kettl, for example, divided accountability into two dimensions: "One is accountability; faithful obedience to the law, to higher officials' directions, and to standards of efficiency and economy. The other is ethical behavior: adherence to moral standards and avoidance even of the *appearance* of unethical actions."[7] After conducting an inventory of the familiar methods for achieving faithful obedience and ethical behavior, they rejected the conventional compliance path to accountability: "In the end, we come back to the recruitment and retention of individuals dedicated to public service, respectful of its call for bureaucratic accountability and ethical behavior, and both knowledgeable about and committed to the constitutional, democratic system."[8]

This capacity-based view of accountability is particularly appropriate for understanding the enactment of the three 1978 reform statutes. With a Democrat in the White House, the Watergate scandal receding from memory, and the taking of American hostages in Iran still two years away, the accepted definition of accountability widened briefly. The Civil Service Reform Act, for example, contained a clear commitment—albeit never fully funded—to performance pay, merit bonuses, and greater stewardship of the government's human

Table 1-1. *Aspects of Accountability*

Characteristic	Definition of accountability		
	Compliance	*Performance*	*Capacity building*
Point of intervention	Post-activity	Mixed pre- and post-activity	Pre-activity
Primary targets	Individuals and accounts	Individuals and programs	Agencies and government
Primary mechanism	Rules	Incentives	Technologies
Role of sanctions	Negative	Positive	Positive
Role of management	Supervision and discipline	Goal setting and reinforcement	Advocacy and stewardship
Role of oversight	Detection and enforcement	Evaluation and bench marking	Analysis and design
Complexity of strategy	Simple	More complex	Most complex
Durability of effects	Short-term	Intermediate	Long-term

capital. The Ethics in Government Act created a financial disclosure process that, while heavily laden with compliance measures, still envisioned presidential appointees coming into office with a greater incentive to perform in the public's interest. And the 1978 IG Act involved a mix of all three definitions of accountability.

The choice of one strategy does not necessarily exclude the need for a second or third. Compliance accountability, for example, is not inconsistent with performance incentives or capacity building and may be essential for assuring the fairness and equity that sometimes undermine employee confidence in performance systems. Nevertheless, considering each definition as separate is useful. In part because of budget pressures, in part because of political incentives, Congress and the president may have created an artificial trade-off among the three, substituting compliance accountability for performance systems and capacity building. Moreover, the three involve different targets, mechanisms, and timetables (see table 1-1).

To compare the methods, start with the point of intervention. Under a compliance model, intervention awaits the activity. Although compliance also assumes some pre-activity deterrence effect, it primarily is a tool for catching mistakes after they have occurred. In contrast, both performance and capacity-based accountability rely on having an impact before something happens.

The definitions also aim at different primary targets, ranging from individuals and accounts at one end of a continuum, to individuals and programs toward the middle, and agencies and government as a whole at the other end. Accepting the imprecision of such a continuum, compliance can reasonably be placed at the individual and accounts end, performance in the middle, and capacity building at the agencies and government side. Investigations, for example, focus on individual violations, whether perpetrated by beneficiaries, contractors, or federal employees.

The primary mechanisms for achieving change are more precise. The common currency of compliance accountability is rules and regulations, whether dealing with procurement, travel, personnel, paperwork, or a specific policy. The rules are reinforced through cumbersome signature and approval systems. In contrast, performance accountability emerges from the establishment of incentives, the most familiar of which are the pay for performance provisions of the Civil Service Reform Act. Capacity building focuses on technologies, broadly defined to include people and the tools of management. In addition, capacity building includes both program and organizational redesign; that is, the development of workable programs and responsive structures.

Consider next the role of sanctions. Compliance accountability places its emphasis on negative sanctions, whether formal or informal. Medicare providers who violate the rules can be debarred, or removed from the program; contractors who cheat can be fined; employees who steal can be prosecuted. Performance accountability puts its focus instead on positive sanctions, notably bonuses and awards, although members of the Senior Executive Service (SES) created under the Civil Service Reform Act also can receive sabbaticals. The problem with positive sanctions, particularly during the 1980s, is inadequate funding. Without funding, pay for performance has a hollow ring. Capacity-based accountability does not involve formal sanctions per se but can be seen as a similarly positive approach to performance incentives. Increases in training budgets, purchase of state-of-the-art technology, and so forth can be powerful inducements for organizational effectiveness.

Managers and overseers play different roles in the three types of accountability. Capacity building views the role of management as one of advocacy and stewardship. Managers are responsible for both securing and maintaining the tools and resources to achieve effectiveness. By comparison, performance accountability requires goal setting and reinforcement, while compliance accountability requires tight supervision and needed discipline. The role of oversight is equally distinct. Compliance accountability demands detection of violations and enforcement of sanctions; performance, evaluation of effectiveness and bench marking, which organizational scholar Janet Weiss defines as "the results achieved by the very best organizations doing the same work"; and capacity building, analysis and design.[9]

The complexity of the strategy for achieving change also varies. Compliance and performance accountability are both relatively simple concepts to implement, while capacity building is much more complex. Holding individuals accountable to clearly stated rules and regulations is one thing, finding and training a new generation of public managers is another.

The durability of each approach flows from the other characteristics. When accountability resides in rules, not the individual or organization, it must be constantly reinforced. When it resides in incentives or organizations, it is more easily remembered. Individuals do the right thing not because they fear detection, but because the incentives and organization lead them, usually over a longer period of time. Compliance, however, is not less valid than capacity building; instead, each method has a different staying power.

The differences do not indicate an inherent trade-off among the three approaches. If Congress saw such a trade-off, as some scholars do, it is not apparent in the statute. The IGs were to play a role in all three, working to assure conformity with internal rules and regulations (compliance), economy and efficiency across a wide range of programs and activities (performance), and more general effectiveness in the management and operation of their departments and agencies (capacity).[10]

As much as Congress hoped the three goals could coexist—compliance reinforcing performance, capacity reinforcing compliance—many IGs were forced to choose. The IGs became instruments of retrospective, or backward-looking, compliance rather than catalysts for either performance incentives or capacity building.

MONITORING TOWARD
ACCOUNTABILITY

Whatever the type of accountability, whether tracking down cheaters or assessing the prospects for efficiency, the IGs have but one tool at hand: *monitoring*. They are to look, not act; recommend, not implement. The IGs were neither created as line, or operating, officers of their departments and agencies nor given any powers to suspend, or otherwise interfere with, program activities. Monitoring can be exercised through traditional financial compliance audits, highly individualized criminal investigations, program evaluation, or policy analysis, but it relies on others for action.

Instead, IGs were given complete access to information—information that Congress wanted, too. The IGs were free to audit, investigate, review, assess, analyze, evaluate, oversee, and appraise every problem, abuse, deficiency, and weakness relating to the programs and operations of their establishments, but they were specifically prohibited from accepting any program operating responsibilities. Ironically, even as Congress began its hearings on ways to reduce the paperwork load imposed on the private sector by government, it signaled its willingness to impose an ever-increasing level of regulatory and reporting requirements on executive agencies and their employees. So, too, did presidents Carter and Reagan, and their Offices of Management and Budget.

At the same time Congress and the president increased the regulation of the federal government's employees, the private sector began to embrace the management philosophy of W. Edwards Deming, which focused on designing quality into a product at the front end of the process, instead of inspecting it in at the back end. Although all of Deming's fourteen points toward quality may be relevant to federal management improvement, the third point is most relevant to the IGs: cease dependence on mass inspection. As biographer Mary Walton explained, "American firms typically inspect a product as it comes off the line or at major stages. Defective products are either thrown out or reworked; both are unnecessarily expensive. In effect, a company is paying workers to make defects and then to correct them. Quality comes not from inspection but from improvement of the process."[11]

Quality, however, does not eschew measurement. Implementation of Deming management is highly dependent on statistical process control and careful performance monitoring that allows managers, not inspectors, to track and tune the process. What makes monitoring different under Deming is its role in the management process. Unlike the American public sector, where monitoring is sometimes an end in itself and is almost always part of individual performance review, the Deming philosophy views monitoring as valid only for checking the progress of an overall management plan. Monitoring is never to be used for assessing employee blame. Evaluation by individual performance, merit rating, or annual review is one of Deming's seven deadly diseases blocking quality in manufacturing.[12]

Table 1-2. *Aspects of Monitoring*

	Monitoring toward		
Characteristic	*Compliance*	*Performance*	*Capacity building*
Findings			
Volume	High	Moderate	Low
Visibility	High	Low	Low
Ease of measurement	High	Moderate	Low
Credit-claiming yield	High	Low	Low
Recommendations			
Dollars and resources	Low	Moderate	High
Goal consensus	High	Moderate	Low
Jurisdictional neatness	High	Low	Low
Time to implement	Low	Moderate	High

Whatever the merits of Deming management, the federal government is not a private entity. No matter how much government managers want to manage, the public demands bureaucratic accountability. The question, then, is not whether to create systems of individual and agency-wide compliance, but how to link those systems to performance and capacity building. Compliance cannot be a substitute for basic investment in human capital and state-of-the-art work-place technologies, careful design of more workable policy, or organizational restructuring to better leverage administrative resources. If compliance monitoring does feed into capacity building, it is useless. Unfortunately, even before the IGs launched their first audit or investigation, the incentives favored compliance (see table 1-2).

To compare the three kinds of monitoring, start with the essential product of any monitoring system, findings—that is, the written conclusions that emerge from, for example, audits, investigations, inspections, and program evaluations.

First, compliance monitoring produces a high volume of findings, the kind that turn into long semiannual reports to Congress and the president, while capacity monitoring often yields far less. After all, how many times can an IG make the finding that an agency's financial system is antiquated or that government is underinvesting in training? Furthermore, investigation of individual targets can be expected to yield more findings than scrutiny of an agency or the whole government. The durability of effects also is at work; that is, short-term effects produce opportunities for similar findings in the near future.

Second, compliance monitoring generates greater visibility. Although the story may remain the same, the names change. Congress, the president, and the media appear to have much greater interest in the products of compliance monitoring than performance or capacity monitoring. Whatever the reason, less of a market appears to exist for findings on declining government capacity, perhaps because the findings have become so familiar or so costly to fix.

Third, success in compliance monitoring is much easier to measure. Knowing when an employee or contractor breaks a rule is simple, provided those in charge of monitoring have the resources to fully audit or investigate. Knowing how individual employees measure up to some objective standard of performance is much more difficult; knowing whether their departments and agencies are succeeding or failing is more difficult yet. This measurement problem resides in the natural ambiguity of the legislative process, the reluctance of managers and leaders to set clear goals for their agents, and, as economist Anthony Downs argued, the imprecision in measuring outputs relative to cost.[13]

Finally, OIG findings vary in their potential for credit claiming by members of Congress and the president. Those who want headlines in the war on fraud, waste, and abuse will find plenty in the narrow stories of graft and corruption that often flow from compliance monitoring. The media appear always willing to report another story on the subject.

Findings are not the only OIG product, however. Most findings are linked to recommendations, small and large, for resolution and improvement—broad proposals for change that emerge from audits, investigations, and evaluations. Once again, compliance monitoring yields more attractive results politically.

Most compliance-based recommendations not only are more likely to be cheaper to implement (creation of new rules and regulations) but also easier to generate (sometimes simply by adding more resources to existing monitoring units). In contrast, performance and capacity-based recommendations are much more likely to be expensive. Fixing the federal pay for performance system, for example, means money, and lots of it. Rebuilding the federal government's antiquated financial management systems, writing new software, recruiting new personnel, and retraining the current employees also would be expensive.

A high degree of political consensus surrounds the simple goal of most compliance recommendations: to punish the cheaters and abusers. Republicans and Democrats rarely disagree; liberals and conservatives have plenty of common ground. But when the issue is one of paying employees for successful performance or recruiting the best and brightest to government, those agreements quickly break down. Why pay for something government workers should produce automatically? Why hire the most capable when the less capable (and less expensive) will do?

Implementing performance and capacity-building recommendations run into messy jurisdictional problems both in OMB and on Capitol Hill. Dealing, for example, with pay for performance in the Federal Aviation Administration is exceedingly difficult without raising questions about the Veterans Administration (VA). Creating a special pay category for police officers in the Federal Park Service inevitably generates questions about security staff at the National Aeronautics and Space Administration (NASA). Performance and capacity recommendations raise tough problems about committee lines of responsibility and budgetary accounts.

Recommendations for improving the capacity of government also take a longer time to implement. A new compliance rule can be drafted in a month or two, a new audit started immediately. To the member of Congress who wants something to take home, the best the capacity builders can say is, "It takes time." In an era of tight budgets and political tension, time is what government lacks.

If compliance monitoring often is good politics, it also is part of a historically dominant paradigm of government management. According to the three basic characteristics of the "bureaucratic paradigm," as public management scholars Michael Barzelay and Babak Armajani argued, government can be seen as a system of authority:

—Specific delegations of authority define each role in government. Officials carrying out any given role should act only when expressly permitted to do so, either by rule or by instructions given by superior authorities in the chain of command.

—In exercising authority, officials should write formal rules and procedures and apply them in a uniform manner. The failure to obey rules should be met with an appropriate penalty.

—Experts in substantive matters—such as engineers, lawyers, enforcement personnel, and social service providers—should be assigned to line agencies, while experts in budgeting, accounting, purchasing, personnel, and work methods should be assigned to centralized staff functions.[14]

Accountability becomes the responsibility of those who make the rules. Drawing upon Max Weber's model of bureaucracy and

Frederick Taylor's vision of scientific management, the paradigm stipulates that workers have no role in accountability except to do exactly what they are told, with supervisors always watching.[15]

Barzelay and Armajani envision a second way of achieving results. The fundamental assumption of their post-bureaucratic paradigm reflects "the notion that government organizations should be customer-driven and service-oriented." According to this alternative view,

A recurring aspiration of public managers and overseers using these concepts is to solve operational problems by transforming their organizations into responsive, user-friendly, dynamic, and competitive providers of valuable services to customers. Thinking in terms of customers and service helps public managers and overseers articulate their concerns about the performance of the government operations for which they are accountable.[16]

Within this paradigm, accountability flows from the interaction between government and its customers. The IGs are steered toward a nontraditional definition of monitoring, one that emphasizes citizen satisfaction, process design, and negotiation. Unlike traditional audit and investigation, in which failure and success are easily measured by long-held standards and formal legal boundaries, the post-bureaucratic paradigm envisions monitoring as focused on "product" design and continuous improvement.

Whether Congress and the president are ready to embrace the post-bureaucratic paradigm is doubtful. Despite growing presidential interest in total quality management, the bureaucratic model still appears to hold and may redouble if voters continue to express anger with all things bureaucratic. Although some scholars have suggested other routes to accountability, the federal government continues to rely on scrutiny as the premier methodology of management, giving little thought to training, system modernization, and other elements of capacity building that might yield greater returns.[17]

Nevertheless, even within the still powerful bureaucratic paradigm, Congress and the president can rearrange priorities and thus alter the course of management improvement. Will compliance monitoring stand as an end in itself or part of a larger process of program redesign? Will IGs be rewarded for longer-term analysis of organizational improvement or short-term statistical accomplishment?

CONCLUSION: AN ERA OF LIMITS

Since the early 1970s, Congress and the president have favored the short-term approach, adding statutes and regulations and limiting bureaucratic discretion. Although the effort to attack the perceived causes of fraud, waste, and abuse in a time of great budget stress can be appreciated, perhaps the National Academy of Public Administration (NAPA) was right in its 1984 call for deregulating federal management. According to the NAPA panel,

> Checks and balances are essential in our form of government, and there have been enough examples of abuse of power to make this clear. The question, therefore, is not whether they are needed, but how much of such protection is required and how it can be brought to bear without impairing effectiveness. The Panel believes that the accumulation of such protections has, in total, become excessive and has often been represented as the answer to poor management in situations where the emphasis should more realistically have been placed on strengthening management.[18]

Many of these administrative checks envision, or demand, an explicit role for the IGs, including auditing the new financial statements required under the Chief Financial Officers Act, responding to citizen-initiated suits under the False Claims Amendments, and investigating complaints under the Program Fraud and Civil Remedies Act. The IGs may even have provided an unwitting excuse for Congress and the president to create more rules than they otherwise could have. Not only do the IGs monitor compliance in much of what government does by way of program delivery, procurement, and financial management, but they also are the key enforcers of a growing inventory of sanctions against those who would cheat the government—and have become leading investigators of white collar crime against the government. Alongside the political pressures leading toward compliance accountability, the legislative agenda may give the IGs little opportunity to do much else.

The IGs' increasing focus on compliance monitoring, however, involves much more than legislative mandates. It reflects the politics surrounding passage of the original statute, the lessons that emerged from the difficulties getting started under Carter, the incentives that unfolded in the Reagan administration's war on waste, the priorities that came with the growing number of investigators-turned-IGs, and the independence that arose from the natural evolution of the IG organizations, all forces that continue to support compliance as the dominant model for management in government.

The Rise of the IG Concept

COMPARED with most bills that were considered and passed in 1978, the Inspector General Act was almost invisible. Reorganizing audit and investigation units into single-headed Offices of Inspector General was hardly the stuff of which major floor debates are made. The language of the IG statute is nothing if not mundane; the legislative debate, if nearly unanimous support can be called debate, is replete with references to the need for better management, not the subject of front-page coverage.

Nevertheless, underlying this noncontroversial history, Congress gave the IGs broad powers.[1] Not only were the IGs to conduct audits and investigations of and relating to the programs and operations of their establishments, but they also were to review existing and proposed legislation and regulations for impacts on economy and efficiency; coordinate relationships between the department or agency and other federal agencies, state and local governments, and nongovernmental entities; and, most importantly, promote the general economy, efficiency, and effectiveness of their departments and agencies.[2] The IGs were mandated to pursue all three paths to accountability—compliance, performance, and capacity. The question was not if IGs had the power, but whether they would use it.[3]

AN INTRODUCTION TO THE IG ACT

At its most elemental level, the IG Act was an organizational device for unifying two simple functions, audit and investigation, into one unit. However, what made the IG Act much more significant was the decision to protect those new units from administrative politics through at least three devices.

First, even though the IG was to be a presidential appointee and removable without cause, each was to be selected "without regard to political affiliation and solely on the basis of integrity and demonstrated ability in accounting, auditing, financial analysis, law, management analysis, public administration, or investigations." Furthermore, the IG, not the president or the head of the establishment, was to appoint an assistant IG for audit and an assistant IG for investigations and was to have full authority to undertake whatever audits and investigations deemed necessary to ferret out fraud, waste, and abuse.

Second, every IG was to have access to all "information, documents, reports, answers, records, accounts, papers, and other data and documentary evidence" needed for an audit or investigation; the right to request assistance from within the agency and information from across government; the authority to subpoena documents (but not witnesses or testimony); the right to hire and fire staff; and "direct and prompt" access to the secretary or administrator whenever necessary for any purpose. Moreover, neither the head of the establishment nor the second in command was to prevent or prohibit the IG from "initiating, carrying out, or completing any audit or investigation, or from issuing any subpoena during the course of any audit or investigation."

Third, each IG was bound by a twofold reporting requirement, one ordinary, one urgent. The first was to be a routine semiannual report, due at the end of April and October, transmitted first to the head of the department or agency. It would include a description of every significant problem, abuse, and deficiency the IG identified during the previous six months, and was to be automatically forwarded to Congress within thirty days, unchanged, along with a separate report containing any comments the secretary or administrator might deem useful in response. The second requirement was an immediate report to the head of the department or agency whenever the IG became aware of "particularly serious or flagrant problems, abuses, or deficiencies." This much shorter report was to be automatically forwarded to Congress as well, this time within seven days, and again with a separate report containing any comments deemed necessary. Since such reports were to be short and immediate, they have come to be known as seven-day letters.

Together, these two reporting requirements constituted a unique dual-channel authority, given protection against any change by the department or agency, or the president. As legal scholars Margaret Gates and Marjorie Fine Knowles argued, "The inspector general is the *only* executive branch Presidential appointee who speaks directly to Congress without clearance from the Office of Management and

Budget. . . . This ability to speak directly to Congress provides a potential source of substantial clout for an active inspector general."[4]

Despite predictable executive branch opposition to such highly insulated, potentially damning units, the IG concept was an idea whose time had come. After establishing the first IG in HEW in 1976, Congress, as indicated by the list in table 2-1, expanded the IG presence in government thirteen times in thirteen years. IGs came to exist in virtually every corner of government.

By 1989, the total number of presidential IGs—those appointed by the president with Senate confirmation—stood at twenty-seven, while the number of small agency IGs—those appointed by the agency head without Senate confirmation—was thirty-four. The Community Services Administration and the U.S. Synfuels Corporation were abolished in the early days of the Reagan administration.

The expansion of the IG concept may have been inevitable. Once an IGship was established at HEW, the concept was easily transferable to the new Department of Energy and the spinoff Department of Education. And following the 1978 government-wide bill, which concentrated on the twelve departments and agencies logically next in line, it was bound to spread to the inner-cabinet of Justice, Treasury, State, and Defense.

A BRIEF HISTORY

To understand the rise of the IG concept and the range of options available to Congress in crafting the 1976 and 1978 bills, historical perspective is needed.[5]

The IG idea can be traced back ad infinitum. For the American experience, however, the scandals surrounding George Washington's colonial army are a good starting point. In one of the first resolutions passed, the Continental Congress established an IG, concluding that it was "essential to the promotion of discipline in the American Army, and to the reformation of the various abuses which prevail in the different departments."[6]

For the next one hundred years or so, the federal government had little need for IGs, or auditors for that matter, never employing more than a handful of auditors at a time. "Their work was principally a laborious task of examining all government vouchers and ledger accounts," wrote GAO experts John Adair and Rex Simmons. "They held their positions at the pleasure of the president—customarily resigning at the beginning of a new administration."[7]

Table 2-1. *Expansion of the IG Concept, 1976–89*

Year	Statute (P.L. number)[a]	Establishment
		Presidentially appointed IGs
1976	94-505	Health, Education, and Welfare
1977	95-91	Energy
1978	95-452	Agriculture, Commerce, Housing and Urban Development, Interior, Labor, Transportation, Community Services Administration, Environmental Protection Agency, General Services Administration, National Aeronautics and Space Administration, Small Business Administration, Veterans Administration
1979	96-88	Education
1980	96-294	U.S. Synfuels Corporation
1980	96-464	State
1981	97-113	Agency for International Development
1982	97-252	Defense
1983	98-76	Railroad Retirement Board
1986	99-399	U.S. Information Agency
1987	100-213	Arms Control and Disarmament Agency
1988	100-504	Justice, Treasury, Federal Emergency Management Administration, Nuclear Regulatory Commission, Office of Personnel Management
1989	101-73	Resolution Trust Corporation
1989	101-193	Central Intelligence Agency
		Nonpresidentially appointed IGs
1988	100-504	ACTION, Amtrak, Appalachian Regional Commission, Board of Governors of the Federal Reserve System, Board for International Broadcasting, Commodity Futures Trading Commission, Consumer Product Safety Commission, Corporation for Public Broadcasting, Equal Employment Opportunity Commission, Farm Credit Administration, Federal Communications Commission, Federal Deposit Insurance Corporation, Federal Election Commission, Federal Home Loan Bank Board, Federal Labor Relations Authority, Federal Maritime Commission, Federal Trade Commission, Government Printing Office, Interstate Commerce Commission, Legal Service Corporation, National Archives and Records Administration, National Credit Union Administration, National Endowment for the Arts, National Endowment for the Humanities, National Labor Relations Board, National Science Foundation, Panama Canal Commission, Peace Corps, Pension Benefit Guaranty Corporation, Securities and Exchange Commission, Smithsonian Institution, Tennessee Valley Authority, United States International Trade Commission, United States Postal Service

Source: Frederick M. Kaiser, "Inspectors General: Establishing Statutes and Statistics," memorandum (Congressional Research Service, Library of Congress, July 10, 1990).

a. Each public law number refers to a separate statute or to the act that contained the respective amendment to the Inspector General Act of 1978.

All this changed in 1921 with the Budget and Accounting Act, which created the first presidential budget system. Frederick Mosher explained its passage:

> To the politicians and the general public, the argument was single and simple—economy in government, to which efficiency and legality would contribute. It was proclaimed that a budget system would lower the costs of government or at least keep them from rising as quickly; it would thus keep taxes down, prevent deficits, and lower public debt. Economy was the great banner of the budget crusaders, and it was so effective that it became almost blasphemy by 1920 to oppose a budget system."[8]

Torn between giving the executive full control over financial management (efficiency) and reserving some role for itself (accountability), Congress elected to separate expenditure of funds from the auditing of accounts. Thus, Congress gave the president a Bureau of the Budget (now the Office of Management and Budget), but it created an accounting and auditing arm called the General Accounting Office for itself. By doing so, Congress took the first of several steps that would lead to the 1978 IG Act.

By 1947, GAO was a vast accounting operation, maintaining more than 400,000 separate accounts; countersigning 60,000 Treasury warrants; auditing 93,000 accounts containing 35 million vouchers; reviewing 1.5 million contracts, 260 million postal money orders, and 57 million postal notes; reconciling 490 million checks; issuing 1,300 reports, and sending 6,200 replies to members and committees of Congress. GAO also was responsible for the compliance audits needed to ensure that agencies were using accepted accounting practices. The workload was staggering. At the height of World War II, for example, GAO employed 14,904 accountants, lawyers, clerks, and associated staff.[9] Much of the expanded workload came with the New Deal (1932–39), when the number of government checks issued jumped from 33 million to 152 million.

The problems with GAO's accounting role were clear. First, critics in the executive branch wondered how GAO could play accountant and auditor simultaneously, especially because auditing often is viewed as an independent check on accounting. GAO not only was duplicating the account management available at Treasury, which had never relinquished its executive accounts, but also was diluting the president's authority to reform and modernize executive financial systems.

Second, critics on Capitol Hill wondered how GAO could do comprehensive, program effectiveness audits about what works and what does not, while maintaining a crushing day-to-day accounting role. The responsibility for accounting exerted an enormous toll on the staff. By 1950, even GAO wanted to let go of the accounting function in return for a selective audit role, one that eventually might involve program evaluation and performance and outcomes auditing.

Third, a growing number of young liberal senators and representatives wondered whether the accounting work was distracting GAO from the broader aims of Congress. With the explosion in personal and committee staffs, and creation of the Congressional Budget Office and the Office of Technology Assessment still to come, increasingly entrepreneurial members of Congress began to view GAO's highly inflexible workload as a serious obstacle to their own legislative work.

Whatever the reason for the change, efficiency won out as Congress in 1950 passed the first major revision of the Budget and Accounting Act, returning the accounting and internal audit function to the executive branch. Almost overnight, GAO employment fell by 9,000. The positions did not disappear, however. They eventually were reestablished in the personal and committee offices of the House and Senate, where staff employment rose from 3,500 in 1949 to almost 12,000 in 1990, creating impetus for the IG Act and potential consumers of AIG information.

A STATUTORY PROTOTYPE

As much as Congress wanted out of the day-to-day accounting business, it still needed information about what the executive branch was doing. No longer reconciling checks and thus lacking the detailed information the task provided, Congress waited less than a decade before establishing the first modern IG as a beachhead back into the executive branch. Created under the 1959 amendments to the Mutual Security Act, the IG was appointed by the secretary of state and held the title of "inspector general and comptroller." Of particular importance for understanding the evolution of the IG concept are the provisions on congressional access to information:

(d) Expenses of the Office of the Inspector General and Comptroller with respect to programs under this Act shall be charged to the appropriations made to carry out such programs: *Provided,* That all documents, papers, communications, audits, reviews, findings, recommendations, reports, and other material which relate to the operation or activities of the Office of Inspector General and Comptroller shall be furnished to the General Accounting Office and to any committee of the Congress, or any duly authorized subcommittee thereof, charged with considering legislation or appropriation for, or expenditures of, such Office, upon request of the General Accounting Office or such committee or subcommittee as the case may be."[10]

As if to emphasize its demand for information, the statute also gave the International Cooperation Administration, in which the IG resided, authority to compel documents from any other agency of government concerned with similar activities.

The legislative report from the House Foreign Affairs Committee does not shed much light on how the issue of access was settled. The report simply explains the relationship between the IG and secretary of state as essential "to provide a means by which information about deficiencies in the operation of (foreign assistance programs) can be transmitted from the operating level in the field where they become apparent to the top echelon of the organization where remedial action can be taken."[11] A best guess is that establishment of the first IG reflected at least two goals—one concerning audit coverage and coordination, the other satisfying a thirst for information on what was happening inside this once easily inspected operation.

If the origins of the first IG are unclear, its eventual expansion is not. Under amendments to the Foreign Assistance Act of 1961, the IG was made a presidential appointee subject to Senate confirmation and given an expanded purview that included the newly created Peace Corps and agricultural trade development. The IG also underwent a name change; becoming the "inspector general, foreign assistance" (IGA); no longer "comptroller."

As with most legislation, these IGA amendments measured considerably longer than the original bill. The 1961 amendments largely built upon the IG's duties and responsibilities and the continuing struggle for information. The new mandate section created a significant oversight role for the OIGs, requiring that they assess whether the programs of assistance were aiding in the attainment of their objectives. Furthermore, the words *economy* and *efficiency* appeared for the first time in connection with IGs. The legislation called upon IGs to determine "the efficiency and the economy with which" foreign assistance was being discharged.

The bill also gave the IG authority to suspend all or part of any project or operation "with respect to which he has conducted or is conducting an inspection," a power never used and never again granted to any future IG. In addition, the IG was given a permanent authorization of up to $2 million a year, which meant that the IG's budget was more or less protected from interference.

As to the need for information, Congress created a tougher reporting requirement, by adding the word *records* to the long list of source demands; ensuring the IG's internal access "to all records, reports, audits, reviews, documents, papers, recommendations, or other material of the agencies of the United States Government" administering foreign assistance; and guaranteeing congressional access to whatever the IG culled under the following time-phased information trigger:

> "Expenses . . . shall be charged . . . *provided*, That such appropriations shall not be charged with such expenses after the expiration of a thirty-five day period which begins on the date the General Accounting Office, or any committee or the Congress, or any duly authorized subcommittee thereof, charged with considering legislation, appropriations, or expenditures under the Act, has delivered to the Office of the Secretary of State a written request that it be furnished any document, paper, communication, audit, review, finding, recommendation, report, or other material which relates to the operation or activities of the Inspector General, Foreign Assistance, unless and until there has been furnished to the General Accounting Office, or to such committee, or subcommittee, as the case may be, (A) the document, paper, communication, audit, review, finding, recommendation, report, or other material so requested, or (B) a certification by the President personally that he has forbidden the furnishing thereof pursuant to such request and his reason for so doing."[12]

In short, either the State Department would provide information or the president would have to invoke executive privilege. Regarding the IG's ability to obtain internal government documents, public administration scholar Thomas W. Novotny noted that the IG's "statutory access to records was a significant first. Since the secretary of state has functional national security responsibility for assistance programs that are housed in DOD [Department of Defense] (such as the military assistance programs, foreign military sales, and security supporting assistance—heavily employed in Israel and Egypt, for example), IGA had cross-agency access that no current IG has. Even GAO did not, at the time, have IGA's access to DOD's records."[13]

Ultimately, whatever the origins of either the 1959 or the 1961 measure, the IGA generally was regarded as a failure and eventually was abolished when the Agency for International Development (AID) created its own nonstatutory IG in the mid-1970s.[14] And despite its clear link to the presidentially appointed IGs of the future, IGA rarely is cited in histories of the concept.[15]

A NONSTATUTORY ALTERNATIVE

Congress was not the only branch of government creating IGs in the late 1950s and early 1960s, however. Indeed, most administrative histories recognize the Agriculture Department as having the first modern IG. Created by Secretary of Agriculture Orville Freeman in the wake of the 1962 Billie Sol Estes scandal, the Agriculture IG was instituted after an exhaustive investigation led by the House Intergovernmental Relations subcommittee, which would author the 1976 HEW and 1978 IG acts.[16]

Subcommittee chairman L. H. Fountain (D-N.C.) headed the investigation, which covered twenty-one days of hearings and generated more than 10,000 pages of testimony and depositions. Estes had built a financial empire by deceiving the Department of Agriculture's grain storage program, dodging one investigation after another by making false statement after false statement. Inasmuch as the subcommittee found no evidence of outright government corruption, Estes had to be either very good at deceiving the government or very lucky at eluding detection.

He was both. According to the subcommittee's final report, "While Billie Sol Estes' record amply demonstrates his talent for deception, his misrepresentations concerning his financial condition succeeded primarily because of shortcomings in the performance of the Department of Agriculture."[17] Moreover, according to the subcommittee, Agriculture personnel "displayed a conspicuous lack of alertness," and none of the myriad agencies investigating the growing allegations had talked with any other: "Had all—or even a few—of the many Federal investigations of Estes' operations been properly coordinated, it is almost inconceivable that his fraudulent activities could have been continued for such a long period."[18]

Why the investigation produced an IG still is unclear. Was the IG forced upon the department by Attorney General Robert F. Kennedy? Was the IG recommended by Fountain? Freeman's testimony suggested that the IG was merely the last in a list of twelve reforms.[19] Freeman referred to the IG more as an illustration of the "types of administrative actions that we have taken to tighten up management and increase efficiency" than as the solution to the scandal. His view was brought into somewhat greater focus during questioning by Fountain and his counsel, James Naughton:

Mr. FOUNTAIN. I think what [we are] talking about is that in the Department, in one office or another, there was information of one kind or another about Mr. Estes. But no single office had all of this information upon which it might make a decision in connection with, say, the grain storage operations. Even though the information they had about Mr. Estes may not have related directly to grain storage, it could have been a circumstance which might have been considered had it been in one central office.

Mr. FREEMAN. I would concur. All of the information was not brought into focus at a given time and place, and it would have been useful if it had.

Mr. NAUGHTON. How much authority are you giving the Inspector General?

Mr. FREEMAN. I think the record here of the committee will show the Secretary's order establishing the post of Inspector General, which is to coordinate, to oversee, to review, as the direct representative of the Secretary, all audit and investigation work that is taking place anywhere within the Department. And as such, to be, let us put it, "Mr. Big," where audit investigations are concerned everywhere within the Department.

Mr. NAUGHTON. Will he report directly to you, or to the Under Secretary?

Mr. FREEMAN. Directly to me.[20]

The Agriculture Secretary's order creating the IG was a model of parsimony when compared with the legislation creating the IGA. The department's administrative handbook identified the IG as "a staff element providing audit and investigative service pertaining to the department, all of its constituent organizations, and all parties performing under contracts, grants, or other agreements with the Department," laying out in short sequence the jobs of the assistant IGs for audit and investigation.[21]

What made the Agriculture IG different from the IGA was that the incumbent (1) served entirely at the pleasure of the secretary and (2) reported only to the secretary. Lester Condon, the first Agriculture IG, said "we brought auditors and investigators together so they did indeed become subordinates of the secretary of the department. They were responsible to the agency, rather than running around the Hill and making alliances with politicians, and too often

not working for the department as a whole. That authority we had
was a powerful and effective one."[22]

With an office staffed by more than 700 employees, Condon used
this authority carefully. As Condon explained in an internal paper
written soon after arriving at Agriculture, he tried to "bring home
to everyone in the Department that the OIG is not a 'Cloak and
Dagger' or 'Gumshoe' outfit; that we are not interested in persecuting
people, or conducting inquisitions. On the contrary, we are proving
that we are in business to assist operating personnel—and to protect
individuals at all levels from false or incorrect accusations or incrimi-
nations in the discharge of their jobs."[23]

Condon also was the strong right arm of the secretary, as described
by Walter Gellhorn in his 1966 book, *When Americans Complain*:

> Without straining too desperately for analogies, one could say
> that Agriculture's Inspector General functions to some extent
> as a sort of departmental ombudsman. His purpose is not puni-
> tive. His findings may absolve as well as condemn. His probings
> seek better practices even when what exists is tolerable. He is
> a mere adviser, but his position adds weight to his advice. His
> job calls for frankness in describing things as they are and for
> boldness in proposing things as they should be, and so he must
> be free from the pulls of other officials. Though separate from
> others, he remains quite properly a member of the Secretary's
> team. His conclusions are therefore not likely to be pushed to
> the point of departmental embarrassment. Moreover, his are not
> the only words that reach the Secretary's ears or eyes; he is
> influential, but his influence is one amongst many and not nec-
> essarily the strongest.[24]

Of particular importance was the decision to give the IG wide
authority to engage in all three kinds of monitoring. The Agriculture
IG was to assure compliance with new rules to prevent a future
Billie Sol Estes scandal, while providing information on broad agency
performance and capacity. The IG was not forced by structure or
mandate to concentrate on short-term compliance as the be-all and
end-all of the job. Compliance monitoring under Condon was linked
to broader questions of departmental effectiveness.

However, as Condon's successor was to learn almost a decade
later in the Nixon administration, the problem with having one
boss and no statutory base is clear: What the secretary giveth, the
secretary can taketh away. Despite the IG's enviable record and
strong endorsement from GAO, Nixon's secretary of agriculture,
Earl Butz, abruptly—some say casually—eliminated the position in

1974, dividing it into the two offices from which it came, audit and investigation.

The task of explaining the decision to Representative Jamie L. Whitten (D.-Miss.), chairman of the House Agriculture Appropriations Subcommittee, fell to Joseph Wright. As deputy director of OMB in the 1980s, Wright was unabashedly pro-IG. But as a New York management consultant turned assistant secretary of agriculture for administration in 1974, he defended the split in pure efficiency terms. As Wright told Whitten, "There was not that much interchange between the investigation side and the audit side [of] OIG when we studied the organization. We found out that we were not getting improved efficiencies by keeping audit and investigation together. We could easily divide up those offices and their responsibilities."[25]

Abolishing the nonstatutory IGship was well within the secretary's authority, an argument Wright made with characteristic bluntness:

> Mr. WHITTEN. . . . for you to come up and recommend that the Office of Inspector General be abolished and left up to you folks in the Secretary's office, it does not strike me as you are on a very sound footing.
>
> What are you up to there?
>
> Mr. WRIGHT. Mr. Chairman, if I could answer that. First of all, by reorganizing the Office of Inspector General—
>
> Mr. WHITTEN. You reorganized it out, didn't you?
>
> Mr. WRIGHT. Into an Office of Investigation and an Office of Audit.
>
> Mr. WHITTEN. In other words, get it where it is dominated by the Secretary?
>
> Mr. WRIGHT. *It could have been dominated by the Secretary if he wanted to at any time.*[26]

Whitten stayed on the attack throughout the hearing, asking Wright at one point, "What in your experience prior to coming here as management consultant leads you to feel that you are an expert in this Department?" Despite the heated exchange, neither Whitten nor any of his congressional colleagues ever moved to give the Agriculture OIG a statutory underpinning, which perhaps condoned the decision.

As Wright later explained, "the decision to split the Office of IG was not to break its back, but to give me back the audit function as part of my job as Assistant Secretary for Administration. I felt I needed audit reporting directly to me if I was to do my job—it was a tenet of good management. Ten years later, I could see the other side of the coin."[27] So, too, apparently could Carter's secretary of agriculture, Bob Bergland, who upon taking office in 1977 immediately reestablished the IG in a brief four-paragraph order.

This checkered history notwithstanding, the Agriculture experience was critical to the evolution of the IG concept, if only to establish the need to give the office some measure of independence. In addition, having moved from Agriculture to HUD in 1969, Condon later convinced Secretary George Romney to create a similar unit in the wake of a housing scandal. The position endured long enough to be brought under the 1978 statute.[28]

Thus, even after its demise at Agriculture, the IG concept continued to gain momentum. It would even arise as a recommendation for the secretive world of counterintelligence through the President's Commission on CIA Activities within the United States (Rockefeller Commission). In a report signed by all eight commission members, including former California governor Ronald Reagan, strengthening of the agency's nonstatutory IG was offered as one option for addressing the domestic surveillance scandal.[29] To demonstrate the limits of commission reports or the resistance of the intelligence community or perhaps a bit of both, the CIA was the last agency to be brought into the IG fold almost two decades later.

CONCLUSION: A BARBED WIRE FENCE

The State and Agriculture IGs gave Congress two substantially different job descriptions for future consideration. In theory, the IGA was designed to be a lone wolf, a tough auditor-investigator, protected by statute, charged with substantial oversight responsibility, given broad information access, and equipped with a "doomsday" sanction in the ability to suspend a program.

The Agriculture IG was a strong right arm of the secretary, one of the family, an important source of inside advice and counsel, as tough as the secretary would permit, someone to dig up the dirt but not spread it.

Congress's eventual adoption of the latter approach, albeit in statute and with a dual reporting relationship, set the IGs on a balancing act that continues today. State Department IG Sherman Funk once described it as straddling a barbed wire fence.[30] But that fence also gave the IGs options they never would have had under the lone wolf model: They could broaden their agendas to include both performance and capacity monitoring. Many IGs, however, stayed on the narrow path.

Designing the Concept

Why Congress Acted

INSPECTORS general can be viewed as both an extension and an outcome of earlier congressional reforms. As an extension, the IGs are another tool for limiting executive branch discretion.[1] As an outcome, they are essential suppliers of the information needed to sustain the earlier reforms, particularly the new budget process and rapidly expanding congressional staff.

Thus, the IG Act has origins well beyond the decline and resurgence of Congress. The legislation's primary author, Representative L. H. Fountain, was hardly a rabble-rouser, and waste, not Watergate, was the main theme of the floor debate. Finding the roots of the IG Act is like making a geological dig, stripping one layer of explanation off another until the underlying stratum is uncovered.[2]

Thus, beneath the traditional explanations of the IG Act as a thirst for accountability or the mere politics of fraud busting, is the burgeoning congressional demand for information. Although some of that demand involved what journalist and scholar Suzanne Garment called "scandal politics," most was more modestly linked to a market created by the rising number of congressional entrepreneurs.[3] With 535 members of Congress, 270 committees and subcommittees, and almost 3,000 professional staff members as their customers, the IGs had ample incentive to favor compliance monitoring.

THE THREE HORSEMEN OF THE IG CONCEPT

The IG Act was a congressional idea. Even though President Carter eventually would hail the 1978 act as "landmark legislation," he came to his enthusiasm reluctantly and only after all twelve departments covered under the act testified in opposition.

To understand why the law was enacted, focus must fall on Congress and what Mark Moore and Margaret Gates characterize as the "unquenchable thirst for accountability that cuts across the political spectrum."[4] However, the IG Act hardly involved an esoteric debate about assuring bureaucratic responsibility. On the contrary, passage of both the 1976 Health, Education, and Welfare IG legislation and the subsequent 1978 expansion would have been impossible without the three horsemen of the IG concept: fraud, waste, and abuse.

1976 Legislation

Just as the Agriculture IG emerged from scandal, so, too, did the HEW IG. The 1976 act can be traced to two investigations. The first, led by Senator Frank Moss (D-Utah) and the Senate Finance Committee, turned up $1.8 billion worth of kickbacks, fraudulent billings, unnecessary care, and inflated charges in Medicaid each year. The second, led by Fountain, found glaring audit and investigatory weaknesses in every corner of HEW.[5] "No one knows how much fraud and abuse in HEW programs are costing the taxpayers," Fountain argued, "but I do not think there is any doubt that such losses have reached literally billions of dollars annually."[6]

Like the 1962 Billie Sol Estes investigation, Congress placed the blame not on loosely designed programs or the individual executives in charge. Instead, as Fountain noted when opening the hearings on the establishment of an HEW IG, the problem was in the organization:

HEW's investigative resources were ridiculously inadequate. Its central investigative unit had only ten investigators with a 10-year backlog of uninvestigated cases.

Information needed by both HEW and Congress for effective action against fraud and abuse was simply not available.

Units responsible for combating fraud and abuse were scattered throughout HEW in a haphazard, fragmented, and confusing pattern, with no single unit having the overall responsibility and authority necessary to provide effective leadership.[7]

Having discovered these parallels to the Agriculture Department weaknesses, Fountain and his staff turned to a familiar solution. But Earl Butz and his decision to abolish the nonstatutory IG post at Agriculture made 1976 different. The dismemberment of the nonstatutory IG had taught Fountain an important lesson about the need to provide some protection, even if that meant making the IG less of a strong right arm to the secretary.

1978 Legislation

Although a single investigation laid the base for the establishment of the HEW IG, selling the IG concept government-wide involved a different strategy. Lacking the resources to do an investigation of each department and agency, Congress had to argue that government was fundamentally flawed, and that only broad reform would do. According to the Senate Governmental Affairs report accompanying the final bill:

> Recent evidence makes it clear that fraud, abuse and waste in the operations of Federal departments and agencies and in federally-funded programs are reaching epidemic proportions. Undoubtedly, the problem is not new. However, increased attention by the press and by government officials has brought to light increasingly disturbing testimony of the magnitude of the problems.[8]

The IG concept, however, was not merely another form of scandal-mongering. At the committee level, where members and staff drafted specific legislative language, the concept reflected a view of government in which coordination and adequate numbers of auditors would create a more effective compliance structure. In this regard, GAO became of critical importance, authoring three separate reports to support the cause.

The first, completed in November 1976, compared the number of auditors in each executive department by two measures—total number of employees and total dollars to be audited—and found the ratios wanting.[9] The second, released ten days later, provided an overview of federal internal audit weaknesses that was sobering at best.[10] The third, released in the summer before final passage of the 1978 act, said that many federal program units were not receiving annual financial audits of their accounts.[11]

None of the reports, however, endorsed the IG concept outright. Although GAO eventually came to support the IGs as a way to strengthen the executive audit function, Comptroller General Elmer Staats was not enthusiastic about the original bills. As one GAO official remembered: "We weren't even asked to testify on the House bill in 1977 because Fountain's staff knew we weren't favorable. Our concern was that creating an IG as the focal point for catching fraud and inefficiency would send the wrong signal to the rest of the departments. Staats simply believed that it was not right to put the burden for fighting fraud and waste on a single office or subordinate when it was everyone's responsibility."

One year later, with the IG Act on a fast track, GAO turned toward compromise. Its decision to release the third report at the Senate IG Act hearings signaled an effort to influence the Governmental Affairs Committee and its chairman, Thomas Eagleton (D-Mo.). Surveying every unit of the federal government, from whole agencies to small program offices, GAO found that almost a third had not had a financial audit since 1974. In unusually dramatic prose on the front cover, the report announced: "One hundred and thirty-three units, with annual funding in excess of $20 billion, told GAO they had not received a financial audit during fiscal years 1974 through 1976."[12] Even accepting the limits of the survey, the findings supported GAO's view that audit was the cornerstone of the IG concept. In its Senate testimony, the GAO would lobby for adding "auditor general" to the IG title:

> The present title suggests that the Inspector General has the investigative function, but does not indicate his responsibility for the full scope of audit, including audits to determine financial integrity and compliance with pertinent laws and regulations, audits to identify inefficiencies or wasteful practices, and audits to assess effectiveness in achieving program goals.[13]

As the GAO witness explained, "We think the name sets the tone of the office. The idea that audit would be brought into the title, I think, would strengthen the audit function." Eagleton was sympathetic to the idea, though he could not help but poke fun at the overall impact of the longer title: "The only argument against it is in terms of abbreviations. You have to have a government short name. IG seems to have an easier ring than IAAG. I guess we could drop the 'and' and make it 'IAG.'"[14] Although the Senate adopted the change to "auditor and inspector general," the new title did not survive the House-Senate conference.

Even without the longer title, the IG concept combined what political scientists Mathew McCubbins and Thomas Schwartz identify as two distinct types of oversight—the more routine, "police-patrol" oversight likely to emerge from audits, and the more dramatic, "fire-alarm" oversight likely to come from investigations.[15] On the one hand, the OIGs gave new visibility and resources to long-neglected audit offices, and represented a very real congressional investment in police-patrol oversight, although delegated to executive branch officials under the dual reporting requirement. On the other hand, the OIGs provided occasional opportunities for sounding fire alarms. According to McCubbins and Schwartz, "a fire-alarm policy enables congressmen to spend less time on oversight, leaving more time for other profitable activities, or to spend the same time on more personally profitable oversight activities—on addressing complaints by potential supporters. Justly or unjustly, time spent putting out visible fires gains one more credit than the same time spent sniffing for smoke."[16]

THE POLITICS OF FRAUD BUSTING

The kind of fire-alarm fraud busting envisioned in the IG legislative record always has been politically viable. As much as blue-ribbon commissions decry those who run against Washington, bureaucrat bashing fits well with traditional public beliefs about waste in government. Rare is the presidential campaign that can resist the occasional punch at overpaid, underworked civil servants and the fat cats who get rich at taxpayer expense.

Alongside Fountain's legitimate interest in the executive branch's ailing accounting and management systems, Congress also embraced the IG concept for its fourfold political promise. The IG Act would guarantee high rates of return—budgetary and political; create a new legislative arena in an era of fiscal restraint; provide protection, albeit minimal, against the growing lack of public confidence in government; and give Congress an opportunity to take a more aggressive role in federal management.

High Rates of Return

Congress likely saw two rates of return in the IG Act. The first was in recovering some of the dollars lost to fraud, waste, and abuse. According to the admittedly loose estimates at the time, the savings from each dollar invested in IG staff was anywhere from two to twenty dollars, depending on the department and the advocate. As Representative Elliott Levitas (D-Ga.) remarked in support of the HEW IG bill:

> If I remember the figure correctly, with 10 staff investigators in the United States during the last year . . . there were approximately 100 cases under investigation that resulted in about $20 million of fraud or program abuse. With 10. Just that fact alone indicates to me that there are literally thousands more cases out there, if there were adequate staff and real determination on the part of the Secretary to do something about it.[17]

Although no one thought the IG Act would close the federal deficit, even small amounts of savings would provide limited budgetary "slack" for new programs, while protecting members of Congress from the kinds of "spend and spend, tax and tax" charges made famous by Reagan in the 1980s.

Second, Congress also likely saw high rates of return in publicity. As Garment editorialized,

> Too many congressional committees have become part of a scandal production system that makes a lot of noises, takes many hostages, does little discernible good, and sometimes makes government distinctly worse. . . . Some committees now have the resources and the will to conduct what must be called a perpetual scandal hunt. They pursue their targets in a spirit of rivalry with the executive branch—a contest less muted than it was in earlier times by customs of civility or restraint from institutional leadership.[18]

Highly entrepreneurial members of Congress also perhaps needed the IGs to generate publicity in the absence of new program opportunities. As political scientist Burdett Loomis argued, the 1970s brought a new American politician to the House, one whose career focused more on individual accomplishment than institutional performance.[19] If information from the IGs could help, so be it.

Representative Henry Waxman (D-Calif.), first elected in the larger, post-Watergate class of 1974, is one example. Rising to chairmanship of the House Health and Environment Subcommittee, before which HHS IG Richard Kusserow testified four times in 1990 alone,[20] Waxman used his position to mine what Loomis called a "rich and controversial lode of issues":

> Waxman demonstrates the potential that a well-staffed subcommittee offers an activist chair. Not only can he promote a pet project, as with his heroin proposal [to provide compassionate use as a pain reliever for the terminally ill], but he can push legislation to fruition through obtaining publicity (orphan drugs), tack on a program to a budget reconciliation bill (maternity benefits), and seek long-term political solutions to intractable policy problems (clean air, acid rain). If Waxman does not always emerge victorious—and he surely doesn't—he always comes to play, and a key subcommittee gives him lots of leeway to find a way to win.[21]

This is not a portrait of scandal politics, but of a serious member of Congress who uses IG input to frame issues for resolution. However, some members of Congress have been less concerned with policy reform, using the IGs instead to score short-term political successes.

New Legislative Opportunities

The IG Act also represented a new area of congressional credit claiming. Budget deficits not only lead to concerns with rates of return, but also limit the creation of new programs. Without money, Congress turned to other sources of legislative activity, in some cases trying to make existing programs work better, in other cases trying to make a name for themselves back home. According to one respondent interviewed by Joel Aberbach for his book on congressional oversight:

> I think the people of the United States are saying: "We don't want any more new programs. We want existing programs to work better." . . . How does that impact up here? It impacts up here politically. . . . In the 1960s I suspect you could not get any credit for going home and saying, . . . "I'm making this program work better," but rather, you had to go back to your district and say, "I passed the new Joe Zilch piece of handicapped elephant legislation," something like that, right? And you've got a new bill on the wall, and that was what you wanted. Well, that's not where the returns are now. The political returns are from oversight.[22]

Not all oversight is driven by scandal politics. Using a variety of indicators, Aberbach shows the rise of incentives for routine police-patrol oversight in Congress, noting that staffs are up to the task despite their relative youth, and "when there is less opportunity to do new things, then fine tuning and correcting the old becomes more attractive." For Aberbach, "In and of itself, this makes a more active information search style more appealing." Furthermore, finding information became cheaper in the 1970s and 1980s in part because legislative staffers are such enthusiastic seekers of it:

> For those who, either by training or experience, have some expertise in the area their committees oversee, seeking information actively is likely a source of personal pride and professional fulfillment. For those who want to make themselves known in the Washington community, and this includes more and more staffers as staff size grows, actively seeking information is one way to project one's presence. This is especially true when, as now, conditions make it difficult for staff to make a mark by working on legislation creating new programs.[23]

The IG Act may even have permitted Congress to legislate far beyond its capacity to oversee. When in doubt about enforcement of new financial management laws, procurement reforms, and so forth, Congress tasked the IGs. For example, in the proposed Government Energy Efficiency Act of 1991, introduced May 9, 1991, by Senator John Glenn (D-Ohio), energy-saving goals would be set for the government and the IGs would be designated as the compliance monitors. Under the act, each IG would be "encouraged to conduct periodic reviews of agency compliance with . . . the provisions of this Act, and other laws relating to energy use reduction." The bill could have moved forward without the IGs, but having the IGs as available enforcers lent the proposal greater credibility.

The Confidence Gap

Beyond these internal explanations, the IG Act created an institutional steam valve against growing public distrust. Having advertised the extent of government fraud, waste, and abuse in hearing after hearing, Congress could not avoid bearing part of the blame. On the heels of Watergate, trust in the presidency was practically nonexistent, and every other measure of trust in government was in decline.

As examples of the confidence gap, consider a sample of the trends in the national election polls conducted by the University of Michigan:

- The number of people who said that "quite a few of the people running the government are a little crooked" increased from 24 percent in 1958, the first year the question was asked, to 42 percent in 1976, the year Congress enacted the HEW IG.
- The number who said that they "could not trust the government to do right most of the time" more than tripled, up from 23 percent in 1958 to 63 percent in 1976.
- The number who believed that "government is run by a few big interests looking out for themselves" escalated from 29 percent in 1964, the first year the question was asked, to 66 percent in 1976.
- The number who said that "people in the government waste a lot of money we pay in taxes" moved from 43 percent in 1958 to 74 percent in 1976.[24]

The IGs were not created as mere political cover, although some scholars have made such a claim. According to public management scholar Robert Behn, for example, "The latest invention for institutionalizing distrust is the inspector general. Having legislators, candidates, journalists, and auditors watching any government agency is not enough. After all, they are all on the outside. How could they catch anything? So, we have decided to institutionalize our distrust even further."[25]

As much as Behn stretches the case, obvious political payoffs can be found in a strong IG concept. Congress not only created an institution to which it could refer complaints but also gained a secondary source of blame when programs went astray. Moreover, public distrust may have led Congress away from the normal solutions to fraud, waste, and abuse—increased audit staff, tighter statutes, clearer standards—and toward a more visible organizational response. In the process, Congress also gained an ally, and occasional scapegoat, for future scandals.

The Management Vacuum

Finally the IG Act allowed Congress to fill a leadership vacuum created by successive presidents and their OMB staffs. In theory, for example, the reorganization of the old Bureau of the Budget into the Office of Management and Budget was designed to reverse decades of neglect, once characterized by public law scholar Marver Bernstein as "a story of inflated rhetoric, shifting emphasis from one fashionable managerial skill to another, and a relatively low level of professional achievement."[26]

If a new era in management was to be the new OMB's mission, the results were less than overwhelming. Looking back over a host of OMB initiatives from the 1970s and early 1980s—Management by Objectives, Productivity Measurement and Improvement, Procurement Reform, the 1972 revision of OMB Circular A-44 (Management Review and Improvement Program), OMB Circular A-117 (Management Improvement and the Use of Evaluation in the Executive Branch), the President's Management Improvement Council, and the Paperwork Reduction Act—GAO reached the following conclusion:

> The history of Executive Branch management improvement efforts since the creation of OMB is characterized by episodic attempts at reform generally of short duration. The initiatives represent a range of efforts to achieve a workable balance between Presidential control and departmental autonomy. While the circumstances surrounding the initiatives vary, they generally share the characteristics of minimal direct interest by the

President or OMB Director; limited attention to implementation strategies; and less than ideal working relationships with
OMB's budget staff.[27]

This story essentially remained unchanged throughout the Reagan
administration.[28]

In such a climate of disappointment, Congress cannot be blamed
for weighing in with its own agenda. Midway through the parade of
opponents at the 1978 IG hearings, Fountain made just such a point.
"I find the same theme running throughout all of the responses from
all of the agencies who are testifying," Fountain said. "That theme
is that once the Congress has established an agency, the agency feels
it is really none of the Congress business how it operates. I find that
the President takes somewhat of the same attitude."[29]

Congress intended the IGs to be a counterweight to the volatility
that came with ever-increasing numbers of short-term appointees
and management fads. A vacuum existed because of longstanding
disinterest in the White House and OMB; Congress's view that merit
existed in a more stable approach to reform was only natural.

THE INFORMATION IMPERATIVE

Neither the GAO seal of approval nor the politics of fraud busting
are enough to explain passage of the 1978 IG Act. Congress had
acted many times without GAO approval and could have continued
its fraud busting without the IGs. Of much greater importance was
the heightened post-Watergate struggle over access to executive
branch information.

The purpose here is not to review the history of executive privilege
or congressional inquiry.[30] Suffice it to say that a struggle for access
always has existed, first expressed in 1789 with establishment of
the Department of the Treasury. To this day, the Treasury secretary
is governed by a dual reporting requirement "to either House of
Congress in person or in writing, as required, on matters referred to
the Secretary by that House of Congress."[31]

Hard and fast truths about executive privilege also are not easy
to come by. The courts have established both Congress's right to
seek information in aid of its legislative and oversight functions—
enunciated in *McGrain* v. *Daugherty*[32]—and the president's right to
withhold executive branch information—supported in *United States*
v. *Nixon*.[33] As public law scholar Peter Shane suggested in a study
for the Administrative Conference of the United States, access to

information is an issue of negotiation: "If law, in the sense of 'rules,' does not directly control the outcomes in interbranch disputes over information in any strong way, then what does? Government officials interviewed for this study typically say 'Politics.'"[34]

To explain the rise of the IG concept, two sides of the information imperative as it shaped the IG Act need to be noted: (1) the conflict over ordinary access to executive branch information, and (2) the market for information created by the rapidly increasing number of potential users—committees, subcommittees, and staffers—on Capitol Hill.

Ordinary Access

The *Congressional Record* during the Nixon years provides easy evidence of the conflict over executive privilege and presidential secrecy. Much of the legislation introduced at the time, however, was designed to assure timely access to information, whether about the Vietnam War or agricultural price supports.

Of particular note in the evolution of the IG concept was H.R. 12462, introduced only days after Nixon's resignation in 1974 and referred to the Government Operations Committee. To amend the Freedom of Information Act to force either the timely release of requested information or the invocation of executive privilege, the bill provoked the opposition of Fountain and future committee chairman, Jack Brooks (D-Tex.).

The problem for Fountain and Brooks was that the legislation codified the president's right to withhold information, a right established by the courts but never given in statute. Fountain's dissent from the legislative report is instructive for understanding his subsequent position on the IG Act:

> Under the provisions of H.R. 12462, a President who wished to do so could easily prevent the Congress from obtaining on a timely basis the information it needs to carry out its responsibilities. Moreover, under the bill, any Federal employee—from Cabinet member to the lowest ranking clerk—could refuse to provide information or answer questions before congressional committees by claiming he "believes" the President might order the information withheld.
>
> I believe H.R. 12462 is a good-faith attempt by its sponsors to limit withholding of information under claim of "executive privilege." However, even if there were no question concerning its constitutionality, in my opinion, H.R. 12462 would still do

far more harm than good. It would weaken—not enhance—the power of Congress to obtain the information it must have to do its job.[35]

Fountain was not the only member of the committee to dissent. Then–committee chairman Chet Holifield, future House Speaker Jim Wright (D-Tex.), and twelve others joined Fountain and Brooks in voting "nay." Although the bill was reported favorably on a largely symbolic 24–16 vote, the combined Fountain-Brooks-Wright-Holifield opposition precluded further consideration.[36]

What Congress needed instead was a practical approach to information collection that simultaneously avoided endless court challenges, and regularized ordinary access. That Fountain came to see the Inspector General Act as one avenue for providing ordinary access is confirmed not only by the reporting provisions but also by the following provisions enacted as part of the 1976 HEW IG Act and proposed for the twelve new IGs in his bill introduced less than a year later:

Section 4(d). The Inspector General (A) may make such additional investigations and reports relating to the administration of the programs and operations of the Department as are, in the judgment of the Inspector General, necessary or desirable, and (B) shall provide such additional information or documents as may be requested by either House of Congress or, with respect to matters within their jurisdiction, by any committee or subcommittee thereof.

Section 4(e). Notwithstanding any other provision of law, the reports, information or documents required by or under this section shall be transmitted to the head of the establishment involved and the Congress, or committees or subcommittees thereof, by an Inspector General without *further clearance or approval.*

Section 5(a). In addition to the authority otherwise provided by this Act, the Inspector General is authorized, in carrying out the provisions of this Act—

(1) to have access to all records, reports, audits, reviews, documents, papers, recommendations or other material available to the applicable establishment which relate to programs and operations with respect to which that Inspector General has responsibilities under the Act.[37]

As proposed, the IG was to serve as a conduit for congressional requests, forwarding any and all information without interference by the secretary or the president. These provisions likely survived in 1976 more because of the scant attention given the HEW proposal by a busy Senate and a weakened Gerald R. Ford White House. Facing more serious opposition in 1978, the provisions were dropped. However, the intent of the early bill, and its link to the struggle over information, is unmistakable.

A Growing Market

Congress's growing thirst for information also was undeniable. Aberbach documented the stunning rise in oversight starting in the mid-1970s, just about the time the IG concept was enacted. According to Aberbach's data, which were based on his careful subject-matter coding of every congressional hearing that was held in odd-numbered, nonelection years between 1961 and 1983, Congress conducted 537 days of oversight in 1977, an increase of 268 percent over 1961. Starting at 146 days of oversight in 1961, Congress became increasingly committed to this task, giving 290 days in 1973, 459 in 1975, and peaking at 587 in 1981. As a percentage of all days spent in hearings, oversight moved from 8 percent in 1961 to 18 percent in 1977.[38]

The rise of the IG concept fits neatly into the expansion of congressional staff and oversight activity. "As the potential for oversight increased," Donald Kettl argued, "so naturally did the practice."[39] Between 1960 and 1980, House committee and subcommittee staff increased from 440 to 1,917, while Senate staff grew from 470 to 1,074.[40] Looking at the year-to-year growth, the sharpest increases in both chambers came in 1974–75, when House staff increased by 353 positions and Senate staff by 329. That growth spurt accounted for almost a quarter of the House expansion and nearly one-half of the Senate increase. At that same time, the arrival of what some congressional scholars have come to see as a new kind of member, one motivated primarily by ambition and publicity, was heralded. This change also affected support for the IGs.

The data in table 3-1 provide a summary of the key staff trends surrounding the establishment of the IGs—the increase in number of standing committees and subcommittees, the growth in staff, and the burst of oversight activity that occurred prior to the institution of the HEW IG and the expansion of the IG concept to the rest of government.

Of equal importance in explaining the rise of the IG concept is the pattern of deployment in those new staffs. While the number of

Table 3-1. *Trends in Committee and Subcommittee Activity,*
1955–83

Year	Standing committees and subcommittees	House committee and subcommittee staff	Senate committee and subcommittee staff	Days of oversight hearings held
1955	225	329	386	. . .
1960	227	440	470	146[a]
1970	247	702	635	. . .
1971	263	729	711	187
1972	263[b]	817	844	. . .
1973	287	878	873	290
1974	287	1,107	948	. . .
1975	302	1,460	1,277	459
1976	302	1,680	1,201	. . .
1977	270	1,776	1,028	537
1978	270	1,844	1,151	. . .
1979	263	1,909	1,269	n.a.
1980	263	1,917	1,191	. . .
1981	271	1,843	1,022	434
1982	271	1,839	1,047	. . .
1983	264	1,970	1,075	587

Sources: Steven S. Smith and Christopher J. Deering, *Committees in Congress* (Washington: CQ Press, 1984), p. 275; Norman J. Ornstein, Thomas E. Mann, and Michael J. Malbin, *Vital Statistics on Congress, 1989–90* (Washington: CQ Press, 1990), p. 136; and Joel D. Aberbach, *Keeping a Watchful Eye: The Politics of Congressional Oversight* (Brookings, 1990), p. 35.
n.a. Not available.
a. This number is from 1961.
b. The number of standing committees and subcommittees is set at the start of each two-year Congress and, therefore, remains unchanged in the second year.

subcommittees grew, their staffs did not and thus remained dependent on outside information to fuel their work. They simply did not
have the capacity to mount deep investigations.

Senate subcommittees dropped from a 42 percent share of total
staff in 1969 to 33 percent ten years later. Even in the House, where
subcommittees nearly doubled their staff during the 1970s, full committee staffers still outnumbered subcommittee staffers by a 57-to-
43 margin.[41] As a result, by the end of the 1970s, subcommittee
staffs were more likely than full committee staffs to be thinner,
more specialized, less experienced, younger, and more dependent on
outside input in setting their agendas; in short, more likely clients
for the IGs.

To operate, this mushrooming staff, whether at the full committee
or subcommittee level, needed fuel—which often came in the form
of executive branch information and sometimes involved nothing

more than scandal. As Garment suggested, the link between staff growth and scandal hunting is clear:

> It has been noted by more than one observer that in this era of the budget deficit, the expanded staffs cannot fully occupy themselves with great, popular, and expensive legislative initiatives. In other words, large numbers of these new people are all dressed up with no place to go. There is little evidence that they have used their increased resources to become more sophisticated supervisors of government management. So what *have* they done? The answer seems to be that most congressional committees deliver the same kind of sporadic performance as before—but more of it.[42]

Not all staff expansion was dedicated to scandal hunting, although malfeasance was the number one factor listed by members and staff when asked how they set the oversight agenda. Even though scandal was the number one factor in setting the general agenda, it was not the most common explanation for the individual hearings Aberbach coded. Far more important were general public concerns about an agency or program, beliefs that programs were not being run effectively, commitments to ongoing oversight of committee programs, and complaints by clientele or interest groups.[43]

The Subcommittee Connection

If the staff and committee growth was linked to IG expansion, three major patterns in congressional-IG activity should be apparent over the years following enactment:

1. The House would use the IGs more than the Senate, if only because House committees outnumbered Senate committees by roughly fifty;

2. Subcommittees would use the IGs more than full committees; and

3. House subcommittees would use the IGs more than House full committees, if only because subcommittees outnumbered full committees by almost 6 to 1.

Assuming that IG appearances before Congress are a valid indicator of use, the IGs did become creatures of House subcommittees. IGs testified 339 times before Congress from 1977 to 1988 (see table 3-2). Of those appearances, 52 percent came in the House and 48

Table 3-2. *IG Congressional Appearances, 1977–88*

Locale	Type of appearance				Total
	Nomination[a]	Appropriation	Program	Other	
1977–80					
House	0	6	12	5	23
Senate	24	8	9	4	45
Full committee	24	0	4	5	33
Subcommittee	0	14	17	4	35
Total	24	14	21	9	68
1981–82					
House	0	11	16	5	32
Senate	10	8	13	6	37
Full committee	10	0	8	3	21
Subcommittee	0	19	21	8	48
Total	10	19	29	11	69
1983–84					
House	0	14	7	9	30
Senate	5	7	9	6	27
Full committee	5	0	8	3	16
Subcommittee	0	21	8	12	41
Total	5	21	16	15	57
1985–86					
House	0	14	12	7	33
Senate	5	8	5	3	21
Full committee	5	0	2	2	9
Subcommittee	0	22	15	8	45
Total	5	22	17	10	54
1987–88					
House	0	18	27	13	58
Senate	2	15	8	8	33
Full committee	2	0	3	5	10
Subcommittee	0	33	32	16	81
Total	2	33	35	21	91
1977–88 *totals (percent)*					
House	0(0)	63(58)	74(63)	39(59)	176(52)
Senate	46(100)	46(42)	44(37)	27(41)	163(48)
Full committee	46(100)	0(0)	25(21)	18(27)	89(26)
Subcommittee	0(0)	109(100)	93(79)	48(73)	250(74)

Source: Congressional Information Service; hearing manifests were searched for any mention of IGs by name.
a. Some early IG nominations involved two hearings—one before the authorizing committee and another before the Governmental Affairs Committee. This practice was not continued into the 1980s. Furthermore, many Reagan nominations were forwarded to the Senate floor without a formal hearing.

percent in the Senate, which confirms the first hypothesis; 250 appearances, or 74 percent, were before subcommittees of either chamber, which confirms the second; and 143 appearances or 81 percent, of the 176 House IG appearances came at the subcommittee level, which confirms the third. As one legislative staffer explained the phenomena, "The IGs are often the number one or number two witness at the subcommittee level, and are always well prepared. With the number of hearings that go on each day up here reaching the dozens, if not hundreds, having a reliable front witness is a big advantage, especially at the subcommittee level where it may be the IG or no one at all."

Four other patterns emerge from the data presented in table 3-2. First, subtracting nomination hearings, which Congress does not control, Senate interest in IGs followed a roller-coaster course. The number of Senate IG appearances was twenty-one in the 95th–96th Congresses (1977–80), rose to twenty-seven in the 97th (1981–82), dropped to twenty-two in the 98th (1983–84), sank further to sixteen in the 99th (1985–86), then moved up to thirty-one in the 100th (1987–88). One explanation for the final rebound could have been the return of a Democratic majority, which may have seen greater value in giving fraud, waste, and abuse in the Reagan administration increased attention.

Second, subcommittee interest in the IGs grew steadily, even as full committee interest fell dramatically. Subcommittee appearances went from a low of thirty-five in the 95th–96th Congresses to eighty-one in the 100th, in part because the IGs may have been suited for the less visible environment of subcommittees. As the number of oversight days increased, the IGs filled some of the open witness chairs.

Third, subcommittees were the primary consumers of IG policy testimony; for example, testimony regarding investigations and suggestions for agency improvement. Excluding Senate nomination hearings (which always occurred at the full committee level) and the "other" category (which generally included oversight of the IG concept or testimony on amendments to the IG Act), while including program appearances and appropriations testimony (which often contained discussions of agency-wide problems, recommendations, and so on), 89 percent of IG policy input occurred at the subcommittee level.

Fourth, the number of program hearings attended by IGs increased between the 96th and 97th Congresses, dropped dramatically in the 98th, grew sightly in the 99th, and then more than doubled in the 100th. The decline may have reflected Democratic suspicion in the House in the wake of Reagan's decision to fire most of the Carter IGs in 1981 and Republican unwillingness in the Senate to expose their new president to criticism. The strong rebound in the 100th Congress could have again been a reflection of Democrats in both chambers preparing for the 1988 presidential campaign.

These four trends appeared to continue into the first years of the Bush administration. In 1990, for example, HHS IG Richard Kusserow testified twenty-three times before Congress. Thirteen of the appearances were before House subcommittees, two before House full committees, six before Senate subcommittees, and two before Senate full committees.

Among Kusserow's topics of discussion were developments in the generic drug industry before the House Aging Subcommittee on Consumer Interests; Medicare Part B claims processing in Georgia and tobacco control before the House Energy and Commerce Subcommittee on Health and the Environment; administrative costs of foster care before the House Ways and Means Subcommittee on Human Resources; and health care fraud in Florida before the Ways and Means Subcommittee on Oversight.[44]

However congressional staff are viewed—as power maximizers, entrepreneurs, risk avoiders, or certainty cravers—information was, and still is, the coin of realm. As a key legislative player said,

> The IG Act basically moved Congress from retail into wholesale. One of the basic reasons for adopting the idea was that we had been busting our butts to cover even a fraction of our agencies. It wasn't that we couldn't get information, but it was always like pulling teeth. The IGs gave us a middleman in the system, someone who would give us regular input through the semiannual reports and irregular access through the development of good working relationships. It wasn't our only source of information by any means, but it cut down on some of the spade work we would have had to do, and let us go directly to more detailed investigations.

The question becomes, however, what kind of business were the IGs in? The answer is that Congress most likely would be interested in compliance monitoring. Compliance monitoring has clear advantages for a Congress composed of highly entrepreneurial members who must operate with few resources. The IG compliance findings are more numerous, carry more visibility in a scandal-conscious Washington, and offer greater chances for credit claiming. As for recommendations, compliance monitoring yields less expensive options with a greater potential for passage and fit more comfortably into existing congressional jurisdictions. Moreover, the advantages are equally well known at the other end of Pennsylvania Avenue, where presidents and their staffs also worry about making headlines, claiming credit, and enacting legislation.

CONCLUSION: THE CHOICE OF COMPLIANCE

Congress made many choices along the way to final passage of the 1976 and 1978 IG acts, not the least of which was one to adopt the strong right arm job description for the IGs. Of all the decisions, however, perhaps none was more important than settling on the primary definition of accountability.

Congress had a number of options for addressing fraud, waste, and abuse. It could have made a major reinvestment in the basic administrative infrastructure through new delivery and accounting systems, computer modernization, reorganization, and so on. It could have invested in government's human capital through salary increases (instead of pay freezes) and new recruitment strategies (instead of hiring caps), as well as provided the dollars for the training and career development opportunities promised under the 1978 Civil Service Reform Act. In short, Congress could have invested in the basic capacity of government, which, for example, could have prevented the savings and loan disaster in the late 1980s. Because neither Congress nor the president acted in time, the IGs were guaranteed to have plenty of grist for their compliance monitoring mill.[45]

In a perverse sense, the rise of the IG concept may have led Congress and the president to ignore the basic elements of program success. Establishment and expansion of the IGs allowed Congress and the president to heap ever greater responsibilities on government, always comfortable in the belief that the new legion of auditors and investigators would make sure everything worked out. By putting their faith in compliance accountability, Congress and the president took the less costly solution. Fixing the program infrastructure would be expensive—closing the pay gap between public and private employees alone would cost the federal government billions—and would not be guaranteed to work.

CHAPTER 4

Creating a Strong Right Arm

DRAFTING the first IG bill fell to two very different members of the House—Benjamin Rosenthal of New York and L. H. Fountain of North Carolina. Both were Democrats, both were members of the Government Operations Committee, and both held key subcommittee posts thereon. But there the similarities ended.

The two differed sharply, for example, on their legislative sympathies. Rosenthal was one of the committee's most liberal members, earning in 1975 a 96 percent rating from Americans for Democratic Action (ADA), 91 percent from the AFL-CIO, and zero from the Americans for Conservative Action (ACA). Fountain was one of the committee's most conservative, receiving 5 percent from ADA, 22 percent from the AFL-CIO, and 79 percent from ACA. In 1975, Fountain also voted in support of the conservative coalition—an alliance of Republicans and Southern Democrats—80 percent of the time.

The two also differed sharply in style. Rosenthal used his chairmanship of the Subcommittee on Commerce, Consumers, and Monetary Affairs as a stage for advocacy of a host of legislative issues, noting that "One congressman with a fair amount of chutzpah can awaken the public conscience." Fountain used his chairmanship of the Subcommittee on Intergovernmental Relations and Human Resources as a quiet platform for more traditional committee work.[1]

Although Fountain would later move forward with his own proposal, Rosenthal was the first member of Congress to draft a bill creating an inspector general at HEW, introducing H.R. 5302 on March 20, 1975. Rosenthal's maverick "showhorse" style may help explain his image of the IG as the lone wolf investigator, while Fountain's more traditional "workhorse" approach may shed light on his view of the IG as a more cooperative member of the president's management team. By opting for the Fountain alternative, Congress gave the IGs the opportunity to be more than just narrow compliance monitors, while providing more opportunities for presidential influence and control.

WHAT MIGHT HAVE BEEN

Rosenthal's vision of the IG as lone wolf is clear from the four cornerstones of his bill. First, Rosenthal's IG would serve for a single ten-year term, removable only by impeachment.[2] Second, the IG would have only one job—investigations; the word "audit" did not appear anywhere in the proposed statute, nor did "economy" or "efficiency." Third, Rosenthal's IG would transmit an annual report to Congress and the secretary of HEW simultaneously, without the prior approval of anyone in the executive branch. Fourth, the IG would have testimonial subpoena power; that is, the power to demand attendance of witnesses and the production of evidence "from any place in the United States at any designated place of hearing within the United States." In short, Rosenthal's IG would be unassailably independent, fully protected against removal, insulated from ambition, and in possession of an extremely potent investigatory tool—the testimonial subpoena, which many of today's IGs still seek to obtain.

Despite these protections and authorities, Rosenthal's proposal was much more limited than Fountain's alternative. Focusing only on investigations, Rosenthal's IG would operate within a narrow compliance mandate, probing only those programs involving federal funds. Out of bounds would have been cases involving third-party providers, Social Security counterfeiters, generic drug manufacturers, steroid sales representatives, or cigarette vendors selling to teenagers, all areas of inquiry chosen for exploration by HHS IG Richard Kusserow. Moreover, by being denied a role for audit, the IG would be deprived of an important source of day-to-day insight on departmental operations and effectiveness.

Nevertheless, HEW opposed the bill. As Under Secretary Marjorie Lynch testified,

> While we recognize the need to strengthen and coordinate our investigative and audit capacity, to clarify regulations and otherwise to assure greater integrity in the use of program funds, we believe that the proposed bill could seriously hamper the Secretary's ability to manage the Department. As a practical matter . . . the Inspector General would not be subordinate to the Secretary of Health, Education, and Welfare, and would not

be directly responsible to the Secretary, or, in fact, to anyone in the executive branch of Government.[3]

Rosenthal was undeterred. As he explained his bill before Fountain's subcommittee, to which the legislation had been referred, insulation from political pressure was the sine qua non of a strong IG:

> Consider HEW, if you will, as a mammoth service-oriented corporation. With a budget of $188.4 billion, HEW has larger revenues than Exxon, General Motors, Ford, Texaco, Mobil Oil, and Standard Oil of California combined.
>
> Now, imagine that each of these six largest industrial corporations in the United States was audited by an accounting firm whose head was hired by the chief executive of the corporation and whose financial report had to be reviewed and approved by the chief executive before being submitted, if ever, to the board of directors. That, obviously, would be ludicrous. It not only does not make sense, but it would violate numerous Federal securities laws.[4]

By May 1976, Rosenthal's proposal had forty cosponsors and had to be taken seriously. But Rosenthal's bill had been referred to the Intergovernmental and Human Relations Subcommittee, making it Fountain's responsibility, and he had very different ideas about what IGs should do.

For one thing, Fountain believed audit should be under the IG purview. For another, he voiced concern about the removal clause, asking Rosenthal point-blank: "Would there be any way to get rid of a person who turned out to be simply incompetent or disabled?" Acknowledging that his bill was "a very strong, very restrictive, and constraining kind of provision," Rosenthal nevertheless argued that

> The person who occupies the Office of Inspector General must be totally free from divisive or political influence, regardless of which branch of Government these influences emanate from. So, in drafting this legislation, we chose to protect that person from caprice or political influences. . . . What we did not want was for the Inspector General to be intimidated by the Secretary of HEW or an Under Secretary or Assistant Secretaries. . . . I wanted to give this Office the maximum amount of independence and freedom from influence, either from outside the agency or in the agency.[5]

After making explicit reference to the disbanding of the Agriculture OIG, Rosenthal offered his rationale for independence: "I want to cement this Inspector General in concrete and steel, so that no Secretary can either intimidate the Office or do away with it."[6]

However, with his proposed consumer protection agency pending in the full committee and needing every vote it could muster to pass, Rosenthal signaled his willingness to abide by the subcommittee's recommendation: "Whether the subcommittee wants to stay with this very restrictive language of impeachment is a matter where the subcommittee can exercise its own judgment, but the mandate to all of us, I think, is the integrity and independence of this Office."

The subcommittee shortly moved forward with a broader measure making the IG more a part of the HEW management team, subject to easier removal by the president, free from any term of office, stripped of testimonial subpoena authority, but reporting simultaneously to Congress and the president. In sum, the IG would have less power, but more oversight territory—an opportunity to go beyond the traditional compliance definition of accountability into performance and capacity building, but without as much insulation against executive pressure.

Fountain's bill did not leave the IGs defenseless, however. The IG would have the seven-day-letter option for reporting "particularly flagrant problems, abuses, or deficiencies" and somewhat clearer reporting responsibilities. Fountain's bill also viewed the IG as a much greater source of information for Congress; (1) providing such additional information or documents as might be requested by either House, (2) transmitting this information without further clearance or approval, and (3) having statutory access to any and all information as needed.

The fine print of the 1976 statute is not as important as the overall thrust. Congress had reached a crossroads on the IG concept and elected to take the broader, quieter path. The decision to make the IG both a strong right arm of the secretary and an independent conduit to Congress created an IG job description of great risk and great potential.

THE IG JOB DESCRIPTION

The HEW IG was operating smoothly by 1977, and a second IG was in the draft legislation creating Carter's proposed Department of Energy. Fountain and his staff had good reason to be optimistic about government-wide expansion. Increasing from one to twelve departments, however, would not happen without objections or compromises.

Objections En Route to Passage

Independence was the most important issue facing the IG legislation. Questions regarding the dual reporting arrangement and the removal clause were being asked at the Department of Justice and in the White House. At the November 7, 1977, cabinet meeting, domestic policy adviser Stuart Eizenstat recorded the following notes from OMB Director James McIntyre. ("Bell" is Attorney General Griffin Bell, and "J.C." is Carter.)

> 1. Gov't Operations passed Reorg. Plan 2.
> 2. Inspector Generals bill. Cut out part re report to Congress and other objectionable items.
>
> J.C.: Less restrictive than one in HEW and DOE. Not think its onerous. Good to have it uniform.
>
> Bell: Unconstitutional re. no removal w/o Congress rep.
>
> J.C.: Good to have if under my control.[7]

The exchange reveals but a small portion of the executive branch opposition. The departments of Agriculture and HUD, which had nonstatutory IGs at the time, also had problems with the bill.[8] As Elsa Porter, then assistant secretary for administration at Commerce, later would write, the opposition resided in the dual reporting provision and the adversarial relationship it created:

> It boggles the mind! Had the legislation merely created the IG's [sic] in GAO's image and left them as the agency's relatively independent auditing and investigating arm, reporting to the head of the agency, I think the model might work. But in forcing dual allegiance (and, therefore, dual dependency) of the IG to both the Executive and the Congress, the legislation creates an enormous problem of trust for the IG's to overcome. Put another way, it plants the seeds of distrust.[9]

The Justice Department also had concerns about the dual reporting channel, calling it "an impermissible infringement on the prerogatives and responsibilities of the Executive."[10] Also objecting to the bill as a dilution of the president's authority under the "take care" clause of the Constitution, Justice disliked three specific provisions:

> (a) *Transmittal of information to Congress without clearance or approval.* Section 4(e) of the bill provides that the information required by the bill shall be transmitted to Congress without further clearance or approval. This clearly conflicts with the

President's power to control and supervise all replies and comments from the Executive Branch to Congress. . . .

(b) *Power of removal.* Section 2(c) provides that, while the President would have the power to remove an Inspector General, he must communicate his reasons for removal to both Houses of Congress. We believe that this restriction, even as limited as it is, constitutes an unconstitutional infringement on the unqualified power of the President to remove officers of the Executive Branch. . . .

(c) *Budget submission.* Section 5(a)(5) would provide that if an Inspector General deems that a budget request for his office has been reduced so as to affect adversely the performance of his duties, he is to inform Congress without delay. This provision is an obvious interference with the disciplined order necessary for effective functioning within the Executive Branch. Does it not constitute a typical example of encouraging, in James Madison's words, the joining of high Executive officers "in cabal" with Congress?

Justice also objected to what it saw as a congressional usurpation of executive functions. "In our view," the Justice Department counsel wrote, "the continuous oversight of Executive agencies contemplated by the bill is not a proper legislative function but is rather a serious distortion of our constitutional system."[11] Furthermore, according to Justice, the semiannual reports violated the president's constitutional privilege to withhold information:

Congress has other legitimate, and fully effective, means of acquiring the information which the bill seeks to make available to Congress. Congressional committees are quite vigilant in seeking the information they require, and the consistent policy of the Executive Branch has been to cooperate as fully as possible with Congressional requests for information. In addition, Congress may utilize the General Accounting Office as it wishes in order to obtain appropriate information on government programs. We believe that these methods have proven fully adequate in the past, and hence no overriding need can be asserted to justify this more intrusive form of inquiry.[12]

Ironically, this opposition was neutralized by one of Carter's own appointees, HEW Secretary Joseph Califano. His department had lived comfortably with an IG for two years, and Califano saw nothing to worry about. Juxtaposed against eight days of complaints, Califano's testimony had a singular impact. As James Naughton, the subcommittee's counsel, later would explain, Califano and his highly respected IG, Thomas Morris, were held in reserve until the ninth and last day of the hearings when their endorsement would make the greatest counterpoint. Witness the following exchange.

Mr. FOUNTAIN. Mr. Secretary, has your Office of Inspector General, as established by statute, in any way impaired your efforts to carry out HEW's mission?

Mr. CALIFANO. No, it has not, Mr. Chairman. It has actually helped greatly.

Mr. FOUNTAIN. Has the existence of a statutory Office of Inspector General in any way inhibited your capability to investigate problem areas in departmental programs and operations?

Mr. CALIFANO. No. Again, it has helped.

Mr. FOUNTAIN. Has Mr. Morris at any time refused or failed to carry out any request you have made for investigations or audits of particular programs?

Mr. CALIFANO. No—despite the fact that I keep calling him up and asking him to do more. It is all underway.

Mr. FOUNTAIN. Have you had any significant problems, in your judgment, which are due to the provisions of law establishing your Office of Inspector General?

Mr. CALIFANO. No, Mr. Chairman.[13]

Although Califano's dutifully noted White House opposition to certain features of the emerging bill, particularly the reporting and appointment clauses, the die was cast.

The Merits of Compromise

The debate surrounding the 1978 IG Act is best viewed as a political dispute between separate institutions sharing power. The issues would not be resolved through discussion of legal precedents, but by balancing presidential and congressional interests.

Congress was willing to test the separation of powers doctrine in more than the IG Act. For example, the 1978 Civil Service Reform Act contained a provision creating an Office of Special Counsel to investigate merit system violations with the explicit authority to "transmit to the Congress on the request of any committee or subcommittee thereof, by report, testimony, or otherwise, information or views on functions, responsibilities, or other matters relating to the Office, *without review, clearance, or approval by any other administrative authority.*"[14]

Congress also passed Title VI of the 1978 Ethics in Government Act creating an independent counsel mechanism for investigating and, if appropriate, prosecuting high-level criminal complaints. Not only would these independent counsels be appointed by a special court (the Special Division), which also determined the counsel's prosecutorial jurisdiction, but they would be removable, other than by impeachment and conviction, "only by the personal action of the attorney general and only for good cause, physical disability, mental incapacity, or any other condition that substantially impairs the performance of such independent counsel's duties."[15] In the event of such action, the attorney general is required to report to both the Special Division and the Senate and House Judiciary Committees "specifying the facts found and the ultimate grounds for such removal."[16]

The independent counsel provisions were sustained by the Supreme Court in *Morrison* v. *Olson*, a case pitting independent counsel Alexia Morrison against former assistant attorney general, and investigatory target, Theodore Olson.[17] Writing for the seven-member majority in 1988, Chief Justice William H. Rehnquist dismissed the idea that the independent counsels were an invasion of executive prerogative. First, Congress had not created for itself a role in the removal of executive officials other than its established powers of impeachment and conviction. Second, and more importantly, Congress had not violated separation of powers in creating the independent counsel mechanism.

The point here is that the compromises on the 1978 IG Act were motivated not by a fear of constitutional challenges, but by real politics. Neither chamber of Congress showed any reluctance to create novel reporting arrangements and restrictive removal clauses, whether in the IG acts, the Civil Service Reform measure, or the Ethics in Government Act. The Democratic Congress had ample reason to accommodate the Democratic president, particularly in his first year of office. And evidence of accommodation exists particularly when comparing Fountain's original bill, H.R. 2819, and the House-passed version, H.R. 8588, authored by committee chairman Brooks. Although the differences are many and varied, four specific changes deserve attention:

PAY. In one of the most puzzling changes, the House-passed bill split the IGs into two tiers, one to be paid at the higher Executive Level IV of the presidential appointee schedule, the other to be paid at Executive Level V. The first tier was composed of HEW, Agriculture,

HUD, Labor, Transportation, and VA; the second, Commerce, Interior, General Services Administration (GSA), Environmental Protection Agency (EPA), NASA, and Small Business Administration (SBA). Although making an argument that the first-tier IGs had an easier time establishing themselves than the second-tier would be difficult, in part because three of the four offices had existed in some form before the 1978 act, the split did create a sense among some of the lower-paid IGs that they had a tougher task creating legitimacy in their agencies. (Congress eliminated the tiers in 1988.)

REMOVAL. The second major change involved the removal clause. After completely eliminating the requirement that the president report the reasons for removal to both houses of Congress, the House compensated only in part by adding the following qualifications for IG appointees: "demonstrated ability in accounting, auditing, financial analysis, law, management analysis, public administration, or investigations." The gesture was largely symbolic, however, because practically any person with an undergraduate degree and a mix of career experience would qualify.

REPORTING. The House-passed bill also softened several key reporting requirements from Fountain's original. First, in a small symbolic change the IG list of duties and responsibilities was amended to remove the phrase "fully and currently" from the requirement to keep Congress and the heads of their departments and agencies informed of fraud and other serious problems.[18] Second, and more significantly by far, the revised bill no longer contained the provision requiring a report to Congress of particularly serious or flagrant abuses. Although the IGs were still required to report those abuses immediately to their department or agency heads, the seven-day letter was gone.

Not all of the changes weakened congressional access to information, however. The House-passed bill substituted a semiannual report for Fountain's annual requirement, and required that each report contain a full list of all flagrant abuse brought to the attention of the department or agency head. The House also required that each report contain a list of all audit and investigative activities by the Office of Inspector General, thereby giving Congress a closer view of what was happening inside the agency.

BUDGET. H.R. 8588 dropped the provision requiring the IGs to inform Congress of any cuts in their budgets deemed to interfere with the adequate working of their offices. This requirement, while short of a simultaneous budget submission to Congress and the agency head, would have been a significant signal that the IGs were to be protected. Instead, the House measure was silent on staff and budget floors, leaving the IGs to negotiate each year's base both with their agencies and the budget examiners at OMB.

These four changes moved the new IGs closer to their agency leadership. Lacking budget protection, for example, four agencies—HHS, Labor, AID, and NASA—later would impose ceilings on OIG staff and budget, while a fifth, GSA, came to set the annual OIG budget through a review board composed of program administrators, whom the IG was tasked to monitor. By 1983, all of the then-seventeen IGs were reporting difficulty getting their budget requests to the agency head, leading GAO to recommend that, at the very minimum, the IGs be allowed to send their budgets in "unmodified" form directly to the top.[19]

All in all, however, the president had done well in the first round of compromise. All three Justice Department concerns were addressed to the full satisfaction of the president, a fact Eizenstat noted in a passing reference at the April 10, 1978, cabinet meeting.

A Step Back Toward Rosenthal?

The final version of the IG Act took shape more like Fountain's earlier, stronger proposal largely because of pressure from two senators—Thomas Eagleton, chairman of the Senate Subcommittee on Governmental Efficiency and the District of Columbia, and Abraham Ribicoff, chairman of the Senate Committee on Governmental Affairs.

The Senate never had been enthusiastic about the IG Act, waiting until July 1978 to hold its first hearings on the measure. Nevertheless, facing a 388–6 margin on final House passage of the bill, the Senate turned its attention to "perfecting" the legislation, strengthening the IG at almost every turn. By the time the bill left the floor, the Senate had restored the semiannual reporting requirement, Fountain's original removal clause, and the seven-day-letter, added whistleblower protections, moved toward an IG for the Department of Defense, established new IG authority to review existing and proposed legislation and regulations, and required all IG reports to be made public within sixty days.

Of all the Senate amendments, however, none appeared more important than the protection against agency interference: "Neither the head of the establishment nor the officer next in rank below such head shall prevent or prohibit the Inspector General from initiating, carrying out, or completing any audit or investigation, or from issuing any subpoena during the course of any audit or investigation." Adding up the changes, the Senate had moved past Fountain's vision of an IG, and if not all the way back to Rosenthal's lone wolf version, then at least to an IG with broader access to information, expanded authority, and greater protection from executive interference.

The Senate Governmental Affairs Committee noted in its legislative report that the final bill balanced independence against the needs of management, taking into account the lingering concerns that "the Inspector and Auditor General may become an adversary of the agency head and undermine his ability to run the agency." Although the committee recognized the need to protect the IG from undue pressure, it also stated its view that "an Inspector and Auditor General's efforts will be significantly impaired if he does not have a smooth working relationship with the department head." In the most significant statement of future expectations in the entire IG Act legislative history, the committee offered the following assessment:

> If the agency head is committed to running and managing the agency effectively and to rooting out fraud, abuse, and waste at all levels, the Inspector and Auditor General can be his strong right arm in doing so, while maintaining the independence needed to honor his reporting obligations to Congress. The committee does not doubt that some tension can result from this relationship, but the committee believes that the potential advantages far outweigh the risks.[20]

The Senate's version of the IG Act emerged almost intact when the final bill cleared Congress. The Senate lost the "inspector and auditor general" title, the associated definitions of audit and investigation, and the Defense IG, but prevailed elsewhere. Because the effective date of the legislation was October 1, 1978, acting IGs were at work before the president made the nominations.

INSTITUTIONALIZED AMBIVALENCE

The IGs were to be neither the lone wolf imagined by Rosenthal nor the strong right arm sought by Fountain. The IGs ended up being a bit of both, ready to fire off a seven-day letter alerting Congress of flagrant abuse while remaining under the general supervision of their secretaries and administrators, empowered to audit and investigate without interference while staying faithful members of the president's subcabinet.

Unfortunately, the dual reporting channel, and the resulting congressional protection, create an unavoidable challenge: "Anybody in the Executive Branch is going to be suspicious as heck if anybody in his employ reports directly to the Hill and there are honest concerns about that." State IG Sherman Funk testified in 1988:

Now, let's multiply these concerns. Suppose an IG gives bad news to the Hill, and someone up here slips it to a newspaper. The next thing, the bad news is blazed on page 1. It is no wonder that we often are regarded with great suspicion. The Hill is worried about the IG's being co-opted by management, and management is worried about our being a conduit to the Hill. We are stuck right in the middle. If we are seen talking to somebody from the Hill, "Ah-huh, the IG's leaking information or giving away stuff about his findings." If we get too cozy with management, we are being co-opted. This is what I call straddling the barbed wire fence.[21]

A classic collision of separation of powers was taking place. How could the IGs serve both Congress and the president at the same time? Moreover, in an era of divided government, when IGs worked for a Congress of the majority party and a president of the minority, how could they serve one without denying the other?

No event more clearly illustrates this ambivalence than the HUD scandal. Tasked as the strong right arm of the secretary and the eyes of Congress, the HUD IG seemingly could do no right. Blow the whistle prematurely, and the Reagan administration would have ample evidence of disloyalty. Blow the whistle too late, and Congress would have a scapegoat.

The problem was that the HUD IG never had been given the authority to "make sure this doesn't happen," as Representative Christopher Shays later put it. As HUD Secretary Samuel Pierce testified, he had refused to act on a March 1988 IG recommendation to suspend the Section 8 Moderate Rehabilitation (Mod Rehab) Program.[22] Asked how he could so "cavalierly disregard" the IG, Pierce said, "I wanted to give the [other staff] a chance. After all, there were other people involved with this who were working on this thing and that was my General Counsel, the Under Secretary as well as the Assistant Secretary of House. These people know something too. *The IG is not God.*"[23]

The IG indeed was but one of many claimants on the secretary's attention. In 1986, for example, HUD had one of the highest per capita concentrations of political appointees of any department in

government, including eight political executives, thirty-one noncareer senior executives, and one hundred Schedule C personal and
confidential assistants covering a career work force of 11,483. In
contrast, the Department of Health and Human Services had thirteen
political executives, fifty-seven noncareer senior executives, and
eighty-five Schedule C assistants covering a career work force of
133,842.

Congress could not expect the HUD IG's office, which had ab-
sorbed a 2 percent staff cut during the 1980s, to keep track of programs that, at the same time, had been converted to give the HUD
secretary greater discretion. The IG alone also could not prevent a
scandal planned by individuals who intended to defraud the government and designed their schemes in anticipation of IG investigations. Regarding misuse of the HUD Technical Assistance (TA)
program, the HUD deputy assistant secretary for program policy
development and evaluation testified that he deliberately shifted
responsibility from headquarters to the field after he looked at the
IG staffing:

> What I would do is, I began to move funds . . . to the field because
> in central headquarters he was very strongly staffed and had the
> capability and staff numbers set aside to review and do pre-
> audits on TA contracts. So what I would do is, I would kind of
> look at his organizational pattern on where he had the fewest
> employees at, and I began to move money because I knew that
> they didn't have the time to do pre-audits. . . . This allowed me
> the flexibility to move funds out of headquarters into the field,
> into area offices where his manpower and resources had to be
> categorized and prioritized, and therefore the TA Program would
> not be one of them they were prioritized for auditing purposes
> as far as pre-audits.[24]

The House Government Operations Employment and Housing
Subcommittee, which investigated the scandal, went so far as to use
the formal audit term "material weakness" to describe what it saw
as "the HUD Inspector General's inability to force an issue at HUD
with Secretary Pierce. This was exacerbated by a HUD management
which was often not responsive to and in some instances antagonistic
to findings and recommendations by the Inspector General."[25]

Of Warnings Made, But Clouded

The warnings in the IG reports covering the Reagan administration
now seem clear. Even in his first semiannual report covering

April–October 1981, HUD IG Charles Dempsey pulled no punches, listing problems under headings such as "Serious Accounting Deficiencies," "Inadequate Monitoring of Program Participants," and "Corrective Actions Promised But Not Taken." The litany of problems never stopped during Reagan's first term (see table 4-1). Nevertheless, as Dempsey later testified,

> I never received as much as a phone call. And if I may say ... at that time, between 1981 and 1984, we investigated the HUD Undersecretary, the Assistant Secretary, the Deputy Assistant Secretary, and three regional administrators. Action was taken against all. We received very heavy publicity in the *Washington Post* and other papers around the country. And I still didn't receive a call. It was reported to the Congress in the semiannual reports but it was also with heavy publicity. I never received a call from a congressional committee.[26]

But as the data in table 4-1 also show, virtually every report offered some reason for hope. As Senator William Roth (R-Del.), chairman of the Senate Governmental Affairs Committee during the first six years of the Reagan administration, remarked, "Frankly, just reading through these, you know, you sort of think there really is not a problem, that it is being taken care of."[27]

First, as with reports from other IGs, every HUD report started with a list of statistical accomplishments, which grew more impressive with each passing year. From the April–September 1981 report that celebrated $24 million in cash recoveries and savings, 1,168 new cases, 111 indictments, and 68 convictions to the end of Pierce's tenure in 1988, progress always was evident. In its first ten years of operation, the HUD OIG reported cumulative recoveries of more than $542 million, "cost efficiencies" of more than $307 million, and convictions numbering 2,840.

Second, and much more importantly, the executive summaries of the IG's report almost always contained a message of progress under way. Save for the report covering the period October 1984–March 1985, which contained nothing but warnings, the rest of the early reports gave Congress and the president some reason, even excuse, to breath easy. "As evidenced by the efforts described in this Semiannual Report," read the October 1981 report in a harbinger of future endorsements, "the Secretary and his staff are fully committed to improving the integrity, efficiency, effectiveness, and responsiveness of HUD management and programs. The support and cooperation afforded our office has been excellent. We are looking forward to further cooperative efforts in the future."

Table 4-1. *HUD Semiannual Executive Summaries, 1981–85*

Warning	*Reassurance*

April 1982

The Department has problems with (1) program management (including planning, executive and monitoring); and (2) resource and asset management. This report deals with a number of major weaknesses in program monitoring and accounting functions. Our prior semiannual reports contained specifics on other aspects of these two broad areas. The Department has had a long history of these problems.

As a matter of perspective, we would like to comment on the unprecedented cooperation we have received from the current management team. We commend the attitudes and actions of those managers who are dedicated to addressing the problems in HUD.

October 1982

As we stated in our last report, the Department has problems with (1) program management . . . ; and (2) resource and asset management. This report highlights a number of major weaknesses in controls over fund management by the Department and its program participants, as well as problems in program management by HUD staff. Also the report provides illustrations of significant abuses of various HUD programs by participants.

HUD managers and employees are cooperating and supporting our work. There has been an increased emphasis by managers on accountability of HUD staff and program participants. . . . We are encouraged by these signs of growing concern for improved management and program integrity.

April 1983

In general, the problems discussed [in the following report] focus on weaknesses in cash management and program compliance by the participants in HUD's programs.

We are working with program managers to resolve and correct these problems.

October 1983

This report summarizes the significant problems noted and recommendations made during the period, and emphasizes our audit focus on weaknesses in the operations of financially troubled Public Housing Agencies.

This effort is continuing and HUD management has been very receptive to our recommendations for improving Public Housing Agency operations.

Table 4-1 *(continued)*

Warning	Reassurance
April 1984	
Our office devoted significant resources to reviewing the public housing program. Within the Department, we examined HUD's operating policies and procedures. Externally, we focused on the overall management of financially troubled Public Housing Agencies (PHAs). While the majority of PHAs operate effectively, there are inherent weaknesses that need attention. The Department must improve its ability to detect problems and assist PHAs in meeting their goals and objectives. We believe there is a pressing need for cooperative efforts at the Federal, State, and local levels to address these weaknesses, thereby improving the public housing program.	Departmental efforts to assess program vulnerabilities, increase employee awareness, and redirect monitoring to high-risk areas clearly demonstrate the Department's commitment to strengthen operations and to minimize fraud and abuse. We commend management for this commitment and strongly urge its continuation.
October 1984	
This report illustrates continued weaknesses in HUD's monitoring of program participants. Although the Department has repeatedly attempted to improve its performance, inadequate monitoring continues to be a persistent problem of significant concern to us.	The Secretary and Under Secretary have taken an active interest in correcting this situation. They have supported changes in monitoring policies and procedures. Their interest is demonstrated in the Department's effort to obtain legislative authority that would make computer matching more feasible and to initiate a quality control system for rental assistance payments.

Source: Department of Housing and Urban Development, Office of the Inspector General, semiannual reports to Congress, 1981–85.

The positive signals also were evident on Capitol Hill. Testifying on his March–September 1985 semiannual report before the House Housing and Community Development Subcommittee, HUD IG Paul Adams had ample opportunity to air his continued frustrations with problems at the department. Instead, after summarizing a long list of serious weaknesses, Adams took a more reassuring tone, balancing his role as strong right arm with his reporting responsibilities to Congress:

Weaknesses do exist in the administration of housing programs, but HUD is taking positive steps to identify and eliminate these weaknesses. Effective, strengthened housing programs depend on HUD's continued pursuit of initiatives to prevent and detect fraudulent activities and programmatic weaknesses. Our office will continue to provide our full support to these efforts and report troublesome areas so they can be addressed timely [sic].[28]

Adams even argued that "we believe the media tends to exaggerate the pervasiveness of the problem," prompting House Banking Committee chairman Henry Gonzalez (D-Tex.) to remark: "Well, you know, you can hardly expect the media not to get excited about those things. I really regret to see [the criticism of the media], because it seems to me that that is more proper from the PR [public relations] Department."[29] Thus, even as Adams testified in 1986, a small band of political appointees at the top of HUD had converted the department into what the House Government Operations Committee called "an agency in total disarray." As the final committee report put it: "During much of the 1980s, HUD was enveloped by influence peddling, favoritism, abuse, greed, fraud, embezzlement and theft. In many housing programs objective criteria gave way to political preference and cronyism, and favoritism supplanted fairness. 'Discretionary' became a buzzword for 'giveaway.'"[30]

Third, many of the reports were just plain boring, so filled with auditese that only the most dedicated staffer or reporter could get through and understand them. As Brookings Institution Governmental Studies director Thomas Mann testified before the Senate's HUD investigating subcommittee,

I listened to Mr. Dempsey and Mr. Adams, and I do not have any doubt that they believe their signals were crystal clear to the Congress, but for someone who is not an aficionado of these reports, I have to tell you they are long, vague, and boring, and they are not likely to get the attention of members of the Congress or of congressional staff.[31]

In addition, most reports were little more than collections of highly individualized findings, often mixing the small and large in seemingly random order. Although Adams in 1989 would look back over the scandal and conclude that ten years of audit and investigative reports "clearly showed a pervasive pattern of inadequate internal controls and financial management systems . . . [that] created a climate in which fraud and abuse can thrive," the reports in fact were a veritable cacophony of trees in which a forest would be almost impossible to spot.

Only in 1989, for example, can a complete description of the term "internal control" and an analysis of the systemic problems that plagued the department be found. Until then, one compliance finding followed another, with no link to the broader performance and capacity questions that might yield lasting reforms.

Omission or Commission?

Ultimately, however, the greatest omissions were not made in semiannual reports, but in the legislative decisions of 1978. Representative Shays was misinformed in his view of the IG's role in the search for accountability: "My impression of the IG's office was that you looked at wrongdoing, found it out, and then you made sure something was done about it." Unlike the original IG, foreign assistance, the HUD IG had but one power; the power to persuade. The HUD IG could not enforce recommendations or suspend programs.[32]

With Congress and OMB uncertain readers of their reports, Dempsey and Adams had only one place to turn for resolution of the continuing problems: Samuel Pierce. The IGs, however, are only as influential as their secretaries and administrators want them to be.[33] They may have guaranteed access, ample staff, and sophisticated organizations, but they have no authority to compel their bosses to respond.

The central question in the HUD scandal is not so much whether the IG reported clearly, but whether the IG can be held accountable for the failure to catch and highlight the problems earlier. To what extent can the IGs be expected to prevent wrongdoing? The answer is that the IGs offer one line of defense, effective only if Congress and the president listen.[34]

Thus, the president and Congress both bear much of the responsibility for the HUD scandal. As the House Government Operations Committee concluded, the scandal reflected a decade-long politicization of HUD as dozens of new appointees were added at the top of the department, high rates of turnover were experienced among those appointees, a lack of commitment to basic programs was evident, and a reverence was apparent for the "revolving door" in which former appointees returned for favors from their political cronies. According to the Senate HUD investigating committee,

With over a third of its top management positions going to noncareer appointments, clearly political appointees were making inroads at HUD. And, as an agency, HUD had a significantly higher number of political SES appointments government-wide.

In comparison to other Cabinet agencies for the last ten years, HUD ranked third in the percentage of its SES members who were political appointees.[35]

Unfortunately, the evidence suggests that as the quantity of HUD appointees went up, the quality went down. As one of Pierce's own lieutenants later testified, "Samuel Pierce got loaded up on him a group of Young Turks who were very political and on a must hire list, and we had no housing skills whatsoever."[36]

Presidents have the right to staff the departments as they wish, but the question remains whether the public interest has been well served by the exercise of this presidential power. According to the report's summary of the Mod Rehab Program,

> Projects pushed and lubricated by politically well-connected consultants and a cadre of ex-HUD officials received the lion's share of these increasingly scarce and valuable mod rehab funds. Some people with little or no experience in housing made a lot of money for a very limited amount of work. Well-connected political consultants such as former Interior Secretary James Watt received hundreds of thousands of dollars for talking to the "right people" at HUD, including Secretary Pierce, to obtain mod rehab funds. The selection process then in place at HUD for awarding mod rehab funds had all the competitiveness of professional wrestling.[37]

Congress committed sins of commission, too. The Senate confirmed many of the Mod Rehab participants on the "must hire list." Moreover, congressional repeal of the so-called fair-share allocation rule opened the process to graft. Congress acted favorably upon HUD's request for the change, even though it knew the extent of petty scandal in the department, a recurring theme in the *Washington Post* and *New York Times* headlines of the early 1980s. Having repealed the requirement, HUD quickly moved to a noncompetitive, influence-based approach, one about which Congress apparently never asked.

There was plenty of blame to go around for the HUD scandal—Congress, the president, the media, the IG, HUD employees. Despite that, a question arises: To what extent is monitoring of any kind, be it compliance, performance, or capacity-based, a substitute for actual investment?

The answer seems obvious. No amount of monitoring can make up for action on recommendations for front-end investment in government capacity. As the American private sector knows, fixing a problem after manufacture is a more expensive, and ultimately less effective, method for assuring quality than designing a product correctly in the first place. The teachings of the private sector's quality experts suggest that post-hoc inspection is no way to ensure quality. It did not work at HUD.

PART 3

Implementing the Act

The Class of 1979

IMPLEMENTING the Inspector General Act was not Jimmy Carter's top priority in 1978, the midpoint of his presidency. By the time Carter nominated the first IGs authorized under the act—the class of 1979—his main concern was saving his administration.

Outside Washington, Carter's honeymoon was over—public approval had fallen to 37 percent, down almost 40 points in two years.[1] Inside Washington, Congress had rejected many of Carter's top legislative proposals, including hospital cost containment, welfare reform, and the $50 tax rebate.[2] Joseph Califano, whose strong testimony in 1977 on behalf of the IG had provided important support, was about to be fired. The administration was into the "cycle of decreasing influence"—declining congressional support, a mid-term loss of seats in Congress—but not yet fully benefiting from the "cycle of increasing effectiveness" that comes with learning.[3]

This was hardly the most promising time for recruiting IGs or establishing their offices. Nevertheless, having signed the IG Act as a "chance to protect the taxpayer's dollar, to root out corruption, fraud, waste, mismanagement in the most effective and enthusiastic fashion," Carter set out to find twelve individuals to fill the new positions created under the 1978 act and one to occupy the Education post established under separate law.[4]

The first years under the IG Act reveal important lessons about how the IGs were accepted, rewarded, and encouraged. The Carter IGs had a remarkably tough time getting under way, in part because the administration was foundering and in part because of lingering resistance from the departments and agencies. The IGs soon discovered that to survive they needed alliances with Congress and the president, and that these alliances would depend in large measure on the IGs' ability to generate the kinds of findings and statistics rewarded on Capitol Hill and in OMB—those most easily generated by compliance monitoring.

CARTER'S CHOICES

The search for the first IGs was a model of deliberateness. As one White House staffer remembered, "Calls went to all the different groups—bar associations, accounting firms, inside players, a lot of seasoned career folks, some of the national groups—looking for women and minorities. We were proud of the process. We wanted to signal the rest of the administration that minorities in particular had a role to play at or near the top."

Once the initial pool of roughly twenty-five candidates was selected, every agency was given two to three names per slot. Although the White House shaped the search, if only by determining the initial pool, the departments and agencies did have a say in the final choices. As a second White House staffer added, "It made no sense to put people in a job where the agency was completely opposed. But we never gave the agencies carte blanche. They could tell us if they were uncomfortable, but had no veto. The minute we let the agencies pick their own people as IG, common sense says they wouldn't be picking heavy-weights."

Whether measured by demographics, career focus, nomination experiences, or frustrations and satisfactions of the job, the Carter IGs look different from those that followed in the Reagan administration.[5] The more conservative Reagan search process moved the IGs in three new directions: (1) toward a more traditional appointee demographic profile, represented by greater education, particularly in private institutions and the Ivy League, (2) toward an inside career path, characterized by a preference for nominees with OIG experience, and (3) toward a demonstrated allegiance to the executive branch, revealed by a changing view of the audience for the IG reports.

A Demographic Profile

If not for the reappointments of Frank Sato and June Gibbs Brown in 1981, the number of Reagan appointments of women and nonwhites would be at or near zero. Because Brown served in two separate posts under Reagan, she counts for two-thirds of the women appointed as Reagan IGs. The Carter appointees were younger, less experienced, slightly less educated, more likely to have backgrounds in the humanities or law enforcement, and more likely to be female or a

Table 5-1. *The IG Demographic Profile, Carter versus Reagan*
Percent

Variable	Carter[a]	Reagan[a]	Total
Age at appointment[b]			
Under 50	50	19	28
50–60	40	31	33
61–70	10	50	39
Gender[c]			
Female	33	7	15
Male	67	91	85
Race[c]			
Nonwhite	17	4	7
White	83	96	93
Highest degree earned[d]			
Bachelor's	46	39	41
Law	36	19	24
Master's	9	39	30
Ph.D.	9	4	5
Undergraduate institution[d]			
Ivy League	9	12	10
Private	46	54	51
Public	46	35	38
Undergraduate major[d]			
Finance, accounting, or business	36	39	38
Humanities	27	19	22
Law enforcement	27	15	19
Political science	9	27	22

a. Data are based on responses from 12 Carter and 28 Reagan (first- and second-term) appointees. Some respondents did not answer every question. Total may not add to 100 because of rounding.
b. $N = 36$.
c. $N = 40$.
d. $N = 37$.

member of a minority than the Reagan IGs (see table 5-1). Only five of Carter's appointees survived into the first Reagan administration—three were white males, one was an Asian male (Sato), and one was a white female (Brown).

Carter's effort to cast a diverse net is reflected in the demographic profiles. As Mary Bass, IG nominee at Commerce, said about her appointment: "I'm a woman, I was General Counsel and Inspector General at a large institution, and I'm good. . . . if someone sought to assemble a list of good women—as they did—my name would come up."[6] Further, while the majority of Reagan's appointees were aged fifty or over, half of Carter's were under age fifty. Paul Boucher was the youngest, thirty-seven at the time of his nomination at SBA, followed by Marjorie Fine Knowles, forty, at Labor.

Two IG characteristics regarding education also deserve mention. First, percentage-wise, substantially fewer Carter than Reagan appointees elected political science as their undergraduate major. Political science majors who later became IGs reported less difficulty mastering departmental procedures and were less likely than finance or humanities majors to experience problems with the short-term orientation of Washington politics or to get frustrated with either the slow pace of decisionmaking in their agencies or statistical measures of success.

Second, separately or combined, the Carter and Reagan IGs had a rather different educational profile from many of the presidential appointees with whom they served. According to the National Academy of Public Administration study, 75 percent of the appointees who served in the Johnson through Reagan administrations, 1964–84, had advanced degrees, compared with 59 percent of the IGs. In addition, 25 percent of the appointees took their undergraduate degrees from Ivy League schools, compared with 10 percent of the IGs.[7]

A Career Profile

The IGs of the two administrations were culled from somewhat different pools, but similarities between the groups do exist (see table 5-2).

Most of the Carter and Reagan IGs were recruited from jobs in the executive branch. Only three Carter IGs came from outside the federal bureaucratic establishment—one from a Washington, D.C., think tank; one from a private law practice, and one from a post as general counsel at a public university. Even here, one of the three, Thomas Morris, was more accurately on sabbatical from a long career as a federal auditor. This recruitment pattern stands in sharp contrast to that of other presidential appointees. According to the NAPA survey, only 41 percent of all appointees had any executive branch career or noncareer experience. The rest came from Congress and its staff, state and local government, or the private sector—15 percent from business and banking, 11 percent from private law, and 11 percent from education and research concerns such as think tanks and consulting firms.[8]

Despite these similarities in lengths and locations of service, the Carter and Reagan IGs identified with different careers. Almost half of the Carter IGs called themselves auditors, financial managers, or administrators, compared with 30 percent of the Reagan IGs. Moreover, while the two sets of appointees contain roughly equal

Table 5-2. *Backgrounds and Opinions of IGs, Carter versus
Reagan*
Percent

Variable	Carter[a]	Reagan[a]	Total
Years served in the executive branch[b]			
Less than 10	17	0	5
10–20	33	29	30
21–30	25	36	33
More than 30	25	36	33
Location of previous job[c,d]			
Inside executive branch			
Administration office			
Same department	7	3	4
Different department	40	15	17
IG office			
Same department	20	27	25
Different department	0	33	25
Program office			
Same department	0	3	4
Different department	13	12	15
Outside executive branch			
Administration office	13	3	8
Audit office	0	0	0
Investigation office	0	0	0
Other IG office	0	0	0
Program office	7	3	2
Self-identified career focus[e]			
Audit, financial management, or administration	46	31	35
Investigations or law	55	46	49
Program management or evaluation	0	23	16
Moving up from within[f]			
1 (Is a conflict of interest)	10	25	21
2	20	32	29
3	30	14	18
4	0	18	13
5 (Is not a conflict of interest)	40	11	18
Waste in government[b]			
1 (Government is very wasteful)	0	0	0
2	8	21	18
3	25	14	18
4	42	39	40
5 (Government is relatively efficient)	25	25	25

a. Data are based on responses from 12 Carter and 28 Reagan (first- and second-term) appointees. Some respondents did not answer every question. Totals may not add to 100 because of rounding.
b. $N = 40$.
c. Data derived from analysis of biographical information on the IGs.
d. $N = 48$.
e. $N = 37$.
f. $N = 38$.

numbers of self-identified investigators and lawyers, one-quarter of the Reagan IGs said they were program managers or evaluators, a career focus none of the Carter group chose.

The most plausible explanation for the higher incidence of administrators under Carter is that the IG offices had not existed prior to 1978 as a training ground for future IGs. Only 20 percent of the Carter IGs were promoted upward from another IG Office, compared with 63 percent under Reagan. The data, however, may overstate the case. Three of the Carter IGs already were sitting IGs—Charles Dempsey at HUD (nonstatutory), Thomas McBride at Agriculture (nonstatutory), and Thomas Morris at HEW (statutory)—while a fourth, Sato, had accepted the nonstatutory VA IGship created in anticipation of the 1978 act; a fifth, James Thomas at Education, had been the nonstatutory HUD IG from 1975 to 1977 before moving for two years to the Interstate Commerce Commission as the director of the Bureau of Accounts; and a sixth, Marjorie Fine Knowles, had been assistant general counsel in the Inspector General Division at HHS, a position technically within the general counsel's office but providing service directly to the IG.

During the first decade that the IG Act was in force, the IGships became important sources of new appointees. Several IGs served as mentors of future talent, working to develop their assistant IGs into full IG prospects. June Gibbs Brown, for example, developed at least four future IGs while at NASA—Robert Beuley, who would later go on to a post at Agriculture; John Layton, Energy; J. Brian Hyland, Labor; and Bill Colvin, NASA. Dempsey developed three while at HUD—John Martin who would move to EPA; Paul Adams, HUD; and Charles Gillium, SBA. Sherman Funk guided Frank DeGeorge, who would move up at Commerce.

Although few IGs expressed concerns about being promoted from a deputy or assistant IG post, perhaps because many came up that way, a substantial number objected to recruiting an IG from a non-IG position within the same agency. According to HHS IG Richard Kusserow, who came from outside the department:

> It seems to me as a general principle that it is a good idea to select your IG's from outside the agencies in which they are going to be an IG. They should not be creatures of the bureaucracy that they are going to later on have to question and oversee. I think, as a general rule with many exceptions, that selecting somebody who is qualified from one department and moving

them somewhere else in the Federal Government would be preferable to promoting them to inspector general in their own agency.[9]

In 1989, notwithstanding these concerns, the new secretary of veterans affairs proposed moving the director of the $15 billion veterans benefits program, Raymond Vogel, into the long vacant IG post.[10] Although his nomination was never forwarded to the Senate, Vogel survived at least two attempts to scuttle the nomination made by the IGs, who believed it involved a clear conflict. The IGs did not believe Vogel could be objective about programs he had administered and personnel he had hired.

The Vogel case and other celebrated Reagan-era conflicts of interest may explain why so many of the Reagan IGs came to oppose promotion to an IGship from a non-IG post within the same agency. When asked to rate how much of a conflict of interest existed in such a recruitment path—where 1 represents a conflict and 5 represents none—more than half of the Reagan IGs chose either 1 or 2, while 40 percent of the Carter IGs selected 5.

On the one hand, IGs from both administrations felt that having had a non-IG post within the same department or agency might help a new IG master program details, a source of some consternation among all the IGs interviewed. On the other hand, a significant number of IGs also felt that such a post might create the appearance, if not outright substance, of conflict of interest, an appearance that warranted a strong stand against such internal promotions. (For many, though not all, of these IGs, such concerns about appearance of conflict did not extend to their eligibility for the senior executive bonuses awarded under law by their department or agency heads.)

In contrast to these divided opinions on non-IG promotions, near unanimity of opinion emerged when IGs were asked whether promotion of a deputy IG in the same agency created a potential conflict. Only 14 percent of the Reagan and 9 percent of the Carter IGs answered "yes." Nevertheless, according to one IG later interviewed in person, moving from the deputy IG spot may not be a conflict of interest but perhaps is unwise: "Being in the IG office in the same department is now the path of least resistance to the top, but if you're in the same agency too long you (1) get to know senior career staff well, and (2) get jaded. It's not human to expect someone not to want to protect friends or skewer enemies they have made along the way, maybe decades ago. It's also not human to expect someone not to get bored from working the same programs year after year after year."

Table 5-3. *The IG Nomination Process, Carter versus Reagan*
Percent

Variable	Carter[a]	Reagan[a]	Total
Sources of news of the nomination[b]			
Department or agency official	60	48	51
Office of Management and Budget	0	18	14
White House personnel office	20	30	27
Other or combination of above	20	4	9
Responsibilities for the nomination[c]			
Department or agency official	46	61	56
Department or agency and White House	18	0	5
Inspector general	9	4	5
Office of Management and Budget	9	18	15
White House personnel office	9	4	5
Other or combination of above	9	11	10
IG nominee contact with sitting IGs[d]			
No	92	64	73
Yes	8	36	28
Weeks between nomination and confirmation[d]			
Less than 11	33	7	15
11–20	33	46	43
21–30	0	21	15
31–40	0	7	5
More than 40	33	18	23
Causes of nomination and confirmation delays[e]			
FBI field investigation	17	29	24
Financial disclosure	33	29	30
Senate confirmation process	33	52	45
All of the above	8	0	3
Other	17	5	9
No delays	25	33	30

a. Data are based on responses from 12 Carter and 28 Reagan (first- and second-term) appointees. Some respondents did not answer every question. Totals may not add to 100 because of rounding.
b. $N = 37$.
c. $N = 39$.
d. $N = 40$.
e. Some IGs answered the question only for their first appointment, while others answered for their multiple appointments. As a result, only the first appointment was coded, reducing the sample size from 40 appointees to 34 individual IGs. Respondents could give more than one answer. $N = 33$.

The Nomination Process

Being picked for an IG post by the White House personnel office is only the beginning of the process. The IG designee also must be told of his or her selection and formally nominated. The bearer of the news is an important indication of who the likely boss will be. When asked who had informed them of their nomination, the Carter and Reagan IGs again had slightly different answers (see table 5-3).

Under Carter, department and agency officials primarily were responsible for informing IG designees, a role reduced somewhat under Reagan. Few Carter IGs were informed by OMB, compared with 1 in 5 under Reagan. This greater OMB presence was the direct result of Reagan's 1981 mass firings of the Carter IGs.

Regardless of the bearer of the information, when asked who was responsible for their appointment, most IGs believed the department or agency had a prominent role in their selection. No matter how rigorous the White House search process, no matter how visible the role of sitting IGs in suggesting names, the process appears to have reinforced the Senate's view of the IG as working primarily for a secretary or administrator as a strong right arm.

Formal nomination is still not the end of the process. All presidential appointees must submit financial disclosure information and resolve any potential conflicts of interest; most must undergo an FBI field investigation; and those subject to Senate confirmation must fill out pre-hearing questionnaires and survive both a committee review and a floor vote. For noncontroversial appointments—those at the assistant secretary level or below, including the IGs—waiting becomes the order of the day, a pattern confirmed by the data in table 5-3.

In general, the Reagan IGs experienced more delays, particularly in the Senate confirmation process. By comparison, the class of 1979 was in office in record time. Almost half of the Reagan IGs waited more than twenty weeks to be confirmed. Because both sets of nominees were governed by the new ethics process required under the 1978 Ethics in Government Act, which added a new layer of delay, the explanation for the slowdown must rest elsewhere.

A first possibility is that the novelty of IG nomination hearings had worn off, relegating the IGs to the back of the nomination queue as authorizing committees disposed of more visible appointments. A second is that the Republican Senate majority, which came into power in 1981 after a twenty-five year interim, needed some time to learn the ropes. A third is that the events surrounding Reagan's mass firings caused enough concern in the Senate for each nominee to be given close inspection.

Despite the delays, most IGs remember the Senate process as being friendly, if somewhat unfamiliar. Most contacts were with congressional staff who were favorable to the IG concept. Given the IGs' career executive branch experience, few made contact with Congress before the nomination, and none appear to have used Capitol Hill connections to secure their appointments, largely because few had those contacts to begin with. As one would expect from a nominee to a Senate advise and consent post, all contacted their nominating committees before their hearings, and three-quarters had further contact with the Senate Governmental Affairs Committee. In addition, almost half made contact with the House, largely as a result of requests from their department or agency legislative liaison unit.

The formal hearings, too, went smoothly: introductions were cordial, opening statements were supportive toward the IG concept, and questions were easy. The IGs who appeared before Governmental Affairs faced Lawton Chiles (D-Fla.), one of the most personable members of the Senate, who asked three standard questions regarding background, any preconditions imposed by the White House, and conflicts of interest. The nomination next was sent to the full Senate for consideration and a vote. Looking back, the process was about as gentle as a Senate confirmation can be.

AN ABBREVIATED TERM

Once confirmed by the Senate, the IGs found their welcome to their departments and agencies far less friendly. The opposition to the IG concept that had shown itself during the 1978 hearings still was strong, particularly among the assistant secretaries for management and administration who had testified so vehemently against the idea. The opposition was similar to that encountered by Orville Freeman twenty years before in establishing the nonstatutory Agriculture IG:

> Finally this morning I called in the Department heads and told them that I had this in mind and had all but made up my mind and asked for their comments. Their comments were quite explosive. Sid Smith, an excellent Administrator, and a good soldier, said I had ruined his Christmas and proposed to cut off his right arm. Other comments were very vigorous. Administrators felt that Investigation and Audit is a part of their management function and a critical and essential tool for them and they resent and resist bitterly it being taken away from them. . . . I'm a little concerned because there could be a kind of revolt on this which could hurt our excellent spirit now. I'm also a bit concerned that the Appropriations Committees may buck a bit on this, but once we have started in this direction I think I must push ahead. And when I reflect on it only a bit, it becomes clear to me that this is a tool and a sort of power that really is critically essential. We'll see how it goes tomorrow.[11]

Allies and Adversaries

Concern about the proper location of the auditing and investigative function was common among the Carter assistant secretaries for administration and management. They had lost, with the introduction of IGs, the capacity to learn about departmental problems first. The following comment is a sample of the climate the new IGs faced:

> My own view is that the IG Act was one of the most destructive bills ever passed. (1) It undermined the secretary's responsibility for taking hold of scandal. I'm the first to concede that past years have produced some lightweights among the ranks of the political leadership, but the answer is to get better secretaries, not to destroy any last incentive for caring about performance. (2) It fragmented assistant secretary responsibility by vesting authority for one of our most important management tools in an adversarial unit. The problems of fraud and waste were certainly real, but the remedy wrong. It just wasn't right to put a do-gooder type in at the assistant secretary rank.

Because by 1979 federal personnel had been converted into a zero-sum game in which gains for one unit meant parallel losses for some other, these assistant secretaries knew that they would never be able to recapture their former roles and understood that they would have to beg for assistance. The establishment of OIGs, with their heavy demand for new staff, forced the agencies to make real choices.

Moreover, the new IGs arrived just as these once career-reserved management posts were being converted into political appointments. Beginning under Carter and continuing in earnest under Reagan, virtually every career assistant secretary for management and/or administration was replaced. To these career executives, the IG Act represented a further weakening of their posts. By 1989, only one of these assistant secretaryships, at the Department of Transportation, was still held by a career civil servant.

Yet many IGs were, and still are, career civil servants, drawn from the ranks of career auditors and investigators. The IGs and assistant secretaries for management had much more in common than either cared to admit. That they never forged an alliance is in part a consequence of OMB's growing sponsorship of the IGs under Reagan.

The Carter IGs could not have started work at a more difficult moment. Personnel ceilings were in effect across government as part of the compromise to win passage of the civil service reform legislation, the new Office of Personnel Management (OPM) was struggling to sort through a host of complicated changes affecting classification and filling of existing vacancies, and Carter was about to fire part of his cabinet.

Furthermore, rules governing the newly created Senior Executive Service (SES) appeared to conflict with IG authority to "select, appoint, and employ such officers and employees as may be necessary for carrying out the functions, power, and duties of the Office." Because the departments and agencies controlled all SES slots under policy guidance from OPM, and because the Civil Service Reform Act technically passed after the IG Act, albeit by a matter of days, the standard interpretation was that the IGs were bound by department-wide procedures, further limiting their ability to move quickly.[12]

At the mid- and entry level, the informal government-wide hiring cap of 1979 soon was converted into a formal government-wide freeze that prohibited the IGs, and the rest of their departments and agencies, from filling any vacancies existing on or after February 29, 1980. As the House Government Operations Committee later argued, "The impact of the hiring freeze was especially severe on those IG offices which experienced a large number of retirements or resignations or had a large number of vacancies on February 29, 1980. The Department of Transportation's Office of Inspector General was particularly hard-hit. Because of the freeze, that office had 94 vacancies in mid-1980 and faced the prospect of having to incur 65 more vacancies before being able to hire a single replacement."[13]

Whatever the obstacles—new SES rules, OPM chaos, hiring freezes, or Carter's plummeting popularity—the opportune time was not at hand to add staff or reorganize agencies. However, that is what many Carter IGs needed to do (see table 5-4). They faced plenty of obstacles to staffing, including inflexibility in personnel regulations and budget authority.

Given the limited amount of time and resources available to complete the major overhaul the Carter IGs deemed necessary, there was still much to be done when most left two years later. Perhaps the best the class of 1979 could hope for was to make the need for additional full-time-equivalent (FTE) positions known and to look for improvement in the second Carter term. Consider excerpts from the last IG semiannual reports under Carter, issued in March 1981 but in progress before the Reagan inauguration and the subsequent firings:

Agriculture: The lack of sufficient resources, both travel and personnel, continued to be a major impediment in terms of

Table 5-4. *Audiences and Operations of IGs, Carter versus Reagan*
Percent

Variable	Carter[a]	Reagan[a]	Total
State of the office upon arrival[b]			
1 (Running very smoothly)	0	7	6
2	25	4	8
3	0	11	8
4	13	32	28
5 (Needed major overhaul)	63	46	50
Need for additional staff[c]			
1 (Enough staff)	17	7	10
2	25	29	28
3	8	18	15
4	8	21	18
5 (Serious shortages)	42	25	30
Problems in recruiting and retaining top staff[c,d]			
Inability to compete on pay	33	54	48
Inability to reorganize	8	7	8
Inflexibility in regulations	50	54	53
Lack of adequate training	33	18	23
Lack of response from staff	25	11	15
Lack of rewards for staff	42	36	38
Turnover among key staff	16	57	45
Primary audience for audits[c]			
Congress	42	29	33
Media	8	4	5
Office of Management and Budget	0	4	3
Program managers	8	21	18
Secretary or administrator	33	39	38
U.S. attorney	8	4	5
Primary audience for investigations[c]			
Congress	25	25	25
Media	8	11	10
Office of Management and Budget	0	0	0
Program managers	0	21	15
Secretary or administrator	17	11	13
U.S. attorney	50	32	38

a. Data are based on responses from 12 Carter and 28 Reagan (first- and second-term) appointees. Some respondents did not answer every question. Totals may not add to 100 because of rounding.
b. $N = 36$.
c. $N = 40$.
d. Respondents could give more than one answer.

operating at the effectiveness and level which was envisioned by our 1981 budget.

Community Services: Hiring freezes prolonged an almost intolerable situation in which the Office of Inspector General was severely hampered in its efforts to effectively meet the mandates of the Inspector General Act of 1978. The Office was forced to set stricter priorities.

Education: The magnitude of our workload, coupled with increasing demands by Congress, the Office of Management and Budget, and the U.S. General Accounting Office makes it evident that the current personnel ceiling of 304 is far below our actual needs.

EPA: The most critical problem facing the Inspector General at EPA continues to be the shortage of manpower necessary to provide an appropriate level of oversight to EPA programs and functions. . . . During the last six months, our staff shortage situation has worsened instead of improving.

Labor: A matter of major concern to the Office of Inspector General as a whole concerns staffing resources. Despite [a] sizable increase, the cumulative effect of the government-wide hiring freezes, in place during much of the past year, prevented anticipated staff expansion. . . . As a result, while there will be an increase in OIG activity over previous levels, there will be reductions in relation to previously planned program levels.

Transportation: Our workload requirements continue to be greater than our resource availability. As a result, there are audit and investigative areas which are not receiving the required attention.[14]

Ultimately, the staff increases arrived, albeit too late to help the Carter IGs and in spite of continuing personnel freezes and budget crises. The IGs, however, continued to complain about too much work and too few FTE employees. A variety of units gave up FTE for the IG expansion: evaluation units, budget offices, policy analysis staffs, offices of legal counsel, equal opportunity bureaus, procurement units, personnel offices, public and legislative affairs branches; in short, virtually every staff unit at the top of most government departments and agencies. Complaints began to emerge about whether those units could do their work, particularly in helping design effective programs, implement policy, or, for that matter, prevent fraud, waste, and abuse in the first place. In essence, Congress and the president took FTE from government offices that worked on the front-end of the policy process to supply the search for fraud, waste, and abuse at the back end.[15]

The Politics of Implementation

The Carter IGs had difficulty getting started because of internal agency resistance and the zero-sum staff game. At least four undercurrents also were working against them.

WHO'S THE BOSS? As suggested by the data in table 5-4, the Carter IGs were much more likely than their Reagan successors to see Congress, not the program managers, as the primary audience for their audit work. Forty-two percent looked to Congress first, 33 percent to their secretary or administrator, and only 8 percent to program managers. Perhaps the assistant secretaries for management were right to worry about divided loyalties. However, this focus on Congress did not extend to investigations, where the Carter IGs saw the U.S. attorneys as the primary audience.

Looking at both audits and investigations, the Reagan IGs were less likely to look outside their departments and agencies. They also were more likely than the Carter IGs to see program managers as the primary audience for investigations, which perhaps is surprising because many investigations uncover problems that must be dealt with at high department or agency levels, if not the FBI or Justice Department.

TOUGH JOBS. The Carter IGs faced enormous pressure to hit the ground running, and some were bound to have trouble. One IG left her post in less than a year, and at least five were slated for replacement after the 1980 elections. The IGs themselves felt they needed a remarkable portfolio of skills to be successful (see table 5-5). Although a relatively small number of Carter or Reagan IGs thought knowledge of White House politics was necessary, a majority of those surveyed checked off every other item as either important or very important.

The Carter and Reagan appointees differed most in two skill areas: (1) The Carter IGs were almost twice as likely to say management skills were very important to success, and (2) the Reagan IGs were more than twice as likely to say knowledge of Congress was very important.

Important differences also existed between the two groups on the difficulties they encountered. The Carter IGs faced greater problems

Table 5-5. *The Nature of the IG Job, Carter versus Reagan*
Percent

Variable[a]	Carter[b]	Reagan[b]	Total
Average work week (hours)			
Less than 51	33	25	28
51–60	33	43	40
More than 60	33	32	33
What an IG needs to know[c]			
Audit skills	58	61	60
Budget process	33	75	63
Department or agency programs	67	57	60
How Congress works	75	86	83
How to manage	92	86	88
Investigation skills	58	57	58
Office of Management and Budget	67	75	73
Organizational politics	75	64	68
White House politics	25	32	30
Most difficult parts of the job[d]			
Dealing with Congress	29	61	60
Dealing with the media	42	39	40
Dealing with the White House and OMB	23	36	33
Mastering budget process	17	29	25
Mastering department procedures	25	32	30
Mastering program details	25	39	35
Organization of the OIG	50	32	38
Short-term orientation	16	39	33

a. $N = 40$ for all categories.
b. Data are based on responses from 12 Carter and 28 Reagan (first- and second-term) appointees. Some respondents did not answer every question. Totals may not add to 100 because of rounding.

with organization of their offices, while the Reagan appointees battled growing problems with congressional interference.

That so many Carter IGs saw Congress as their primary audit audience may provide a partial explanation. Having set a "Capitol Hill comes first" tone in 1979–80, Congress perhaps was unwilling to let the Reagan IGs go in a different direction. Congress also may have become more interested in the IGs as the organizations grew and matured.

DIFFERENT WORLDS. Whether the strong right arm of their secretaries or not, IGs drawn from the top of the career service did not share many of the goals that other political appointees traditionally bring to their jobs. In many ways, the IGs looked more like career civil servants than political appointees. Many started out in government as civil servants and retained SES fallback rights in the event they ever wanted to return to their career posts.

Table 5-5 (*continued*)
Percent

Variable[a]	Carter[b]	Reagan[b]	Total
Sources of frustration[d]			
Agency resistance to change	50	46	48
Congressional interference	25	46	40
Lack of resources to do job	58	32	40
Lack of time to plan	17	18	18
Media visibility	17	18	18
OMB interference	17	18	18
Slowness of government decision making	42	50	48
Statistical measures of success	8	29	23
Turnover of political appointees	42	39	40
White House interference	0	4	3
Satisfactions from being IG[d]			
Being catalyst for change	50	57	55
Dealing with challenging problems	67	43	50
Enhancing public respect for government	50	29	35
Finding fraud, waste, abuse	25	43	38
High visibility of the job	8	4	5
Improving programs care about	16	11	13
Increasing government efficiency	50	75	68
Serving admired president	0	7	5
Serving secretary or administrator	17	25	23
Working with interesting people	17	4	8

c. The figures represent the percentage of respondents who considered the item important or very important. Respondents could give more than one answer. For "how to manage," 58 percent of the Carter and 32 percent of the Reagan inspectors general (IGs) said very important; for "how Congress works," 25 percent of the Carter and 57 percent of the Reagan IGs said very important.

d. The numbers represent the percentage of respondents who mentioned the item. Respondents could give more than one answer.

The IGs may not have even shared the common work schedule of political appointees. Although the IGs worked hard, they were biding time compared with political appointees. According to NAPA, only 27 percent of the 1964–84 appointees worked less than 60 hours a week, another 35 percent worked 61–70 hours, while 38 percent worked 70 hours or more.[16]

In addition, the IGs gained their greatest satisfaction from dealing with challenging problems, increasing government efficiency, enhancing respect for government, and rooting out fraud, waste, and abuse. Presidential appointees often find fulfillment elsewhere, although they, too, like to take on complex problems (see table 5-6). The IG focus on increasing government efficiency stands in direct contrast to the much more prominent concern with programs and objectives among other presidential appointees.

The two groups also represented substantially different careers,

Table 5-6. *Presidential Appointee Goals, 1964–84*
Percent

Satisfactions from being appointee	Mentions[a]
Dealing with challenging problems	76
Accomplishing important public objectives	76
Meeting and working with stimulating people	51
Participating in important historical events	35
Serving an admired president	26
Helping to save taxpayers' money	10
Learning new skills	9
Other	4
Enhancing career opportunities	2

Source: National Academy of Public Administration, 1985 presidential appointee survey; table drawn from G. Calvin Mackenzie, ed., *The In-and-Outers: Presidential Appointees and Transient Government in Washington* (Johns Hopkins University Press, 1987), p. 187, table 9-8.
a. N = 536.

educational backgrounds, training, goals, and long- and short-term motivations. The IGs were not of a political mold, nor were they supposed to be. As a result, they did not share many of the frustrations or achievements of normal appointee life. Although the IGs and the appointees could commiserate about the slow pace of decisionmaking—roughly half in each group found it a source of constant frustration—they could hardly share a general complaint about the efforts of organized interest groups to reshape public policy (mentioned by 47 percent of the 1964–84 presidential appointees).[17]

Unfortunately for the IGs, if anyone to talk with existed in the executive suite, it would have been the assistant secretaries for management and administration, who often shared similar training and goals. But because they still were opposed to the IG concept, the conversation never got started, and the IGs remained estranged from their natural allies.

EARLY NOTICES. Alongside the normal tensions inherent in establishing turf, precedents set in the first report by the HEW IG may have caused enough controversy to worry even the most trusting political staff. Operating under the 1976 HEW statute, which required one annual report but not the thirty-day waiting period enacted in 1978, Thomas Morris elected to send his document directly to Congress with only the briefest opportunity for the HEW secretary to respond.

The report included a controversial inventory of HEW fraud, waste, and abuse that showed $6.3 billion to $7.4 billion in annual losses. Although the figures were carefully presented as "no more than an initial inventory" that was a "conservative measure" of a project that was not yet finished, the first section of the document nevertheless presented a single table summarizing the fraud, waste, and abuse for each HEW program.

The firestorm was less about the inventory, its underlying statistical assumptions, and the resulting press coverage, which was brief if intense, than about how the report was released. After all, Morris owed his job to Secretary Califano. Under pressure from Senator Herman Talmage (D-Ga.) to appoint a favored staffer to the IG post, Califano had fought hard for Morris instead. At one point Califano remarked to Carter that he would much rather appoint his own mother to the job than the Talmage candidate; Carter replied, "Your mother, not mine."[18]

Morris wrote the report without input from the secretary, and made his draft available only days before its scheduled release to Congress and the press. As Morris remembered,

> The Secretary and I had no prior agreement about what would be an adequate lead-time for him to review the report; it just hadn't occurred to either of us that this would be a problem. Normally, we wouldn't have had a problem, but I used up every day of time in writing the document. Our objective in the first report was to make it as complete and current as we could. . . . That's what caused part of the problem; an overzealousness in wanting to be current, which led us to use up our lead-time in writing and prevented others from having an adequate review period. I finished the report and had it ready to go on the 29th and hand-delivered it that evening to the Secretary's Office.[19]

Under law, Morris did exactly what he was required to do. Unfortunately, given the time constraints he faced drafting the report, Morris had to make a choice between his two bosses:

> The Secretary in effect did not have a chance to put comments on the report unless they were done in a very fast turnaround of a few hours. I had a last minute choice to make between my commitment to Congress, who was one of my two bosses, and giving the Secretary more time to look at the report, and I elected the former because I felt it was more important. With the law being so explicit I didn't want to be in the position of missing my deadline, especially as this was our first report. We were a brand new office under a brand new law with a committee looking at everything we were doing day-by-day, and there could have been negative repercussions that the IG was dragging its

feet, being influenced, or not revealing information promptly as
required by law. . . . I was determined, in short, to meet that
deadline; even if the Secretary asked me to hold up, I think I
would have gone ahead.[20]

Given that Fountain's watchful staff alter-ego, counsel James
Naughton, already had called to make sure the report would be on
time, Morris made the right choice. However, it created enormous
ill-will among the Califano political appointees, particularly the
press and congressional liaison staffs who had less than forty-eight
hours to get in front of the report. As Califano's executive assistant,
Ben Heineman, Jr., recalled,

First, we had to show what the number $6 [billion] to $7 billion
really meant. . . . Second, I wanted to be sure we got credit, if
you will, for having instigated the report. I did not want this to
come off as an exposé of what I had done, or our administration
had done; I thought it was important to drive across the point
that we had ordered this, were taking a hard-nosed look at fraud
and mismanagement, and that this is where we came out.[21]

Being the secretary's strong right arm was, and still is, an extraordinarily difficult role, particularly if the IG was to be an independent
monitor on behalf of taxpayers and Congress. Furthermore, the individual goals of the political team did not mesh with those of the IG
and the OIG staff. These lessons could not have been lost on others
in government as they prepared for the arrival of their first IGs.

CONCLUSION: TOO MUCH TO DO,
TOO LITTLE TIME

All things considered, the Carter IGs were lucky to prepare any
reports at all. Their staffs were beleagured, and their time was
limited. Moreover, as the Carter administration moved into reelec-
tion gear, the IGs moved off the president's personnel agenda. Morris
left HEW on September 28, 1979; no replacement was nominated
for eleven months. Marjorie Knowles left Labor in May 1980; her
post remained vacant until the end of the term.

The Carter IGs did make headway in building their offices. Brown
and Dempsey recruited many future IGs, and they and their colleagues stitched together the office structures that would form the
locus for a remarkable expansion during the 1980s. The IGs left the
Carter years, however, painfully aware that staff and dollars were

needed to succeed, resources that were not likely to come from the budget process within their departments and agencies.

The IGs also decided that their success was to be measured in long lists of highly individualized audit and investigatory findings, which were more easily generated from traditional compliance monitoring. The Agriculture IG in 1980, for example, reported more than 1,000 audit and investigative reports in the preceding year, as well as $80 million in recoveries and 235 convictions; Commerce claimed $3.7 million in savings and $600,000 in "cost avoidance or deferrals," plus $3.1 million in identifying risky loans; HHS celebrated $200 million in audit savings, 137 indictments, 145 convictions, and $4.7 million in fines, recoveries, and restitutions; HUD opened 1,089 investigations, referred 277 cases for prosecutions, and questioned $363.6 million in agency costs, resulting in recoveries of $14.2 million.[22]

Although true IG savings—actual dollars returned to the U.S. Treasury—likely totaled far less than $100 million, the class of 1979 created enough momentum to propel the IG concept through the 1980 election and into the beginning of an administration hotly committed to the war on fraud, waste, and abuse. The IGs had ample reason to look forward to their glory days. What they could not and did not predict was that they all would be fired on inauguration day, an action that set the stage for further reinforcement of the compliance monitoring model.

Glory Days

THE 1980 campaign held no hint of the controversy that would befall the IGs in the first days of the Reagan administration.[1] As a candidate Reagan seemed absolutely committed to a full-scale war on fraud, waste, and abuse, the kind of war that would feature the IGs. His speeches were peppered with remarks, for example, that referred to "tens of billions of dollars that is lost in fraud alone," and his platform promised a $195 billion savings from a full-scale attack on waste.[2]

However, in his second act as president—the first having been to impose a federal hiring freeze—Reagan wrote the Speaker of the House and the president pro tempore of the Senate to inform Congress of his decision to "remove from office the current appointees to the position of Inspector General." His reason was simple: "As in the case with all positions where I, as President, have the power of appointment by, and with the advice and consent of the Senate, it is vital that I have the fullest confidence in the ability, integrity and commitment of each appointee to the position of Inspector General." Nevertheless, all of the Carter IGs were fired.[3]

If the purpose of the firings was to mark the president's commitment to "meaner junkyard dogs," as press secretary James Brady later explained, the action had the opposite effect. As one Carter IG put it, "Everybody wants a strong IG operation until it starts investigating them. The administration may start out thinking they want junkyard dogs, and what they may end up getting is French poodles."[4]

The firings reminded the IGs of their dependence upon the president, not Congress, for their institutional survival. Whether in winning new staff for their offices or career security for themselves, the IGs were influenced by the president's values. The IGs would soon find that this president, and his surrogates in OMB, placed greatest value in the kinds of statistical accomplishment closely linked to compliance monitoring. The administration was not likely to be interested in broad findings and recommendations on performance and capacity. Its agenda was one of budget cutbacks and reductions in force, not higher pay for civil servants, more money for training, or increases in government employment.

FEAR OF FIRING

Many Carter IGs had expected a weeding out of the ranks with the new administration. As HUD IG Charles Dempsey commented in House hearings almost ten years later, "On the plus side—in 1980, some IGs had become or gave the image and appearance of being political appointees; this is a violation of the IG Act. If a few had been fired it might have resulted in some class action suits; therefore, I believe to fire all and rehire some perhaps was the best way to clean house."[5] OMB Deputy Director Edwin Harper said as much at the time in testimony before the House Government Operations Committee. As to why all the IGs had to be fired to get at the few, Harper offered a more curious argument: "There is no reason to jeopardize the reputation or career of a person who had done a marginal job which would have been good enough in a less important post. Thus, it is humanitarian not to single out those who did a less than outstanding job."[6]

Given the firestorm of negative publicity that followed, Reagan likely regretted the decision, telling one House Republican that it could have been done better. Representative Elliott Levitas wondered whether the "meat-ax" firing signaled a preference for "political hacks who are simply going to blow in the political winds of the time," while L. H. Fountain and Jack Brooks both promised hearings, privately fuming that they had not been forewarned.[7] The IGs had not been forewarned either. Inez Reid, the EPA IG, explained as follows: "I learned that I was 'fired,' as the news media put it, by watching the evening television news at the end of the working day. No one had informed me by telephone or in writing prior to the news broadcasts that I was to be removed." Furthermore, some of the letters were misaddressed, and all were signed by machine—the White House personnel director's name was misspelled as E. Pendelton (not Pendleton) James.[8]

Nevertheless, the firings marked the beginning of the glory days for IGs. For the few IGs rehired, and the new IGs recruited, the message was clear: The more statistical accomplishments produced in the war on waste—measured by dollars saved and cheaters caught—the more the IG office will grow and prosper. Compliance monitoring was the route to the resources the Carter IGs had found wanting.

GETTING STARTED . . . AGAIN

The future must have seemed bleak to the IGs at the beginning of the Reagan years. If any silver lining existed in the firings of these "obscure public officials," as syndicated columnist Jack Anderson called them, it was that Reagan was forced to fully commit his administration to the war on waste. In a February 18, 1981, address to Congress, Reagan renewed his campaign pledge to ferret out the waste:

> Now, let me say a word here about the general problem of waste and fraud in the Federal Government. One government estimate indicated that fraud alone may account for anywhere from 1 to 10 percent—as much as $25 billion—of Federal expenditures for social programs. If the tax dollars that are wasted or mismanaged are added to this fraud total, the staggering dimensions of this problem begin to emerge.
>
> The Office of Management and Budget is now putting together an interagency task force to attack waste and fraud. We're also planning to appoint as Inspectors General highly trained professionals who will spare no effort to do this job.[9]

Four weeks later, Reagan created the President's Council on Integrity and Efficiency (PCIE) to lead the battle. Composed of IGs and chaired by the deputy director of OMB, the PCIE would quickly become a continuing source of leverage as the IGs fought for resources within their agencies.

A Chilling Effect

Still, 1981 could only be viewed as a chilling time for the new IGs. Although the OIGs were too young to take a share of the blame for the government fraud, waste, and abuse highlighted in Reagan's campaign rhetoric, the firings put future IGs on notice that they would be asked to make the grade by producing dollar savings and convictions in steadily rising amounts.

As Harper noted, C-plus performance might be good enough for many government jobs, but not for the IGs. Those who dug out fraud, waste, and abuse in sufficient amounts would be rewarded;

those who did not would be fired or ignored. Beyond the emerging focus on short-term statistical results, the firings produced at least three other likely unintended consequences.

First, despite Reagan's pledge to hire new IGs quickly and Harper's accelerated search, many positions remained vacant for the first half of the year. The new HHS IG was not nominated until May 5; Agriculture, June 9; Interior, July 10; Transportation, July 17; EPA, July 23; GSA, August 5; Energy, September 23; and Commerce, September 29. The SBA IG was not nominated until March 16, 1983. For the five rehired Carter IGs, renomination was not faster—James Thomas at Education and Dempsey at HUD were not told they were staying until May 27; Frank Sato was not notified that he was moving to VA until May 29; Thomas McBride that he was moving to Labor until June 1; and June Gibbs Brown that she was moving to NASA until June 10.

The IGs were not singled out for delays, however. Harper could do only so much to speed up the process. According to G. Calvin Mackenzie, every administration since Kennedy has been later than its predecessor in getting top positions filled, and Reagan was no different. Whereas Kennedy took roughly two months to nominate his cabinet and subcabinet, Nixon took four, Carter almost five, and Reagan almost six.[10] Whether the delays came because of the Senate, the FBI, the ethics act, or the crush of resumés from anxious Republicans, the IGs were caught in the backlog. Despite a pre-election transition planning operation designed to speed up the appointment process, no evidence existed that the Reagan planners ever thought that IGs would need to be appointed.

Second, the firings may have scared future appointees, especially those asked to serve in the final days of an administration. "Even now, nearly 8 years later," the Government Operations Committee reported in its ten-year review of the IGs, "there is a sense of concern and uncertainty in the inspector general community of the 1981 removals."[11] "The firings introduced a new element to IG life," one sitting Reagan IG reported in 1989. "It set a precedent for the next President. You can bet that I had my form 171 [used in applying for government jobs] ready in 1988 just in case. And it didn't matter whether I thought Dukakis or Bush was coming. I was just getting ready."

This fear of firing was lessened for IGs with the option of going into the federal Senior Executive Service. If fired from their IG posts, fallback rights guaranteed automatic placement at only a slight reduction in pay. This right, as Dempsey explained, "was of great importance to IGs, particularly for independence—as this places IGs in what I've always referred to as the 'Go-to-Hell' club. When an IG was being squeezed by a political appointee or anyone, the worst thing that could happen was he/she would be fired, become a 'hero' to many, and have fallback rights. It's a position that stiffens one's backbone."[12]

Third, the firings may have encouraged the Department of Justice to revisit the debate it had lost in 1978 over IG investigative authority. According to a draft policy agreement presented to the new IG nominees at an OMB-hosted retreat on June 3, 1981, the IGs were to relinquish their criminal cases to the FBI. For any IG worried about how those cases turned out, Justice committed the FBI to "furnish a written summary at the conclusion of an investigation on the nature of judicial action, if any." And for those concerned about management issues, "the FBI and the prosecutor will attempt to provide for the Inspector General's use, an analysis of any underlying problems in the federal program or procurement procedures that were uncovered during the course of the investigation and which need corrective action."[13] In short, Justice proposed the de facto abolishment of the IG criminal investigative function. Although Congress explicitly created assistant inspectors general for investigations, Justice urged the IGs to focus on auditing.

Whatever the motives, whether concern for duplication or worries about competition, the Justice strategy failed. Although the IG concept had been temporarily weakened by the firings, none of the IGs would agree to the formal memoranda of understanding required to implement the proposal. Not only did the IGs doubt the FBI's commitment to white collar crime, particularly given the rising workload created by the war on drugs, but they also already had established some skill at finding small-scale fraud that neither Justice nor FBI would ever pursue; that is, cases in the $25,000–$100,000 range that fell between the cracks.

The Beginning of a Very Close Friendship

Despite these early setbacks, the 1981 firings proved enormously positive, particularly if measured by staff and resources. Needing someone to put out the congressional brushfire, the White House turned to Ed Harper and his staff. That Harper may have single-handedly rescued the IG concept—with a degree of prodding from Congress—is evident in the praise he received from the House Government Operations Committee nearly eight years later:

Although the subcommittee is not in a position to make an

informed judgment about every [new] nominee on an individual basis at this time, it is clear that the nominees as a group have excellent qualifications and experience. The obviously high quality of the nominee has helped considerably in alleviating concern that the removal of the former IG's was the first step in a plan to 'politicize' the offices. OMB Deputy Director Harper and those who assisted him in the selection process deserve to be commended for this achievement."[14]

Along the way, Harper and OMB became the primary sponsors and protectors of the IGs. They provided a counterweight to continued department and agency opposition. Whereas the Carter OMB had not taken much interest in the IGs, the Reagan OMB now claimed outright ownership, which was evident in several ways. The IGs had regularly scheduled meetings with Harper and occasional meetings with OMB Director David Stockman; the PCIE was established as a kind of executive branch trade union; and photo opportunities and briefings with President Reagan were arranged for the IGs. "Having those early pictures with the 'Prez' was critical," one new appointee noted. "You could hang it on the wall back at the office, put it in the house organ, spread it around." Such symbols of presidential support could not hurt at the agency, especially given how strongly the Reagan appointees identified with their admired president.

OMB ownership also created an entirely new search process for selecting future IG nominees. OMB not only took charge of the IG search but also often had the final say, putting it at odds with the Reagan administration's overall centralization of appointments in the White House.

By 1982, the IGs themselves had earned a remarkable place in the process. Instead of a recruiting pool drawn from sources within OMB, Harper and his successor, Joe Wright, created an informal recruiting committee composed of only IGs to screen names and recruit candidates. Until the end of the Reagan administration, this three-member screening committee was the primary source of IG nominees. Not surprisingly, therefore, the IGs endorsed the OMB sponsorship as the key to their success. And if Harper had rescued the IGs after the mass firings, Wright provided the support and freedom to strengthen IG operations.

The White House was not completely removed. A cursory political check continued, as did Carter's practice of giving the departments and agencies a limited veto. However, while the president's signature still was required on every nomination, OMB was in charge. If an

IG candidate did not pass muster with Harper, that IG was not appointed.

The OMB's ownership involved more than the appointment process, however. It also generated resources for the IGs. Because the budget side of OMB controlled personnel allocations for the entire government and the management side of the war on waste, and because Harper was in charge of both management and budget, he could cross-walk staff from one side to the other to the benefit of the OIGs.

In the normal budget process, OMB establishes a personnel ceiling and allows departments and agencies to allocate full-time-equivalent slots on their own. In the case of IGs, however, OMB earmarked FTE to go only to the Offices of Inspector General. Because the federal government still was under the personnel freeze imposed by Reagan on January 20, 1981, most staff lines reserved for the IGs involved a reallocation from somewhere else in the department or agency. In short, OMB was exercising real power. Absent Harper's intervention, the IG glory days would not have begun.

Over time, this informal process grew into a "special director's review" designed to set the staffing levels for each OIG. As Wright explained the process as it still existed in 1988, "[W]e review the IGs original request, the agency's recommended level, and the budget and management staff recommendations. After reviewing this data, the Director and I set the resource levels."[15] Thus, absent Wright's continued involvement and his leverage as OMB deputy director, the glory days would not have continued. Had Harper or Wright been at the associate director level or below, merely representing the IGs from the management side of OMB to the budget side, the IGs likely would have had to take whatever the departments and agencies wanted to give. The impact of the special reviews is evident from the data in table 6-1.

The OIGs thrived during this period of OMB sponsorship, averaging a 23 percent increase in staffing from 1980 to 1986. In comparison, civilian employment government-wide went up only 1 percent, mostly in Defense. (The IGs did equally well in budgeting, with an increase from $248 million in 1981 to $500 million seven years later.) Overall, the IGs and their offices were the most frequent winners in the zero-sum personnel game, surpassing their departments in staff employment and forging far ahead of the career SES. Even when the OIGs lost ground—at Agriculture, Education, GSA, HUD, NASA, and SBA—they experienced fewer cuts. The message was unmistakable: the IGs were protected.

The table also includes data on the gains and losses for three

Table 6-1. *IG, Civilian, and Political Appointee Growth, 1980–86*
Percent

Department or agency	IG staff employment	Civilian employment	Career SES	Noncareer SES	Schedule C positions
Agriculture	−9	−12	−11	37	40
Commerce	20	−29	−12	6	−3
Defense	15[a]	10	19	23	7
Education	−4	−38	−20	25	82
Energy	42	−23	−26	−31	27
EPA	83	−5	−7	−17	27
GSA	−32	−39	−9	167[b]	283[b]
HHS	41	−14	−11	24	−20
HUD	−2	−30	−14	29	−1
Interior	53	−4	1	−15	33
Labor	28	−25	−17	21	3
NASA	−2	−6	−6	c	−100
SBA	−3	−16	−7	7	27
State	46	8	80	33	29
Transportation	2	−15	11	17	42
VA	17	5	d	−57	50
Total[e]	23	1	−5	13	13

Source: General Accounting Office, *Federal Employees: Trends in Career and Noncareer Employee Appointments in the Executive Branch*, GAO/GGD-87-96-FS (July 1987), p. 9.
a. The Defense OIG was created in 1982.
b. GSA noncareer SES increased from 6 to 16; GSA Schedule C, from 6 to 23.
c. NASA noncareer SES went from zero to 8.
d. VA does not have a career SES.
e. Totals include many more agencies than the ones cited here.

classes of top government executives: career members of the SES, noncareer (or political) members of the SES, and Schedule C personal and confidential assistants (also political). The Reagan administration invested heavily in both the control and monitoring of the executive branch. Defining noncareer SES and Schedule C appointees as monitors, growth at those personnel levels reflected a deliberate strategy to control the levers of government through the careful picking—and packing—of appointees.

The issue here is not whether politicization is right or wrong. Some scholars, such as Terry Moe, argued that politicization is nothing more than a president's desire to gain control of the executive establishment.[16] Others, such as those involved with the National Commission on the Public Service (Volcker Commission), argued that politicization limits room at the top and, therefore, reduces both career opportunities and presidential access to institutional memory.[17]

Table 6-2. *Career and Noncareer Appointee Growth, 1980–90*

| | 1980 | | 1990 | | |
Category of employee	Number	Percent of total	Number	Percent of total	Percent change
Presidential appointees	488	5.5	557	6.1	14
Noncareer SES	582	6.5	675	7.4	16
Schedule C appointments	1,456	16.4	1,700	18.6	17
Career SES	6,379	71.6	6,190	67.9	−3

Source: Office of Personnel Management monthly reports.

Regardless of these theoretical arguments, the figures indicate a general thinning of the career layer of leadership, a conclusion confirmed by the data in table 6-2.

At first glace, a 3-percentage-point drop in career SES is not dramatic. However, when coupled with the strengthening of the IGs, rising congressional oversight, and increased OMB presence in regulatory, budgetary, and administrative processes of government, the change may be more significant. As one senior career executive explained,

The reviewer-to-doer ratio has never been higher—congressional staff, bright people who know how to keep busy; GAO folks who know how to get into people's knickers; increased IG capability, department superstructures decimated, a lot of new units mandated by OMB, including more staff in its own Office of Information and Regulatory Affairs, and a stack of multiple reporting requirements—bundle it all together and get a bunch of program managers together and you'll get a common refrain: "I wish I had as many people doing as I have reviewing."

The IGs did well under Reagan, particularly with the help of OMB, but Congress played a role in the glory days, too. Harper was strongly criticized on the resource issue in the Brooks-Fountain post-firing hearings, which led the House Government Operations Committee to recommend that the Reagan administration: "(a) to the extent feasible and appropriate, take immediate steps to meet urgent needs of Offices of Inspector General for additional resources; and (b) take appropriate action to assure that adequate resources are requested for Offices of Inspector General in the future."[18]

Thus Government Operations used the firings to leverage more IG staff, first noting that total employment in the sixteen IG Offices was less than 5,500 FTE (including the State Department, which established an OIG in late 1980), then calling the numbers "grossly inadequate" and pointing out the high rates of return from each employee hired. The committee expected an increase. And increase the OIGs did. By the fifth year of the Reagan administration, IG staffing already had grown by almost 1,500 FTE employees, with no signs of a slowdown.

In an absolute sense, an increase of 1,500 in a civilian work force of 2.2 million seems insignificant. However, even a small absolute increase looms large when compared with the general growth trends highlighted in table 6-2, even larger given the fact that total government employment grew by only 14,427 during the period, and larger still given the general declines at the headquarters level of most departments, where OIGs and other staff units compete for staff and resources.[19] Seemingly trivial changes in IG staffing can have large impacts. As one OMB staffer argued, "Management offices have given up a great deal to the IGs. At the headquarter's level, small shifts in total FTE can have a real impact on total staff allocation. You take 30 FTE from management and shift it over to the IGs, and you've really done something." Thus, even discounting the new IGship at Defense, which grew by almost 1,000 from 1983 to 1986, the IGs took the lion's share of new staff.[20]

THE SEEDS OF ALLIANCE

Ultimately, OMB and the IGs were drawn together because each could benefit from the alliance. As long as the IGs produced ever-larger statistical accomplishments, OMB could claim success in the war on waste. And, as long as OMB allowed the IGs to regulate their own enterprise, the IGs could build a measure of internal independence. If not the strong right arms of their secretaries and administrators, the IGs perhaps would become the strong right arm of OMB.

The problem with the alliance, however, was one of institutional loyalties. Just as the dual reporting relationship to Congress may have undermined trust in their departments and agencies, so, too, did the strong connection with OMB. As the 1980s progressed, OMB became just as intrusive in monitoring, regulating, and micromanaging the executive branch as Congress. By casting their lot with OMB, the IGs may have weakened their potential influence within their own establishments. Nevertheless, the incentives for alliance were irresistible.

The OMB Invitation

On the management side of OMB, where the Reagan war on waste was fought, the agency saw the IGs as a more reliable source of information and leadership than the assistant secretaries for management and administration. The career assistant secretaries who had not been replaced were generally seen as too loyal to their agencies to be trusted with reform, whereas the new and growing corps of political assistant secretaries were seen as too inexperienced to lead the charge. Looking for an experienced, yet still presidentially accountable source of leadership, the OIGs became an increasingly popular vehicle for the Reagan reform agenda, if only occasionally the primary implementors, then certainly almost always the key compliance monitors.

In many ways, the lack of confidence in the assistant secretaries reflected the quality of Reagan's own appointments, which were made either at the White House or the departments and agencies. As the Reagan personnel process replaced the career assistant secretaries, the positions often became little more than a holding pattern for political appointees looking for a better job. Those at OMB who worked closely with the President's Council on Management and Efficiency, which was composed primarily of assistant secretaries for management, and the PCIE almost uniformly reported the PCIE as more effective in tackling the Reagan administration's management agenda. Such was the price of the administration's own politicization.

This is not to argue that the IGs had no interest in leading the reform campaign. As one OMB staffer remarked, "With the IGs it's generally an issue of them pushing too hard. We end up having to pull them back. With the PCME group, it's exactly the opposite. They've got nothing but questions. We end up having to hassle them constantly."

Nor is this to suggest that the White House only was to blame. OMB also played a role in weakening the assistant secretaries for management, providing uncertain signals about the administration's reform agenda and unstable leadership. The Reagan administration's primary management initiative—titled "Reform '88" in the hopes that all improvements would be completed by the end of the second term—was more a collection of disparate compliance ideas than an integrated philosophy of new incentives for performance, such as fully funded merit pay, or needed investments in capacity, such as financial system modernization. Furthermore, launched in 1983,

Reform '88 allowed the agencies only five years to repair problems that had been decades in the making.

The contracting-out initiative provides a good example of the problem with Reform '88. The plan was designed to encourage government to contract out when the same job could be done at less cost in the private sector. The formal process required under OMB Circular A-76, however, was extraordinarily burdensome, calling for employee-by-employee cost studies, "a millstone around our neck," as one assistant secretary for management described it. According to GAO, "The strategy OMB used evolved from one of laissez-faire to one of inflexibility: OMB set goals for the number of positions to be studied, and agencies were expected to meet them. If they did not meet them, budget cuts were threatened. In fiscal year 1985, for example, OMB attempted to stimulate A-76 implementation in two ways—by establishing cost study goals for each agency and by cutting agencies' budget requests at the beginning of each budget cycle."[21] It is no wonder the assistant secretaries asked questions.

These kinds of problems with the reform agenda were only the beginning. Despite its commitment to a five-year effort, the management side of OMB showed anything but stability. From 1981 to 1989, four different associate directors for management were installed, and six reorganizations of the overall operation took place. In 1981, OMB had four management subdivisions; in 1982, two were abolished, and two more were created; in 1983, two were combined into a Management Reform Division, and two more were created; in 1984, two were abolished, the Management Reform Division was renamed, and a new management secretariat was created; in 1985, the secretariat was abolished; in 1987, the whole operation was reorganized into two divisions, Government Operations and Financial Management.

Whereas the IGs had consistent leadership at the higher deputy director level, where Wright stayed in the job for more than six years, the assistant secretaries for management had constant change among the associate directors just below. Just as Wright's tenure in the deputy directorship was a significant factor in the IGs' success, his failure to keep an associate director for Management for more than a year or two helped account for the fitful relationship with the assistant secretaries.

Moreover, looking at OMB staffing figures, it would be remarkable if the assistant secretaries felt anything but poorly led. As Congressional Research Service expert Ronald C. Moe reported, in 1970, the management side of OMB had 224 full-time employees. By 1980, the number was down to 70; by 1988, 46. While the number of staff

Table 6-3. *Status of Reform '88 Proposals, 1987–89*

	Number			
Subject	*Proposed*	*Enacted*	*Pending*	*Defeated*[a]
Financial management	10	3	4	3
Fraud prevention	9	5	0	4
Paperwork reduction	2	1	0	1
Procurement	9	2	0	7
Productivity	7	1	3	3

Source: General Accounting Office, *Managing the Government: Revised Approach Could Improve OMB's Effectiveness*, GAO/GGD-89-65 (May 1989), p. 89.
a. Includes those dropped.

dedicated to financial management reform and fraud control steadily grew, the number working on basic management fell. "During the 1980s," Moe wrote, "OMB systematically subordinated its remaining management capabilities to support its budgetary and financial systems priorities. They believed that if they conducted enough financial management improvement projects, this would equal a management philosophy."[22] As Moe also noted, OMB increasingly had to rely on short-term staffers "detailed," or loaned, from the departments and agencies for management leadership.

Even with sustained leadership at the deputy director level, the assistant secretaries for management would have been hard pressed to produce the kind of statistical success stories OMB was looking for. The assistant secretaries and the IGs had very different marching orders from OMB. The former were given responsibility for productivity and quality improvement, procurement reform, contracting out, and privatization, all of which were exceedingly difficult to implement, while the latter were given leadership on fraud busting and compliance monitoring. For an OMB increasingly preoccupied with short-term indicators of success, the IGs promised greater returns.

Throughout the Reagan administration, fraud busting remained the easier reform to implement and, coincidently, the most popular initiative with Congress. Of the 37 legislative proposals connected to Reform '88, fraud control bills were the most likely to be passed by Congress, while productivity improvement, financial management, and procurement trailed far behind (see table 6-3).

Ultimately, the IGs may have been most attractive to OMB because they represented something of a budget-cutting success in the wake of a mounting federal deficit failure. Testifying before the

House Government Operations Committee, Wright provided an explanation of the IG staffing increases that can be seen as one example of how the IG numbers played in the Old Executive Office Building:

I think, Mr. Chairman, I have got to say—I'm looking back on the history—that this is a real success story for the Federal Government. There are numerous accomplishments. In fiscal 1982, the IG's reported $11.5 billion in recoveries, savings, and avoidance of unnecessary expenditures. Last year they reported $20 billion. That's an 80-percent increase.

In fiscal 1982, they reported 2,099 convictions; last year, 4,365. That's a substantial increase.

Mr. Chairman, it's not the fact that anything has gotten worse in the last 8 years from the standpoint of fraud, waste, and abuse—I would look at it as the fact that the IG's are doing a much better job in their fight to go ahead and prohibit these types of practices.[23]

Since 1981, the IGs had averaged about sixty-eight convictions, twenty-six administrative sanctions, and $308 million in savings every week. For every $1 spent on staff and operations, the IGs returned $45 in better government. As Wright concluded, "I don't think you can find that in too many cases around the Federal Government."[24] Although the numbers included a huge amount of "funds put to better use" and were sometimes suspect, the IGs provided a brief ray of sunshine in an otherwise disastrous OMB portfolio.

The IG Embrace

As OMB considered the IGs more reliable sources of information and accomplishment, the IGs considered OMB a more reliable source of freedom. Although many IGs successfully established good working relationships within their departments and agencies, OMB provided a reservoir of protection, whether against Congress, political appointees, or career civil servants.

For IGs fighting their departments over access, resources, or audit resolution, OMB offered a final court of appeal. For IGs "straddling the barbed wire fence" between Congress and the president, OMB served as a "wire cutter," an effective way to pass the congressional pressure to a well-defended ally. And for those working in departments and agencies where the top leadership did not care, OMB had encouragement and resources.

Ironically, as OMB became less flexible toward the executive branch on management reform, paperwork reduction, regulatory review, personnel, and budgets, Harper and Wright became more willing to let the IGs take the helm on fraud, waste, and abuse. Perhaps this was a consequence of OMB's role in the selection process and the belief that good IGs had been picked. Moreover, having the IGs align with OMB made sense. Looking back to the Carter administration's IG coordinating body, which had been chaired by the attorney general, HHS IG Richard Kusserow explained the advantage of having OMB in charge:

> I think we are probably better off with the OMB for two reasons. One is that the Office of Management and Budget is in fact the management arm of the President, and they are supposed to look across the entire government. The Deputy has a major role in management; therefore, in one respect it's good for that so that we can get the perspective of the entire government. Second—and, again, I guess this comes from pecuniary interests of an IG—and that is if we go out and do work and we find there is something wrong government-wide, who should have to take the action? It should be OMB. So what we do is kind of lay an egg right at their doorstep and then, by the fact that they chair the process, I think that it puts a little more impetus behind them doing something about it. So I think it works to our advantage.[25]

If OMB forgot about watching the IGs, so much the better. As Kusserow explained in 1987, "I think a little benign neglect as far as watching the IG's is probably desirable. We don't want [OMB] running our program—we run it ourselves."[26] In this regard, Reagan's IG class of 1981 was remarkably skilled in establishing precedents for managing itself.

The glory days were characterized by a new-found liberty. For example, with OMB's full blessing, the IGs were given the lead role in investigating allegations of wrongdoing among their peers. In interviews, the IGs mentioned at least two such investigations—one of Agriculture IG John Graziano, one of EPA IG Michael Novak—and hinted at a minimum of four others. On the surface, the process had obvious problems. Every profession—whether doctors, lawyers, or IGs—has some incentive to protect itself from public disgrace, particularly when one highly visible scandal could undermine the legitimacy of the entire class.

Another, and much more important, example is the responsibility for recruiting IG nominees. As Dempsey explained, the new search process began with a request from Wright:

Table 6-4. *Location of Job Held before Becoming IG, First and Second Reagan Administration Appointees*

Location of previous job	First Reagan administration (1981–85) appointees	Second Reagan administration (1985–89) appointees
Inside executive branch		
Administration office		
Same department	1	0
Different department	3	2
IG office		
Same department	3	6
Different department	6	5
Program office		
Same department	1	0
Different department	3	1
Outside executive branch		
Administration office	1	0
Audit office	0	0
Investigation office	0	0
Other IG office	0	0
Program office	1	0
Total	19	14

Source: Data derived from analysis of biographical information on all the Reagan IGs. Community Services Administration IG not included.

We sent out letters to selected persons requesting the names of possible candidates and we also sent questionnaires to Deputy IGs and Assistant IGs. We had over 75 responses. The [three-member IG committee] gathered information on background, education, and special skills of those named and computerized it. After we had data sheets on these 75 the committee selected 14 of the most highly skilled, experienced nominees. From 1984 to date, seven of the latest eight nominees came from this list.[27]

The process also resulted in a clear inbreeding of the IGs. According to the data in table 6-4, eleven of the fourteen IGs selected from 1985 to 1989 came from IG offices. In addition, one of the two non-IGs, June Gibbs Brown, had previously been an IG before leaving government for private business. Returning to NASA in 1986 as associate administrator for management, she was nominated as Defense Department IG one year later.

The IGs clearly used the process to reward deputy and assistant IGs, cutting down on administrators and almost completely eliminating program managers from the pool, whether coming from posts within the same department or not. The one exception was William Barton, who had been deputy director of the U.S. Secret Service before becoming IG at the General Services Administration.

The recruitment process also was essentially hidden from view. Secretaries and administrators had only one option if they did not like the initial candidate: Draw another name, which was likely to resemble the first one, from the IG-generated list. If diversity of race, gender, or career did not exist at the assistant or deputy IG level, it likely did not exist in the candidate pool.

Although the second Reagan administration IGs still were presidential appointees, at least twelve originally had been selected and groomed within the IG community. While some deputy secretaries and assistant administrators eventually did rise to the top of their agencies, particularly toward the end of a presidential term, the IGs had remarkable influence.

CONCLUSION: A MATCH MADE IN HEAVEN?

The early 1980s were not always good to the IGs, however. Serious problems arose with the IGships at State, EPA, and Interior.

At State, for example, a 1982 GAO report argued that the IGship created under a 1980 statute was less independent, and therefore less effective, than the offices created under the 1978 act. According to GAO, the State IG was performing inspections of foreign posts traditionally reserved for management, while a non-IG management unit (the Office of Security) was performing investigations usually done by inspectors general.

Moreover, the IG was almost entirely dependent upon a temporary staff of Foreign Service officers to conduct its audits and inspections, leading GAO to warn of a loss of independence because "(1) these staff members routinely rotate between the IG office and management positions within the organizations they review, and (2) major decisions affecting their careers are determined by the State Department rather than by the IG Office."[28] Questions were asked regarding objectivity and effectiveness, which led to transfer of the Office of Security into the IG office and the recruitment of a stronger IG, Sherman Funk, in 1987, who created a much larger and more independent staff.

In a much more serious 1983 case at EPA, the IG was implicated in the widening Superfund scandal involving top agency officials and EPA Director Anne Burford Gorsuch. According to GAO's investigation, the IG's office apparently harassed an internal critic of the agency's toxic waste policy, prematurely closed a number of investigations implicating the agency's political leadership, and ignored at least three accusations of wrongdoing received anonymously through the EPA fraud hotline.[29]

GAO also argued that EPA was not doing enough big-ticket investigations and audits. Looking back over the period leading up to the Burford resignation in 1983, GAO found that "investigators spent a substantial amount of time investigating relatively minor matters that could be handled by program officials, and doing administrative work that could be done by clerical persons. Twenty-six percent of the investigative time spent on cases closed during fiscal year 1982 involved either dollar losses of $500 or less or administrative matters."[30]

The EPA IG allegedly had not done his job, either ignoring wrongdoing by his bosses, harassing inside critics, or directing the office away from more serious cases onto more trivial work. Long before the GAO report was released, however, the IG, Michael Novak, had resigned and was replaced on an acting basis by Dempsey. The change may have signalled an attempt to embrace a more professionalized image of the IGs.

Finally, at Interior, the IG was severely criticized in 1984 for mishandling of an investigation arising out of the Power River Basin coal lease sale of 1982, specifically the unauthorized disclosure of proprietary coal leasing data prior to the sale. Although the Interior OIG issued three separate reports on the allegations of wrongdoing, GAO minced no words in concluding that the investigations were flawed:

> GAO's examination of the three OIG reports issued in connection with the investigation disclosed deficiencies in each of the reports which are sufficiently serious to render the reports incomplete and unreliable. GAO found that a sufficient basis existed to initiate an investigation long before GAO's April 20, 1983, referral [of the case to the Interior OIG]. Furthermore, the OIG terminated the investigation prematurely, did not pursue leads concerning leaks of Interior data, and did not reconcile discrepancies in the information which was obtained. Several leads suggesting potential leaks were identified in the OIG reports, but they were either dismissed or not followed to a reasonable conclusion.[31]

Once again, however, the scandal produced a gain for the IG concept. The IG in charge of the questionable investigations, Richard

Mulberry, one of two Reagan IGs without federal experience, resigned in September 1984 and was replaced by James Richards, a former assistant U.S. attorney and later IG at Energy. In turn, Richards was replaced at Energy by John Layton, a former deputy IG at NASA under Brown. The net result was a further endorsement of IG experience as a prerequisite for service, and a confirmation of the dangers in bringing an outsider into the community. Like the situations at State and EPA, the message from the Interior case was to give the IGs greater independence to do their compliance work. The IGs seemingly could not lose.

As the IGs gained greater independence from their home departments and agencies, they moved closer to OMB. In return for yearly gains in statistical accomplishments—which could be translated into immediate press releases to counter a rising sea of red ink—the IGs would get additional staff. OMB would get the good news it needed to take the edge off the burgeoning deficits; the IGs would get the resources they wanted.

The risk was that some future deputy director would lose interest. By banking so heavily in one source of support, the IGs also were gambling that OMB would remain faithful. Moreover, having established themselves as steady sources of statistical accomplishment, the IGs also were counting on OMB to continue to value their products.

CHAPTER 7

Backlash

DESPITE the 1981 firings, and in part because of them, the IGs clearly prospered under Ronald Reagan. By 1985, they virtually controlled their own succession, their offices were running smoothly, and they continued to strengthen and expand their audit and investigation staffs. Government's capacity for compliance monitoring never had been higher, and OMB continued to promise staff and resources in return for more ammunition in the statistical war on waste. Although L. H. Fountain had retired from Congress in 1983, a need no longer seemed to exist for a strong congressional champion, especially with OMB Deputy Director Joe Wright in office. Year after year, the IGs were front and center in the annual budget document, allocated more staff and acknowledged for their work.

Moreover, the incentives for statistical accomplishment remained in place: The more the IGs produced by way of savings, administrative sanctions, "funds put to better use," indictments, prosecutions, and convictions, the bigger they would grow. The compliance definition of accountability, measured in purely fraud, waste, and abuse terms, was at work. In January 1987, for example, the PCIE chose three charts to depict the "highly significant impact on improving Government operations and reducing vulnerabilities." One showed a steady rise in yearly dollar savings, which totaled $84 billion over the 1981–86 period; a second showed a similar increase in successful prosecutions, which totaled 18,801 during the same time frame, and a third showed a fourfold increase in sanctions against contractors—6,118 sanctions put into effect from fiscal 1982 to fiscal 1986.[1] The report made no mention of IG accomplishments under the Carter administration.

THE CLASS OF 1985

The evolution of the IG concept into a strong right arm of the president and OMB is evident in the background and attitudes

Table 7-1. *The IG Educational Profile, by Class*
Percent

Variable[a]	Class of 1979[b]	Class of 1981[b]	Class of 1985[b]
Highest degree earned			
Bachelor's	46	41	33
Law	36	24	11
Master's	9	35	44
Ph.D.	9	0	11
Undergraduate institution			
Ivy League	9	11	11
Private	46	47	67
Public	46	41	22
Undergraduate major			
Finance, accounting, or business	36	35	44
Humanities	27	18	22
Law enforcement	27	12	22
Political science	9	35	11

a. $N = 37$.
b. Data are based on responses from 12 Carter, 18 Reagan first-term, and 10 Reagan second-term appointees. Some respondents did not answer every question. Totals may not add to 100 because of rounding.

of the class of 1985. Screened by their mentors in the IG community, the class represented the ideal IG.

First, an IG should come from an assistant or deputy IG position. Whereas 85 percent of the class of 1985 were drawn from assistant or deputy IG posts—half within their own department—only 45 percent of their Reagan predecessors were, compared with 20 percent of the Carter appointees. The class of 1985 also reflected recruitment biases in place years before the 1978 act was enacted; all of the Reagan second-term IGs were white, and all but one were male.

According to the data in table 7-1, members of the class of 1985 were more likely than either the Carter or first-term Reagan IGs to have advanced degrees and less likely to have gone to public institutions. In some ways, second-term Reagan IGs looked increasingly like the "average" presidential appointees who served from 1964 to 1984.

Second, an IG should have undergraduate training in finance, accounting, and business. This preference may be a byproduct of the IG selection process. Although all of the IGs were involved to some extent, the formal process was run by a three-member committee composed of Brown (an auditor), Dempsey (an investigator), and Sato (an auditor).

The drift toward auditors was almost inevitable, when Brown's mentoring of IGs also is considered. Having earned a master's in

Table 7-2. *Backgrounds and Opinions of IGs, by Class*
Percent

Variable	Class of 1979[a]	Class of 1981[a]	Class of 1985[a]
Years served in the executive branch[b]			
Less than 10	17	0	0
10–20	33	22	40
21–30	25	33	40
More than 30	25	44	20
Self-identified career focus[c]			
Audit, financial management, or administration	46	24	44
Investigations or law	55	53	33
Program management or evaluation	0	24	23
Moving up from within[d]			
1 (Is a conflict of interest)	10	22	30
2	20	28	40
3	30	11	20
4	0	28	0
5 (Is not a conflict of interest)	40	11	10
Waste in government[b]			
1 (Government is very wasteful)	0	0	0
2	8	17	30
3	25	16	10
4	42	33	50
5 (Government is relatively efficient)	25	33	10

a. See table 7-1, note b.
b. $N = 40$.
c. $N = 37$.
d. $N = 38$.

business administration at Cleveland State University, Brown started out as a staff accountant, eventually moving up to director of internal audit for the Navy Finance Center in Cleveland. Although her position immediately prior to appointment as the first Interior Department IG was a combination of administration and finance, Brown boasted impeccable accounting credentials. She eventually would recruit five IGs, most of whom had finance or accounting backgrounds; they, in turn, would recruit other IGs. Her background and her mentoring helped shape the future IG job description.

The number of IGs whose self-identified career focus was audit, financial management, or administration increased between the class of 1981 and the class of 1985, while investigations or law enforcement declined (see table 7-2). The change perhaps reflected Brown's influence in both assembling the pool of candidates and making final choices.

Together, these two criteria also may have resulted in somewhat younger IGs, which, in turn, may have favored those with somewhat less executive branch experience than the early IGs. The IG offices had existed as a training ground for only five to eight years, and auditors were less likely than investigators to have served in other federal agencies. Many investigators worked for another law enforcement agency—the FBI, Bureau of Alcohol and Firearms, Immigration and Naturalization Service—before joining an OIG, while the auditors usually started work with an OIG and stayed throughout their career. That the Reagan second-term IGs found greater fault with those who would become IG after serving in a non-IG post in the same department is not surprising given this career path.

In an unexpected turn, the data reveal that the new IGs saw government as more wasteful than past IGs. The differences among the three classes are not so extreme as to suggest that the final Reagan appointees were more cynical or harsher critics. The number who ranked government as very wasteful remained constant at zero across all three groups. Rather, the new IGs may have (a) seen more waste from their assistant and deputy posts, (b) been swayed by the continuing Reagan rhetoric on government mismanagement, or (c) reflected a lack of long-term experience that might temper views of waste.

The final Reagan IGs clearly benefited from the work of those who came before them. They saw less need for major overhauls of their offices and less shortages in their staffing (see table 7-3). One reason for this greater comfort level is that almost half of the second-term Reagan IGs helped build the office they directed.

Ties to Congress also weakened over time. As Congress became less of a primary audience for reports, the program managers grew in importance to the IGs. Seventy percent of the class of 1985 saw its primary audience as within their own departments or agencies, compared with 56 percent of the class of 1981 and 41 percent of the class of 1979.

Were the IGs finally being embraced by their own establishments? One answer is that the reports may have gone to the program managers, but the statistics went to OMB. A second is that good evidence exists, particularly in the congressional effort to strengthen the resolution of audit and investigative findings, that the primary audiences were not always listening. Reporting problems and winning resolution are different things.

The same trend toward an internal audience holds for investigation reports. Half of the final Reagan IGs identified the secretary or administrator or the program managers as their primary audience, compared with 23 and 17 percent of the earlier Reagan and Carter

Table 7-3. *Audiences and Operations of IGs, by Class*
Percent

Variable[a]	Class of 1979[a]	Class of 1981[a]	Class of 1985[a]
State of the office upon arrival[b]			
1 (Running very smoothly)	0	11	0
2	25	0	10
3	0	0	30
4	13	39	20
5 (Needed major overhaul)	63	50	40
Need for additional staff[b]			
1 (Enough staff)	17	6	10
2	25	33	20
3	8	11	30
4	8	28	10
5 (Serious shortages)	42	22	30
Problems in recruiting and retaining top staff[c,d]			
Inability to compete on pay	33	39	80
Inability to reorganize	8	0	20
Inflexibility in regulations	50	50	60
Lack of adequate training	33	17	20
Lack of response from staff	25	16	0
Lack of rewards for staff	42	33	40
Turnover among key staff	16	56	60
Primary audience for audits[c]			
Congress	42	33	20
Media	8	6	0
Office of Management and Budget	0	0	10
Program managers	8	17	30
Secretary or administrator	33	39	40
U.S. attorney	8	6	0
Primary audience for investigations[c]			
Congress	25	33	10
Media	8	11	10
Office of Management and Budget	0	0	0
Program managers	0	17	30
Secretary or administrator	17	6	20
U.S. attorney	50	33	30
Problem getting attention for reports[e]			
1 (Great difficulty)	17	0	0
2	17	18	22
3	25	24	22
4	25	24	22
5 (No difficulty)	17	35	33

a. See table 7-1, note b.
b. $N = 36$.
c. $N = 40$.
d. Respondents could give more than one answer.
e. $N = 38$.

Table 7-4. *The Nature of the IG Job, by Class*
Percent

Variable[a]	Class of 1979[b]	Class of 1981[b]	Class of 1985[b]
Average work week (hours)			
Less than 51	33	33	10
51–60	33	33	60
More than 60	33	34	30
What an IG needs to know[c]			
Audit skills	58	66	50
Budget process	33	78	70
Department or agency programs	67	72	30
How Congress works	75	95	70
How to manage	92	89	80
Investigation skills	58	61	50
Office of Management and Budget	67	78	70
Organizational politics	75	78	40
White House politics	25	33	30
Most difficult parts of the job[d]			
Dealing with Congress	29	61	60
Dealing with the media	42	33	50
Dealing with the White House and OMB	23	39	30
Mastering budget process	17	28	30
Mastering department procedures	25	39	20
Mastering program details	25	50	20
Organization of the OIG	50	39	20
Short-term orientation	16	28	60

a. $N = 40$ for all categories.
b. See table 7-1, note b.
c. The figures represent the percentage of respondents who considered the item important or very important. For "how to manage," 58 percent of the class of 1979, 39 percent of the class of 1981, and 20 percent of the

IGs, respectively. Debate continues on whether this inward focus is proper for investigatory reports.

The class of 1985 benefited from earlier efforts to gain attention for the semiannual reports. The Carter IGs reported much greater difficulty than either class of Reagan IGs. However, even the most important warnings can be ignored, misread, or so circumscribed by caveats that they are missed entirely.

The class of 1985 took their jobs seriously, working a bit harder than their predecessors and perhaps having less difficulty in most parts of their jobs (see table 7-4). The third class of IGs differed most from their predecessors in worries about program details, organizational politics, and technical management skills, perhaps because

Table 7-4 *(continued)*
Percent

Variable[a]	Class of 1979[b]	Class of 1981[b]	Class of 1985[b]
Sources of frustration[d]			
Agency resistance to change	50	61	20
Congressional interference	25	44	50
Lack of resources to do job	58	33	30
Lack of time to plan	17	17	20
Media visibility	17	11	30
OMB interference	17	28	0
Slowness of government decision making	42	61	30
Statistical measures of success	8	28	30
Turnover of political appointees	42	33	30
White House interference	0	6	0
Satisfactions from being IG[d]			
Being catalyst for change	50	61	50
Dealing with challenging problems	67	39	50
Enhancing public respect for government	50	28	30
Finding fraud, waste, abuse	25	44	40
High visibility of the job	8	6	0
Improving programs care about	16	11	10
Increasing government efficiency	50	72	80
Serving admired president	0	11	0
Serving secretary or administrator	17	33	10
Working with interesting people	17	0	10

class of 1985 said very important; for "how Congress works," 25 percent of the class of 1979, 67 percent of the class of 1981, and 40 percent of the class of 1985 said very important.

d. The figures represent the percentage of respondents who mentioned the item. Respondents could give more than one answer.

their needs changed. The final Reagan IGs also did not put as high a premium on knowledge about Congress.

These IGs also stood apart in what they found most difficult about their jobs. They were far less likely to say mastering program details and the OIG organization, but much more likely to mention dealing with Congress. They also listed congressional interference as one of the greatest sources of frustration.

The members of the class of 1985, meanwhile, were less troubled by the slow pace of decision making and agency resistance to change. More importantly, they were significantly more likely than any of their predecessors to mention the short-term orientation of Washington politics as a problem.

Ironically, the IGs may have reinforced the short-term pressure through the search for immediate statistical accomplishments. Unfortunately, even though Congress and OMB doubled IG funding between 1980 and 1988, neither branch could find the money for an integrated financial management system to replace the approximately four hundred antiquated, uncoordinated setups that caused so many of the problems unearthed by the IGs. Although the IGs did not favor this trade-off, it was forced by budget pressures nonetheless.

As an ideal type, the class of 1985 may best represent the decade-long shift toward alliance with OMB. According to the data in table 7-4, the IGs were individuals increasingly motivated by the desire to promote government efficiency, although many also indicated an interest in dealing with challenging problems and being a catalyst for change. Overall, IGs moved from having an *external* orientation—a goal of enhanced public respect, a primary audience outside the executive branch, fewer worries about congressional interference and the media—to an *internal* perspective—a goal of increased efficiency, a primary audience inside their departments and agencies, greater worries about congressional interference and the media.

FINE-TUNING

Despite the notable progress toward institutionalization, the evolution of the IG concept was not over. Still lacking IGs were two members of the inner-cabinet (Justice and Treasury), several major independent agencies (the Federal Emergency Management Agency [FEMA], the Nuclear Regulatory Commission, the CIA, and the Office of Personnel Management), and a host of small agencies, quasi-independent enterprises, and independent commissions. According to GAO testimony before the Governmental Affairs Committee, ninety-nine federal entities—some large, some small, some visible, some forgotten—were operating without the benefit of a statutory IG in 1988. Although the Senate did not want ninety-nine new presidential IGs, if only because it would have to confirm them all, the House and Senate staff generally agreed that the thirty-three agencies with budgets greater than $100 million or independent commission status ought to be brought under the IG blanket.

Other refinements in the IG concept needed to be made. The two-level pay structure never had been fixed; the deputy IG at HHS still was a presidential appointee subject to Senate approval; some confusion lingered over the IGs' authority to appoint their own staff to the Senior Executive Service; and problems existed with reports and budgets.

Some argue that Congress likes nothing better than to improve upon a successful idea. With the OIGs running relatively well, the notion of expanding the IG concept seemed the logical next step. Thus, as the 1978 act approached its tenth anniversary, Congress prepared to amend. Working with the first Democratic Senate in six years, Jack Brooks's House Government Operations Committee staff met with Democratic Ohio Senator John Glenn's new Governmental Affairs Committee staff to map out a strategy for securing passage of a comprehensive reform.

Securing Justice

The ultimate challenge was to create an IGship at the Justice Department. In the Senate, the former chairman of the Judiciary Committee, Strom Thurmond (R-S.C.), remained opposed to IG reform legislation. With Thurmond promising a "hold" on any such bill, the two committee staffs agreed that the Justice IG would have to originate from the House.[2] Glenn and the Senate Governmental Affairs Committee would develop the Treasury proposal, which appeared to be more of a problem in the House. At the risk of oversimplification, the Senate would recede to the House on Justice, and the House to the Senate on Treasury.

Justice was not willing to concede the issue, however. The department drew the line clearly against H.R. 4054, Brooks's version of the Inspector General Act Amendments of 1988, raising a series of long-rejected arguments against the IG concept in general and the Justice IG in specific. Not surprisingly, the House Government Operations Committee was not swayed. Having passed legislation creating a Justice IG four times only to have it ignored each time in the Republican Senate, the committee was unmoved. An IG was inevitable. As the committee tersely noted in its final report accompanying the Justice IG bill,

> The constitutional issues raised by the Justice Department are aimed at provisions contained in the 1978 Act and the acts which established inspectors general in the then–Department of Health, Education, and Welfare, and in the Department of Energy. These arguments were presented to the Congress prior to passage of those laws, but were not accepted. Moreover, the President signed the laws containing the questioned provisions and the committee knows of no effort to overturn them in the courts.[3]

Congress did give Justice one major concession: The Office of

Professional Responsibility (OPR), which held primary responsibility for investigating allegations against U.S. attorney's offices across the country, would be left out of the IGship. Although it was a high price to pay, particularly given that OPR since has been embroiled in controversies surrounding its investigatory independence, opponents of the compromise simply did not have the votes to prevail.[4]

Smaller Changes

Once the Justice agreement was ready, the rest of the 1988 amendments fell into place. Glenn would get IGs at the Nuclear Regulatory Commission and Treasury; Brooks would get Justice; the IGs at Executive Level V would move up to IV; and the OIGs would get their own appropriations accounts. The net result of the amendments was to further strengthen the OIGs in the competition for scarce resources, particularly dollars and staff, and to increase the potential for readership. Two other changes toward those ends merit further review.

REPORTS. After ten years of confusing, jargon-filled reading, Congress finally felt compelled to legislate on the structure and content of the IG reports, enacting a long subsection titled "Provisions to Ensure Uniformity and Reliability of Reports." Although the IGs later complained about the intricate reporting requirements, the provisions seemed warranted by the flurry of meaningless data being submitted in the semiannual reports. On top of the flood of billion-dollar claims and almost complete lack of agreement on basic terms, each IG had adopted a separate reporting format. As a result, comparisons across departments and agencies were nearly impossible. Accordingly, the IGs now were to add data on "questioned" versus "unsupported costs" of management failures, summaries of each "particularly significant report," a summary of each audit report "for which no management decision has been made," tables showing the status of all recommendations, and information concerning any disagreements with management.[5]

Congress, however, could do little to strengthen the IG reports as a basic warning device, as was amply demonstrated in the HUD scandal. No way existed to enforce a requirement for simple, direct language. But as much as the IGs can be criticized for their reporting style—one congressional staffer remarked that "the IGs could obscure the Revolutionary War"—little evidence exists that most members of Congress care enough to read even the more scintillating text.

SMALL AGENCIES. The 1988 amendments also expanded the IG concept to thirty-three small agencies.[6] The term "small agency" casts a wide net, given that it includes the U.S. Postal Service with its 800,000 employees. Most of the agencies were truly small, however. For example, the Board for International Broadcasting had seventeen employees; the Federal Maritime Commission, 225; and the Federal Election Commission, 243. Because many of the OIGs at these agencies would consist of one or two professionals plus clerical staff, the agency head would make the selections in accordance with applicable laws and regulations, the positions would not be presidential appointments, and the Senate would not have to vote to confirm.

For protection, the agency head was prohibited by statute from interfering in the IG's work and was required to report to both houses of Congress the reasons for firing the IG. Nevertheless, the lack of Senate confirmation meant these small agency IGs would be different from their Executive Level peers. Most would be career officers; many would be buried in small agencies almost unknown to most members of Congress, as well as the White House. Moreover, the small agency IGs would not be covered by separate appropriations accounts or required to establish assistant IGs for audit and investigation.

The small agency IGs would be called IGs nonetheless. By retaining the titles, the House and Senate were betting that these new IGs would succeed in spite of their size. They were also hoping that a black mark against the small agency IGs would not be interpreted as a black mark against the Senate-confirmed IGs.

INTO THE BUSH YEARS

As a result of passage of the 1988 amendments, the first Justice and Treasury IGs had to be nominated and confirmed; thirty-three small agency IGs had to be hired; and every IG report had to be reformatted. Just as in 1980, however, there was no hint of the controversy that was about to befall the IG concept.

Within months of the Bush inauguration, the IGs were embroiled in questions of authority, battles for visibility, and a full-scale scandal of their own. It still is not clear what went wrong, although a number of possible reasons arise: the 1988 election and the arrival of a new administration; the size of the task; bad timing with the emergence of the HUD scandal in early 1989; the need for each new administration to establish its own priorities. Having been so closely identified with the Reagan war on waste, the IGs may have paid a price in a new White House seeking ways to distance itself from its predecessor.

Whatever the cause, the emerging backlash against the once-protected OIGs was felt in four separate waves over the first year of the Bush administration: (1) numerous small problems in implementing the small agency provisions, (2) confusion regarding the new leadership at OMB, (3) a sweeping effort by the Department of Justice to limit IG authority, and (4) an attack from the staff of a Senate Governmental Affairs subcommittee.

Small Agency Problems

Of all the changes enacted in 1988, none caused more headaches for the presidentially appointed IGs than the creation of the thirty-three small agency IGs. They shared the same name, but not the same resources or statutory authority. Without separate appropriation accounts, minimum staffing requirements, and Senate confirmation, the fledgling IGs had few protections. The result was uneven implementation at best.

Many small agency IGs had little or no staff, while others suffered a string of embarrassments getting started, not the least of which was trying to obtain a formal mail-stop on the internal delivery routes. Save for the U.S. Postal Service, the size issue bedeviled small agency IGs. Moreover, according to a survey of the small agencies, the new IGs faced serious problems with resources and basic operating support, which could distract Congress from the needs of the big agency IGships.[7] Some could not get office space; others had trouble with telephones and office furniture.

Not all of the problems were small, however. The Government Printing Office (GPO), for example, with its 5,000 employees, $1 billion in revenues, and $1 billion in contracting, clearly warranted an IG presence. Although the new IGship experienced the usual start-up pains, it had forty-two full-time employees by 1990 and seemed to be well on its way toward routine operations, that is, until a new public printer, Robert Houk, informed Congress that he had decided to fire the incumbent IG. He noted only that "Because the incumbent in this position reports directly to the Public Printer and is responsible for analyzing and making recommendations pertaining to the overall management efficiency of the agency as well as other sensitive and significant matters, I have decided that I wish to appoint a candidate of my own choosing to this position."[8] His action was legitimate under the small agency provisions.

Inspector general advocates on Capitol Hill might not have challenged Houk, except he also sought to eliminate twenty of the IG's forty-two positions and appoint as IG a relatively inexperienced former police instructor who had served from 1984 to 1990 as FBI liaison to the White House personnel office. The problems with the new IG began immediately:

> On June 27, GPO's personnel office began a classification review of all IG audit positions to see which ones could be downgraded.
>
> On July 3, the new IG changed the titles of his audit directors from deputy assistant inspectors general to supervisory auditors.
>
> On July 11, a proposal was made to reduce the IG's staff allocation from forty-two full-time-equivalent positions to twenty-two, and the new IG agreed.
>
> On July 20, the IG reported to his staff that he had no control over the personnel decisions because he had not been in his position long enough to have any reason to question the wisdom of the public printer.
>
> On July 23, in accordance with civil service rules, other units in GPO began recruiting the OIG staffers about to lose their jobs in the reduction in force.
>
> On August 1, the chairmen and ranking members of the House Government Operations and Senate Governmental Affairs committees wrote the House and Senate Legislative Branch Appropriations subcommittees requesting a separate budget line supporting forty-two positions at GPO.

The situation at GPO is less an illustration of the difficulties in convincing a small agency about the merits of a quasi-independent IG and more a lesson about the lengths to which Congress had to go to protect the small agency IGs. Whatever the value of the small agency expansion, Glenn and his staff were forced to run from one brushfire to the next, investing time and energy that might have been better spent protecting large agency IGs from greater challenges.[9]

Uncertain Allies

The glory days ended for the IGs in a remarkably short span of weeks and months starting the day after Bush was elected. The IGs never appeared to be a priority in the White House personnel process and clearly were less of a concern for the new OMB.

Thus, even though Justice and Treasury acted quickly in creating their OIGs, the White House was slow in making the first nominations. The Treasury IGship remained vacant for nine months, while Justice was open for well over a year. These were not the only IGships that needed to be filled, however. By March 1990, more than a year into Bush's term, five of the twenty-six presidential IGships were still without nominees—CIA, FEMA, Labor, Transportation, and Veterans Affairs—while three had nominations pending before the Senate—Agriculture, Justice, and the Resolution Trust Corporation.

More importantly, even though the House and Senate had pushed hard for immediate reappointments, the incumbent IGs were left in limbo throughout much of the period. They were neither fired nor hired. The Bush White House told them that they would be subject to reappointment somewhere down the line, but not renominated per se. Some later said they would have preferred being fired to the lingering review. As Sherman Funk told the Senate Governmental Affairs Committee in September 1989, "If matters had moved quickly then, there would be no problem today. But matters did not move quickly. The process went on for many months. I have to tell you that the appointment process for everybody, as you know, has not been marked by blazing speed, so it was not just the IG's. But the IG's being in kind of a funny position, feeling under the gun, quite a number felt that this was making their life a bit too difficult." [10]

No matter the cause, the delays sent a message. Brown offered the following description of the slow, but steady, erosion of IG confidence as the reappointments failed to come:

> At first, there was not much discussion, and I think all of the IG's went on with business as usual. Then in March we were advised that our status was being reviewed. I think that is always appropriate, and that IG's need to be reviewed on a regular basis. However, every month this was reiterated at meetings of the President's Council on Integrity and Efficiency, and the IG's began to operate under a greater cloud of uncertainty. [11]

The IGs also lost their role in screening new nominees. Although the informal three-member screening committee still was in business in 1989, it had little influence. Twice at VA, for example, the screening committee rejected the department's choice of the incumbent chief benefits director as IG. Twice, the screening committee strongly noted its concern about moving someone so tightly linked to the internal operations of the department into the IG's post. And twice, the nomination survived. Only after the Senate and House both raised objections did the White House relent.[12]

These changes said something about the new regime at OMB. The deputy director, William Diefenderfer III, arrived late in his job and was not as interested in management or IGs as his two predecessors, Joe Wright and Ed Harper. As much as Frank Hodsoll, the new associate deputy director for management, supported the IGs, he had dual responsibility as the budget program director for national security programs, essentially working both sides of OMB, and lacked the clout of a deputy director. Thus, with Diefenderfer heavily engaged in budget policy, and Hodsoll at the wrong level to cross-walk resources, the IGs had no one to argue their case as the White House regained control of the IG appointments process.

Other precedents were abandoned with remarkable ease in the first days of the Bush administration, perhaps the inevitable product of the decade-long expansion. As the number of presidential IGs steadily increased—from one in 1976 to fifteen in 1978 to twenty-six in 1989—the highly unusual screening process was bound to be tested. However, absent OMB pressure, the White House began to treat the IG jobs like any other presidential appointment, allowing greater input from the secretaries and administrators and permitting the occasional marginal candidate as a political favor.

As one IG who served under Reagan and Bush said,

> All of us anticipated that the bloom would fade from the rose. We enjoyed great favor under Joe Wright, but that was bound to change. However, the decision by the White House to let the agencies choose their own IGs was a disservice and a violation of the spirit of the law. It was the first of many shots, maybe the natural result of folks not being able to take their shots during Wright's tenure. Wright was able to create the perception that taking a shot at an IG was akin to taking a shot at the Director of OMB and the President.

Questions of Authority

The problems at the small agencies and the changing of the guard at OMB might not have mattered but for a much more serious question regarding IG operations: Did the IGs have the authority to conduct some of their most visible investigations? Asked by the Justice Department's Office of Legal Counsel (OLC), the question signalled another attempt to revisit once-resolved IG issues. This time, however, with congressional supporters spread thinly defending the new

OIGs, and OMB an uncertain ally, the Justice Department's answer, written by Assistant Attorney General Douglas Kmiec in early 1989, seemed to stick.

LIGHTING THE FUSE. The dispute leading to the "Kmiec memo" began as an isolated incident almost two years before in the Department of Labor. The Labor IG, J. Brian Hyland, was working to consolidate the department's criminal investigatory activities under the OIG banner. Although many units in Labor had authority to investigate criminal complaints, their staffs were overburdened, undertrained, or both.

Thus, as Hyland began rounding up the memorandums of understanding transferring criminal investigations to his office, he encountered little resistance. Indeed, the Pension Welfare Benefits Administration (PWBA), which was responsible for overseeing almost 900,000 private retirement plans, seemed genuinely delighted at the prospect, a conclusion supported by a January 1987 PWBA staff memo:

> As you know, PWBA has vast civil investigative responsibilities under Title I of ERISA [Employee Retirement Income Security Act]. Discussions are now under way which, if successful, will allow us to concentrate all our available resources on civil fiduciary investigations along the lines proposed in our recently promulgated Enforcement Strategy Implementation Plan. Thus, we do not foresee any of PWBA's resources being available to assist in fulfilling whatever criminal investigatory responsibilities the Secretary may have either under the Comprehensive Crime Control Act of 1984 or under previous legislation.[13]

That is, if the IG wanted to undertake PWBA's criminal investigations, so much the better. The Occupational Safety and Health Administration (OSHA) and the Wage and Hour Division of the Employment Standards Administration, also expressed interest in similar transfers.

The problem with the delegation of duties was one of legislative intent. If Congress had wanted the IG to handle all PWBA criminal investigations, it might have said so in statute. Instead, this program operating responsibility was explicitly assigned to PWBA. If Congress had intended the IG to have program operating responsibilities, it might not have enacted Section 9 (a)(2) of the 1978 act to prohibit the transfer of any "program operating responsibilities" to an Office of Inspector General.

Whether PWBA was or was not able to handle its criminal caseload was never the issue. Few ever doubted the need for somebody to take on the work at Labor or the IG's superior investigative capacity. The question was whether the IG had the authority to accept long-term investigative responsibilities that appeared to be assigned to other entities: Did PWBA, OSHA, and Wage and Hour criminal investigations constitute a program operating function and, therefore, a specific exception to the IG's broader responsibility? Congress clearly did not want the IGs in the business of delivering basic program services—for example, granting OSHA permits. Whether Congress also prohibited the IGs from investigating criminal complaints regarding delivery of program services was uncertain.

That the issue even reached the point of a formal Labor Department request for an OLC opinion, however, revealed two features of the internal politics at work. One was the enmity between Hyland and the Labor Department solicitor, George Salem. For reasons still unclear, the two were at odds from the beginning of Salem's brief tenure as the fourth Labor solicitor under Reagan. The dispute should have been resolved without resort to OLC intervention.

The other was the territorial jealously that lurks at or near the surface of any agency, large or small. Encouraged from above, PWBA, OSHA, and the Wage and Hour Division all fought to reclaim their lost turf, even when they were no more interested or qualified to run criminal cases in 1988 than they had been six months before when they fully supported Hyland's idea.

AN OPINION IN SEARCH OF A CASE? With no intervention from OMB or the secretary by the end of the Reagan administration, the issue was destined to be resolved by the legal scholars at OLC. Originally, however, OLC appeared less than enthusiastic about the case, responding to the September 23, 1988, Labor Department request for an opinion by asking for the facts of a specific dispute, thereby narrowing the case to a single question.

Instead, the solicitor replied in December that the legal question "is not now presented to you, either in the context of, or as a result of, a difference of opinion about any particular investigation. . . . Our Office of Inspector General claims the general authority to investigate any violation of statute administered and enforced by the Department." [14] In setting the issue in a larger context, the solicitor invited OLC to direct its opinion not just at the IG at Labor, but also at the concept in general.

No one knows why OLC persevered, especially because it would have been easy to leave the controversy to the new Labor secretary and her team. But the opinion was released as the Justice Department was being dragged against its will into the IG community, leading some to wonder about the circumstantial connection. As Senator Glenn said in April 1990:

> Why now? Why does DOJ [Department of Justice] move after 12 years of excellent work by the IGs and all those thousands of cases referred to Justice which have been prosecuted? Why now? Why move after 12 years of excellent work with the IGs to so seriously limit their ability to continue?
>
> Well, I cannot authoritatively answer that question, but it does seem to me a strange coincidence that DOJ would move so forcefully against the IG community after the IG Act coverage was extended to cover the Department of Justice itself, coverage very strongly fought by the Department of Justice.[15]

In defense of OLC, the opinion regarding the Labor Department was not the first time it had weighed in on IG authority. It had been asked a similar question about passport and visa fraud five years before by the State Department. The resulting 1984 OLC opinion laid the groundwork for Kmiec's later memorandum by suggesting that Congress intended the IGs to conduct investigations only of activities *directly connected* to their establishment, whether through federal employees or funds.[16] The 1984 opinion never received any press, however, in part because it was tightly restricted to passport and visa fraud and in part because the next State Department IG, Funk, reportedly did not know about it until it was mentioned in a Kmiec memorandum footnote.

A QUESTION OF INTENTIONS. Whatever the disposition of the 1984 opinion, its 1989 relation was much more difficult to ignore, for it took a very large and highly visible bite at the IG investigatory apple.[17]

As the second paragraph of the nineteen-page opinion concluded:

> As set forth below, we conclude that the Act does not generally vest in the Inspector General authority to conduct investigations pursuant to regulatory statutes administered by the Department of Labor. Rather, Congress intended the Inspector General to be an objective official free from general regulatory responsibilities who investigated the employees and operations of the Department, as well as its contractors, grantees, and other recipients of federal funds, so as to root out waste and fraud. Thus, the Inspector General had an oversight rather than a direct role in investigations conducted pursuant to regulatory statutes: he may investigate the Department's conduct of regulatory investigations but may not conduct such investigations himself.[18]

That is, if the statute did not involve a federal employee or a federal dollar, and was therefore regulatory in nature, the IG was not to be concerned.

The opinion was based on two broad conclusions regarding the legislative history of the 1978 act. The first was tightly bounded by the facts of the case: Congress had not intended the IGs to exercise long-term program operating responsibilities. Because the IG's proposed absorption of PWBA, OSHA, and Wage and Hour criminal investigations easily could be defined as an operating responsibility, OLC said no to IG authority. After dismissing various statements by Fountain on congressional intent, OLC turned to a single paragraph in the formal legislative report accompanying the original House measure:

> While Inspectors General would have direct responsibility for conducting audits and investigations relating to the efficiency and economy of program operations and the prevention and detection of fraud and abuse in such programs, *they would not have such responsibility for audits and investigations constituting an integral part of the program involved.* Examples of this would be audits conducted by USDA's Packers and Stockyards Administration in the course of its regulation of livestock marketing and *investigations conducted by the Department of Labor as a means of enforcing the Fair Labor Standards Act.* In such cases, the Inspector General would have oversight rather than direct responsibility.[19]

Had Kmiec closed his opinion with that quote, the fight might not have ensued. The IGs likely would have found a way around the restrictions, and the opinion would have found a resting place on some dusty executive branch shelf alongside its 1984 companion. Unfortunately, the second part of the opinion raised much broader concerns. According to the memo, Congress also had intended the IGs to investigate only those activities involving either federal employees or federal dollars, not those involving regulatory statutes.

Here, Kmiec drew heavily on a single incident in the legislative history of the 1978 statute. The Senate version of the bill had contained detailed definitions of audit and investigation. According to OLC's reading, the Senate dropped those definitions as nothing more than "surplus language," thereby proving that Congress did not want the IGs to reach broadly in their work. The reality of the record was quite the opposite, however. Congress deleted the language in conference because it was seen as unduly narrow, expressing its intent to give the IGs the fullest possible investigatory range.

Recall, too, that Congress also prohibited any official from interfering with any OIG audit or investigation. Finally, the statute clearly used the words "relating to the programs and operations of the establishment" to describe the OIG's responsibility, not "only inside the establishment" or "only involving dollars or employees of the establishment." Congress explicitly chose its words to give the IGs running room.

SURVEYING THE WRECKAGE. Flawed or not, the OLC memo wreaked havoc in the IG community. James Naughton produced a twenty-four-page single-spaced, point-by-point refutation, complete with ninety-eight footnotes. Naughton's analysis of the opinion began as follows:

> The authors of the OLC memorandum clearly are not lacking in self-confidence, in imagination, and in willingness to enunciate bold, far-reaching conclusion. However, an abundance—or even an overabundance—of those characteristics cannot compensate for an absence of facts and a pervasive lack of knowledge of the subject matter.[20]

As Naughton noted, however, the memo was not a crippling blow to IG investigative range. "Any IG who can't figure out how to investigate anything that needs investigating, including violations of regulatory statutes," Naughton concluded, "is too dumb to be an IG."[21] By itself, the opinion was easy to ignore. The OLC had no enforcement powers, and the opinion was just that, an opinion.

The question, however, was not whether the OLC opinion was enforceable, but whether the IGs could ignore such a prominent attack, which was widely seen as the beginning of a growing anti-IG movement. Thus, even before the opinion was released, Hyland highlighted the state of affairs on the first page of his March 31, 1989, semiannual report:

> I fear that the OIG has been experiencing something of a significant shift that may not bode well for future cooperation in audits and investigations. Where speedy cooperation was once encouraged by top-level Department of Labor management, our requests for information or assistance are now too often subjected to a protracted delay. Today, questions about OIG authority, requests for clarifications, requests for opinions or rulings from the Solicitor or DOJ, or other such actions are routinely used to frustrate any audit or investigative activity that does not fit the current, narrow view of OIG authority that has been held by certain departmental officials.[22]

The IGs also developed a long list of doomsday scenarios about the impact of the opinion on ongoing investigations. Testifying before the Senate Governmental Affairs Committee the following year, Kusserow (HHS), Richards (Interior), and Funk (State) offered one example after another of potential setbacks in the war on fraud. Glenn and Richards also engaged in the following tongue-in-cheek colloquy regarding misuse of seals, logos, and letterhead:

> Mr. RICHARDS. Another area was one . . . touched upon briefly—and a lot of us have done these cases over the years—that is the illegal use of the logo, of the letterhead. There was a case that—somebody impersonated an astronaut.
> Chairman GLENN. Now, that is getting real bad there.
> Mr. RICHARDS. Yes, it is. In order to entice organizations to pay him money to speak to them. Certainly there is no connection with an agency employee or appropriated funds there, but naturally the agency turned to the Inspector General to investigate that. Those are the kinds of things that we do instinctively and the agencies refer them to us instinctively.[23]

Still, Naughton's earlier conclusion regarding long-term effects of the opinion seemed valid. Most investigative cases continued unabated, no investigators were laid off. The best course of action may have been to dismiss the opinion as an aberration, particularly because the IGs had ample alternative authorities, including the Program Fraud and Civil Remedies Act, to investigate all of the issues raised in the hearing. Although Program Fraud restricted sanctions to administrative penalties, an IG could refer a case investigated under the statute for further criminal prosecution.

DENOUEMENT. Whatever its impact on real investigations, as a tool to be applied in bureaucratic turf battles, the OLC opinion took its toll. The Kmiec memo prompted the HHS secretary to suspend an IG investigation of generic drug approval at the Food and Drug Administration (FDA). At the beginning, Kusserow's team of investigators had restricted themselves to cases involving the outright corruption of FDA officials by manufacturers seeking approval of their products. However, under the secretary's broad delegation of Food, Drug, and Cosmetic Act investigatory authority, the investigation began to spread. According to Kusserow,

> We began to see that some of these companies did not even need to bribe officials, that in fact that they might be able to obtain the same benefit through criminal acts on their own such as

falsifying data to support their application, fabricating the attestation of what the product can do, maybe even having product substitution, and in effect committing a fraud, and finally, it did not necessarily have to involve Federal employees in a culpable fashion, that they could be fooled.[24]

At some point, the investigation expanded past the last federal employee and last federal dollar and reached the first of many not directly connected to the government. Nevertheless, things were going well, according to Kusserow, until FDA investigators read the OLC opinion and reclaimed their territory. Under pressure from Justice, the secretary rescinded his delegation of investigatory authority in early 1990, and Kusserow was called off.

The turn of events was "to the delight of disgruntled staff attorneys within the HHS Office of General Counsel," the House Energy and Commerce Subcommittee on Oversight and Investigations later concluded in a report titled *Naked Reverse.* "The net result," according to the subcommittee, "has been to leave the Food and Drug Administration susceptible once again to the same kinds of fraud that have threatened much of the Nation's supply of generic drugs."[25]

Of particular interest was the inability or unwillingness of OMB to resolve the dispute. Meeting with the various players at the White House on December 1, 1989, Associate Deputy Director Frank Hodsoll made little headway in forging an agreement. Whether the deputy director of OMB could have done better will never be known. However, not surprisingly, Hodsoll, a third-level OMB officer at Executive Level V, was unable to persuade an HHS under secretary at Executive Level II, a general counsel at Executive Level IV, an IG at Executive Level IV, and a Labor Department chief of staff representing a secretary at Executive Level I to work out their differences.

Ultimately, the firefighting fell to Glenn and his Governmental Affairs Committee staff. The dispute came to a head when Glenn introduced S. 2608 on May 10, 1990, a bill giving each IG "authority to determine—(A) the persons subject to, and the nature, scope, and purposes of, audits and investigations conducted by the Inspector General relating to programs and operations administered, carried out, financed, or conducted by his or her establishment, including programs and operations under regulatory statutes; and (B) the authority of the Inspector General to conduct those audits and investigations." In short, the IGs would be given authority to determine their own limits.

Although the bill had twelve cosponsors, it was more bargaining chip than legislative possibility. The ranking Republican on the Governmental Affairs Committee, William Roth, opposed the bill and was on the record supporting the general thrust of the OLC opinion.

The denouement of this legal drama was not to be found in legislation, but in a simple coincidence: Barr was nominated to be deputy attorney general. With that nomination pending before the Senate Judiciary Committee, Glenn expressed his intent to place a hold on further consideration, halting floor action until the OLC issue was resolved. Less than two weeks later, Barr hammered out the needed compromise. Not only could the IGs conduct criminal and other investigations so long as those investigations were related to the agency's programs and operation, but they also were authorized to conduct criminal and other investigations of "individuals and entities who are not agency employees and who do not receive federal funds" in three specific circumstances:

a. When an external party is suspected of having acted in collusion with an agency employee or a recipient of agency funds.
b. When the IG is investigating an external party under the Program Fraud Civil Remedies Act in connection with the possible imposition of administration penalties under that Act.
c. When, in an application for a federal benefit or in a document relating to the payment of funds or property to the agency, an external party has filed, attempts to file, or causes or conspires to be filed a false fraudulent statement with the intention of deliberately misleading an employee or official of the agency or of committing a fraud upon the agency. . .[26]

In addition, Barr's modification allowed the IGs to conduct "spot checks" of regulatory statutes, leaving future IGs to figure out what that meant.

Some in the IG community argued that Barr's compromise was hollow. Barr did not rescind OLC's narrow reading of the original statute. However, given the politics of waging a legislative battle that Glenn could not win, particularly with members of his own committee divided on the issue, Barr's proposal was the best available solution to two years of bitter infighting. Two weeks later, Barr was confirmed.[27]

An OIG Scandal?

The final chapter in the backlash began in a subcommittee of Glenn's Senate Governmental Affairs Committee, with a report authored by the staff of Democratic Tennessee Senator James Sasser's Subcommittee on General Services, Federalism, and the District of Columbia. Although never released or approved by either the subcommittee or full committee as required by the rules, the report was shared with the *Washington Post*. The *Post* took note of the report in a September 15, 1990, editorial titled "Watching the Watchdogs."[28]

What concerned the subcommittee staff were allegations, many later proved unfounded, of widespread wrongdoing in IG protection of whistleblowers. According to the report,

The most frequently heard, and substantiated, complaints were that the IGs—
- routinely disclose confidential identities without first obtaining whistleblowers' consent as required by law. There are current no provisions for criminal sanctions or civil remedies to address such violations.
- fail to investigate clearly strong cases; or, if the cases are investigated, fail to conduct thorough and proper investigations or simply white-wash the final reports.
- initiate phoney investigations against the whistleblowers themselves in apparent attempts to intimidate or discredit them, and/or to set examples for co-workers.[29]

Not all of the staff recommendations for reform were hostile to the IG concept; for example, a five-year staggered term of office and removal only for just cause. However, overall the allegations were damning. As with the Kmiec memo, the substance of the Sasser staff report was not as important as the impact. Glenn had no choice but to launch a full committee investigation, which meant more delays in clearing the IGs.

The report also may have called into question Glenn's ability to protect the IGs. With Brooks having moved as chairman from Government Operations to Judiciary in 1989, and his successor John Conyers (D-Mich.) distracted throughout most of 1989 with a futile bid to become mayor of Detroit, IG leadership fell to Glenn. He was the most senior IG sponsor left in the leadership position in either chamber but he was preoccupied with the Senate Ethics Committee investigation that eventually exonerated him of charges that he had done favors for Charles Keating, former president of Lincoln Savings and Loan, in return for major donations to Glenn's campaigns. Furthermore, the report came from a subcommittee of the committee that Glenn chaired, which must have left the IGs wondering who they could turn to for help. If not Glenn, forced into a full committee investigation, and if not OMB, still confused about who was responsible for the IGs, then who?

CONCLUSION: UNCERTAIN FUTURES

The first years of the Bush administration gave the IGs further reason to focus on highly individualized compliance monitoring. Whatever the clarifications surrounding the Kmiec memo, the IGs knew that broad expansions of their investigations would be closely monitored by Justice, especially with Wright gone from OMB. Indeed, Wright's departure may have created the conditions for backlash. As the Bush administration sought to carve its own identity separate from Reagan, the IGs moved down the list of priorities. Having been trained to fight waste during the Reagan administration, the IGs now were without a war. In many ways, the government fraud issue had been played out; Congress and the media lost interest, and the savings and loan failures and other scandals took center stage.[30]

Although the IGs were removed from the president's management agenda, program evaluation was added. OMB was becoming more interested in program evaluation, issuing a government-wide call for renewal. The invitation was contained in the fiscal year 1992 budget, in a section titled "Improving Returns on Investment." It made absolutely no mention of the IGs: "The Administration supports a systematic and sustained investment in more rigorous evaluation—as an aid to both the Executive Branch and Congress in planning, monitoring, and assessing program results, and in determining future program needs."[31]

Being invited to evaluate is different from being able to respond. However, some IGs already were developing this capacity. None was willing to abandon compliance monitoring as the primary focus, and some of the strongest IGs on evaluation also were the most intent upon expanded law enforcement authority. But evaluation was emerging as a new, albeit fledgling, IG product line in which monitoring toward performance and capacity building was more likely and was to be rewarded.

PART 4

Organizing for Accountability

CHAPTER 8

A Drift toward Investigation

O F all the organizational innovations in the IG Act, none was more challenging than merging auditors and investigators into a unified workforce. Auditors and investigators speak different languages, follow different clocks, and pursue different targets.[1] "Audits are done of programs and operations, and are general in nature," wrote Interior IG James Richards, "while investigations are done of allegations of waste, fraud, and abuse, and are specific in nature."[2]

More important for the working relationship, auditors and investigators are hired under separate—some auditors might argue unequal—personnel classifications and, therefore, receive different pay and benefits. Because their work is sometimes hazardous, most investigators receive special pay and retirement benefits, as well as overtime and limited use of government cars. Although the overtime is trivial and the vehicles hardly luxurious, they are perks nonetheless.

These two professions may even favor different kinds of office environments. At the HHS OIG field office in San Francisco, for example, the auditors are housed in standard-issue government offices—green paint, old furniture, venetian blinds, fluorescent lighting—while the investigators have modern cubicles with a badges motif—personal badges dangling from pockets, bigger badges framed on the walls, flags in every corner. "We could just as easily be in Oakland," one member of two staffs remarked about the need for proximity.

However oversimplified these differences, the rivalry may help explain the rising emphasis on compliance monitoring and statistical accomplishments. Had the two professions stayed in separate units, as they existed before the IG Act, they might not have been so easily convinced of the need to continuously increase savings and convictions. Pitted against each other in the internal, and possible universal, organization struggle for resources, each may have lost sight of the broader IG mandate.

AUDITORS AND INVESTIGATORS

Differences between auditors and investigators as IGs translate into meaningful understandings of the attitudes and values of their staffs discussed below, yielding some indication of what the increasing number of investigatory staff may be doing to future IG operations. Auditor and investigator IGs bring different skills to their jobs, seek different audiences for their work, and come to their IG appointments with different goals and satisfactions.

Given their professional backgrounds, these differences are hardly surprising. Auditors tended to be older at the time of their first appointment, with much deeper federal experience, and less likely to have an advanced degree (see tables 8-1 and 8-2).

Equally important, the two professions differed on basic audiences and operations (see table 8-3). The investigators were more likely to say they inherited an office needing a major overhaul, albeit only slightly more likely to see a need for additional staff. Dissatisfaction with the state of the office does not vary much whether an investigator followed another investigator or an auditor, perhaps reflecting a general impatience with the pace of government.

In a similar vein, the investigators said they experienced much greater difficulties getting attention on their reports and action on requests for Department of Justice deputizations of their agents. Because most OIGs do not have blanket law enforcement authority—that is, authority to make arrests, serve warrants, and carry firearms—they ordinarily request special deputization from the U.S. Marshals Service, which until recently involved a long and drawn-out clearance process.

On audiences for their reports, the choice of an investigator or auditor as IG may not matter much. On audit reports, 42 percent of the auditors saw their primary audience as external to the department or agency (Congress), compared with 50 percent of the investigators (Congress, the media, and the U.S. attorney). On investigations, the same pattern emerges: 66 percent of the auditors (Congress and the U.S. attorney), and 63 percent of the investigators (Congress, media, and the U.S. attorney) also looked external. The question is whether the bad news goes to Congress, the media, or a U.S. attorney first. What is clear is that investigators tended to prefer the most visible external audience (the media) much more than the auditors.

Table 8-1. *The IG Demographic Profile, by Career Focus*
Percent

Variable	Auditors[a]	Investigators[a]
Age at first appointment[b]		
Under 50	8	20
50–60	47	42
61–70	50	33
Gender[c]		
Female	8	19
Male	92	81
Race[c]		
Nonwhite	8	6
White	92	94
Highest degree earned[c]		
Bachelor's	50	25
Law	8	33
Master's	42	38
Ph.D.	0	6
Undergraduate institution[c]		
Ivy League	0	6
Private	67	50
Public	33	44
Undergraduate major[c]		
Finance, accounting, or business	75	25
Humanities	8	13
Law enforcement	8	38
Political science	8	25

Source: Data are based on individual responses to the IG mail survey. "Auditors" included those who identified their career focus as "auditing," "financial management," "budget," "accounting," and general "administration." "Investigators" included those who identified their career focus as "law enforcement," "investigations," and general "law." Thirty-five percent of the IGs fell into the audit category; 49 percent, investigations; and 16 percent, program management or evaluation.

a. Data are based on responses from 12 auditors and 16 investigators. Some respondents did not answer every question. Totals may not add to 100 because of rounding.

b. $N = 27$.

c. $N = 28$.

This penchant for visibility carries its own risks, amply illustrated in 1989 when Richard Kusserow almost lost his IGship as a result of an interview with ABC's Chris Wallace. The interview, which appeared on the September 20, 1990, installment of "Primetime Live," involved allegations that Kusserow and his Office of Investigations had set a bounty for Medicare and Medicaid provider fraud.

The bounty, which came in the form of annual performance bonuses linked to quotas, was real; investigators were rewarded for bringing in a set number of cases against providers. The bonus highlighted in ABC's story was for increasing sanctions against health

Table 8-2. *Backgrounds and Opinions of IGs, by Career Focus*
Percent

Variable	Auditors[a]	Investigators[a]
Years served in the executive branch[b]		
Less than 10	0	13
10–20	25	44
21–30	50	19
More than 30	25	25
Previous public service[b]		
Executive branch	83	81
Other	17	19
Location of previous federal service[c]		
Different agency from IG	50	69
Same agency as IG	50	31
Moving up from within[d]		
1 (Is a conflict of interest)	27	33
2	27	20
3	9	13
4	18	13
5 (Is not a conflict of interest)	18	20
Waste in government[b]		
1 (Government is very wasteful)	0	0
2	17	13
3	25	13
4	50	44
5 (Government is relatively efficient)	8	31

Source: See table 8-1.
a. See table 8-1, note a.
b. $N = 28$.
c. $N = 23$.
d. $N = 26$.

care providers by 10 percent a year. By itself, the bounty system was hard enough to defend. However, the case against a New York "country doctor" named William Diefenbach was Kusserow's first media crisis in almost ten years as IG.

According to the OIG files, Diefenbach was removed from the Medicare provider rolls for poor record keeping. In the televised interview about a series of bounty cases, an exhausted Kusserow offered additional information:

WALLACE: Your office reviewed—
Mr. KUSSEREAU [*sic*]: That's right.
WALLACE: —the peer review organization investigation of Dr. Diefenbach—
Mr. KUSSEREAU: We reviewed the paperwork, yes.

WALLACE: —and ruled that he should be excluded—kicked out of—Medicare and Medicaid.

Mr. KUSSEREAU: There was evidence that in a number of cases, that he was an impaired physician—he was suffering from drug abuse—and that as a result of that, he was considered unwilling or unable to change his practice.

WALLACE: Drug abuse?

Mr. KUSSEREAU: Yes.

WALLACE: Where? I mean, I must say, he was never charged with that.

Mr. KUSSEREAU: This person was providing second-class medicine. He did not belong in the program.

WALLACE: Well, you know, the only reason I ask—and we will go back and check, and if there's evidence—

Mr. KUSSEREAU: More than happy. Sure.

WALLACE: —of drug abuse, that's certainly something that we—

Mr. KUSSEREAU: You can jam it down my throat.

WALLACE: —absolutely unaware of.

Mr. KUSSEREAU: Jam it down my throat.[3]

No evidence of drug abuse existed in the OIG files or in Diefenbach's file at the hospital. Wallace asked Diefenbach's wife about the charge:

WALLACE: The Inspector General says that one reason your husband was kicked out of the government programs was because he was an "impaired" doctor, because he had a drug problem.

Ms. DIEFENBACH: Are you serious? He said that?

WALLACE: Yes, he did.

Ms. DIEFENBACH: That man is—is—it's a total, complete, utter, devastating lie. He had better have proof of that.

WALLACE: [voice-over] Primetime asked to see the Inspector General's proof. A week later, KUSSEREAU issued this statement. He still claimed Bill Diefenbach was a bad doctor, but said "After examining the official file I must retract my original statement about Dr. Diefenbach being drug impaired. The issue of drug use played no role whatsoever." KUSSEREAU declined to do another interview.

But Bill Diefenbach gave up the fight to clear his name. His family says from the day he was blackballed from Medicare he slowly sank into a deep depression from which he never recovered. Three months ago he shot and killed himself.[4]

Table 8-3. *Audiences and Operations of IGs, by Career Focus*
Percent

Variable	Auditors[a]	Investigators[a]
State of the office upon arrival[b]		
1 (Running very smoothly)	9	7
2	18	7
3	18	0
4	38	9
5 (Needed major overhaul)	46	46
Need for additional staff[c]		
1 (Enough staff)	0	6
2	33	31
3	17	6
4	8	25
5 (Serious shortages)	42	31
Problems in recruiting and retaining top staff[c,d]		
Inability to compete on pay	42	56
Inability to reorganize	17	6
Inflexibility in regulations	42	56
Lack of adequate training	25	25
Lack of response from staff	25	13
Lack of rewards for staff	25	25
Turnover among key staff	17	44
Primary audience for audits[c]		
Congress	42	25
Media	0	13
Office of Management and Budget	0	0
Program managers	8	19
Secretary or administrator	50	31
U.S. attorney	0	12

Armed with the ABC transcript, the American Medical Association (AMA) joined the American Hospital Association and thirty-eight state medical associations to demand Kusserow's resignation. According to the AMA's joint letter to the HHS secretary:

Although the ABC Prime Time [*sic*] Live telecast of September 20, 1990 was the immediate impetus for the AMA's decision to ask the President to act, Mr. Kusserow's performance on that program merely exemplified a pattern of conduct. The qualities in him that made his performance an outrage to thousands of physicians have been exhibited by Mr. Kusserow throughout his tenure. In his nine years as Inspector General, Mr. Kusserow has failed to demonstrate the balance, objectivity, and sound

Table 8-3 (*continued*)
Percent

Variable	Auditors[a]	Investigators[a]
Primary audience for investigations[a]		
Congress	33	13
Media	0	19
Office of Management and Budget	0	0
Program managers	8	25
Secretary or administrator	25	12
U.S. attorney	33	31
Difficulty getting attention for reports[e]		
1 (Great difficulty)	0	13
2	0	31
3	30	25
4	40	13
5 (No difficulty)	30	19
Difficulty getting deputizations for investigators[f]		
1 (Relatively easy)	11	8
2	33	8
3	11	8
4	33	54
5 (Very difficult)	11	23

Source: See table 8-1.
a. See table 8-1, note a.
b. $N = 24$.
c. $N = 28$.
d. Respondents could give more than one answer.
e. $N = 26$.
f. $N = 21$.

judgment essential to the effective performance of his job. He has been lax in circumstances calling for vigorous prosecutions, zealous in circumstances that counseled moderation, and inept in developing consistent, appropriate, and timely guidelines for program enforcement. As a consequence, the Inspector General has not achieved Congress's goal of ensuring that Medicare and Medicaid programs are efficiently and effectively enforced.[5]

Kusserow survived, in part because the AMA campaign was widely seen as a "red badge of courage" among his congressional supporters. Nevertheless, the incident showed how visibility cuts both ways. Publicity can expose the IG to increased hostility from career civil servants, political appointees, and the congressional authorizing committees, particularly if the scandal involves sacred projects.

Table 8-4. *The Nature of the IG Job, by Career Focus*
Percent

Variable[a]	Auditors[b]	Investigators[b]
Average work week (hours)		
Less than 51	8	44
51–60	67	38
More than 60	25	19
What an IG needs to know[c]		
Audit skills	58	56
Budget process	43	75
Department or agency programs	58	63
How Congress works	52	88
How to manage	67	94
Investigation skills	75	50
Office of Management and Budget	75	75
Organizational politics	58	75
White House politics	17	31
Most difficult parts of the job[d]		
Dealing with Congress	92	50
Dealing with the media	58	25
Dealing with the White House and OMB	42	38
Mastering budget process	8	31
Mastering department procedures	17	38
Mastering program details	17	50
Organization of the OIG	33	50
Short-term orientation	25	31

Source: See table 8-1.
a. *N* = 28 for all categories.
b. See table 8-1, note a.
c. The figures represent the percentages of respondents who considered the item important or very important. For "department or agency programs," 33 percent of the auditors and 18 percent of the investigations said very

Nevertheless, as indicated by the data in table 8-4, investigators-turned-IGs have a much stronger external orientation than their auditor colleagues. Asked what an IG needs to know to succeed, the investigators were more likely to mention Congress, the White House, and organizational politics, while the auditors thought knowing how to investigate was vital. If the responses also pointed to problems experienced by the IGs, investigators faced their greater challenges internally. They were much more concerned with how to manage as a basic skill, a likely product of their lesser federal experience and lack of administrative training.[6] Asked about the most difficult parts of their jobs, the investigators found external relations easiest, particularly in comparison with the auditors.

What emerges is an inside-outside pattern for auditors and investigators. Auditors seem more comfortable with the internal aspects of

Table 8-4 (*continued*)
Percent

Variable[a]	Auditors[b]	Investigators[b]
Sources of frustration[d]		
Agency resistance to change	50	56
Congressional interference	58	38
Lack of resources to do job	33	44
Lack of time to plan	8	6
Media visibility	33	19
OMB interference	8	25
Slowness of government decision making	33	63
Statistical measures of success	25	6
Turnover of political appointees	25	50
White House interference	0	6
Satisfactions from being IG[d]		
Being catalyst for change	83	44
Dealing with challenging problems	33	44
Enhancing public respect for government	33	50
Finding fraud, waste, abuse	25	63
High visibility of the job	0	6
Improving programs care about	8	6
Increasing government efficiency	50	69
Serving admired president	8	6
Serving secretary or administrator	17	13
Working with interesting people	8	6

important; for "audit skills," 33 percent of the auditors and 18 percent of the investigators said very important; and for "budget process," 8 percent of the auditors and 37 percent of the investigators said very important. Respondents could give more than one answer.

d. The figures represent the percentage of respondents who mentioned the item. Respondents could give more than one answer.

the IG job—that is, with mastering program details and departmental procedures, the organization of their offices, the budget process—while investigators seem on stronger footing outside—that is, with Congress and with the media.

The internal-external pattern also applies to IG frustrations. Auditors faced their greatest hindrances outside the OIG, with congressional interference and the media. Investigators-turned-IG felt at ease with external relations but experienced a more general lack of patience for the slowness of government decision making. This impatience helps explain the difficulties investigators had getting attention for reports and deputization for their special agents (see table 8-3).

Auditors and investigators show their greatest differences when asked about the satisfactions of their jobs. On the one hand, the auditors-turned-IG were highly motivated by being a catalyst for change, which may not be evident in a single term or a single semi-annual reporting period, and which cannot be easily measured by statistical accomplishments. On the other hand, the investigators-turned-IG were energized by finding fraud, waste, and abuse; increasing government efficiency; and enhancing public respect for government. All were goals that can be more readily measured or detected.

These differences may explain why auditors and investigators choose alternate routes to reform. Offered a list of possible changes in the IG concept, the investigators were much more likely to endorse reform, whether in areas affecting their investigatory staff—testimonial subpoena power, weapons authority, and law enforcement authority—or their own job security—a fixed term of office and removal only for cause (see table 8-5).

Overall, the auditors appear to fit their introspective, technically oriented stereotype, going about their business with a diligence and quiet persistence characteristic of their profession, willing to let the facts do the talking to Congress and the secretary or administrator. Perhaps they felt less need for job protection as a result of their method of operation. Facts are facts—either the audit has or has not been done correctly, either the methodology has or has not been properly applied using generally accepted government accounting standards.

In contrast, the investigators appear to match their gung-ho, go-for-broke stereotype, moving at high speed to catch the thieves, recover the goods, and restore the public faith, willing, if need be, to bring the media and the U.S. attorney in on the case. Perhaps, as such, they felt more need for removal protection. Given the range of discretion needed in both choosing investigatory targets and convincing a U.S. attorney to prosecute, and the risks involved in sanctioning someone such as Diefenbach, investigators likely would feel vulnerable.

Determining whether auditors or investigators are better IGs depends on the nature of the IG task in the particular agency. One conclusion, however, is clear: Having an investigator at the top of the OIG does not ensure favoritism for investigators, and having an auditor at the top does not automatically mean increases in staffing for auditors. According to the data in table 8-6, having an auditor as IG almost always produced a cut in audit staff and an increase in investigation, while having an investigator almost always brought about no change.

The data in table 8-6 also call into question the investigators' enthusiasm for major office overhauls. While investigators say their

Table 8-5. *Support for IG Reform, by Career Focus*
Percent

Variable	Auditors[a]	Investigators[a]
Provide testimonial subpoena power[b]		
1 (Greatly strengthen IG)	25	44
2	33	19
3	25	19
4	17	6
5 (Not greatly strengthen IG)	0	13
Provide weapons authority for agents[c]		
1 (Greatly strengthen IG)	0	25
2	27	25
3	9	13
4	0	6
5 (Not greatly strengthen IG)	64	31
Provide full law enforcement authority[c]		
1 (Greatly strengthen IG)	18	31
2	55	38
3	9	6
4	0	0
5 (Not greatly strengthen IG)	18	25
Create a fixed term of office[c]		
1 (Greatly strengthen IG)	0	47
2	50	13
3	8	20
4	8	13
5 (Not greatly strengthen IG)	33	7
Provide removal only for cause[c]		
1 (Greatly strengthen IG)	33	60
2	8	20
3	42	7
4	0	7
5 (Not greatly strengthen IG)	17	7

Source: See table 8-1.
a. See table 8-1, note a.
b. $N = 28$.
c. $N = 27$.

offices needed reworking, auditors were more likely to take action. Auditors may know more about the internal mechanics of organizing—a byproduct of their deeper experience—as well as ways to stretch staff. The auditors-turned-IG certainly had mastered the departmental and agency procedures for cutting staff.

Table 8-6. *IG Staffing Decisions, by Career Focus*
Percent

Variable[a]	Auditors[b]	Investigators[b]
Change in administration staff		
Cut more than 5%	0	0
Cut 1–5%	11	29
Cut or increased less than 1%	89	71
Change in audit staff		
Cut more than 15%	11	0
Cut 11–15%	22	0
Cut 6–10%	11	7
Cut 1–5%	11	7
Cut or increased less than 1%	33	86
Increased 1–5%	11	0
Change in investigation staff		
Cut more than 15%	0	0
Cut 11–15%	0	0
Cut 6–10%	0	7
Cut 1–5%	11	7
Cut less than 1%	44	79
Increased 1–5%	33	0
Increased 6–10%	0	7
Increased 21–25%	11	0
Change in evaluation staff		
Cut 1–5%	11	0
Cut or increased less than 1%	88	75
Increased 1–5%	0	18
Increased 6–10%	0	6

Source: The figures were derived from asking each respondent for an approximate percentage of staff deployment in the Office of Inspector General when first becoming inspector general and at the time of departure. See table 8-1.
a. $N = 23$ for all categories.
b. See table 8-1, note a.

THE INVESTIGATORY IMPULSE

Differences at the top of IGships result in different organizations below. Offices dominated by an audit culture will be distinctive from those dominated by an investigator mentality. However, whatever the precise mix and match of staff, differences in histories, norms, and operating methods can easily create obstacles to effective teamwork. As one OMB official remembered the first IG retreat in late 1979, "The problem was that the accountants and investigators sat on opposite sides of the room. After every break we would rearrange the name cards and chairs to get the two sides mixed up, and as soon as they came back into the room, they moved the chairs back."

The story captures a continuing problem caused by forging these two disparate disciplines together into a single unit. Unlike the U.S. Postal Inspection Service, which labels its auditors and investigators as "inspectors," the 1978 act may have created a barrier by establishing the two assistant IGs, one for audit and one for investigation.

Professional rivalry is not a threat to the IG concept, and a multidisciplinary approach to improving government management is not a misplaced priority. Indeed, some IGs even use the spirit of competition as a way to stimulate productivity. "There's a climate of dog-eat-dog here at HHS," one IG staffer reported. "The units could benefit from some cooperation, but there is a Mason/Dixon line right now. It's even obvious at the Christmas bake sale. We've been trying to break those differences through team-building work, retreats, that kind of thing. Try to get an auditor to close his eyes and fall off a step-ladder into the trusted arms of an investigator sometime."

A large part of the problem in working together involves worries that the more visible investigatory role would somehow swallow up auditing. For this reason the Senate Governmental Affairs Committee added the formal definition, later dropped, of audit and investigation to its bill to protect the auditors, changing the title from "inspector general" to "inspector and auditor general." Perhaps GAO was not so far off target in its assessment of the debate in the House-passed bill:

> During House debate on the bill, Congressman after Congressman rose to praise the bill on the grounds that it would create offices to detect fraud in the Federal Government. The message the present Inspectors General are getting from the bill and from reading the *Congressional Record* is that their offices are to be used primarily to detect fraud and abuse in the Government. . . . There are many, Mr. Chairman, who will favor using most of the audit resources of the Inspector General for investigative work. In our judgment, shifting extensive resources away from audit work to investigative work is not likely to be beneficial to the Government. What will be lost will be the benefits of auditors' suggestions for improving governmental efficiency and economy, recovery of overpayments to contractors and grantees, and identification of ineffective activities and programs.[7]

As the IGs entered the 1990s, GAO's concerns remained valid. Auditors were not being used as investigators, as GAO feared, but

Table 8-7. *Audit versus Investigation Staff, 1983 and 1990*
Number of staff unless otherwise specified

Department or agency	Audit[a]		Investigation[b]		Change (percent)		Investigation as percent of total	
	1983	1990	1983	1990	Audit	Investigation	1983	1990
Agriculture	387	398	256	265	3	4	40	40
AID	92	208	26	32	126	23	22	13
Commerce	115	100	39	25	-13	-35	25	20
Defense	451	597	146	388	32	166	24	39
Education	74	166	59	80	124	35	44	33
Energy	81	127	23	53	57	130	22	29
EPA	123	194	34	60	58	76	22	24
GSA	210	159	102	89	-24	-21	33	34
HHS	540	766	134	460	42	243	20	38
HUD	304	252	83	80	-17	-4	21	24
Interior	297	292	36	58	-2	61	13	20
Labor	194	196	173	193	1	12	47	50
NASA	33	64	13	39	94	200	28	38
SBA	55	51	49	39	-7	-20	47	43
State	26	79	4	34	204	750	13	30
Transportation	316	321	61	75	2	23	16	19
VA	205	246	60	82	20	37	23	25
Total	3,503	4,216	1,298	2,052	20	58	27	33

Source: Data include only the number of professional staff available to conduct audits or investigations; clerical and other administrative staff generally are not counted. The 1983 data come from a survey of inspector general staff year capacity conducted by the Veterans Administration in "Workload Assessment and Staffing Requirements Profile," April 20, 1983. The 1990 data were gathered from a phone survey.
a. The average for 1983 was 206; 1990, 248.
b. The average for 1983 was 76; 1990, 121.

they lost staffing shares to investigations nonetheless. If the trend continues, it portends an OIG more and more oriented to the investigator culture: a focus on highly visible, quick-hitting results and perhaps less tolerance for alternative views of accountability beyond individualized compliance monitoring.

The Numbers

Organizations have many ways to signal their priorities. Some point to mission statements; others to long-range plans. For IGs, the best indicator may be the investments made in audit and investigatory staff. The relative gain or loss in one or the other shows the value placed in each and provides a sense of how the IGs saw the future of their organizations.

Both audit and investigations gained ground during the 1980s (see table 8-7). The number of staff devoted to each increased 653 and 754, respectively. However, investigations gained in overall proportion, moving up from 27 percent of total staff to 33 percent. Nevertheless, the average OIG still contained twice as many auditors as investigators and much of the increase came under auditors-turned-IGs.

A wide variation in growth and change took place among the different IGships. Not all OIGs were created equal. Some, such as Commerce, HUD, and GSA, lost staff during the 1980s; others grew dramatically. Some, such as NASA, SBA, State, and Education, remained relatively small, even though NASA and State experienced significant percentage growth. Others, such as Defense and HHS, started out large and expanded rapidly. Indeed, these two OIGs alone account for almost a third of all staff in both years.

The impact of individual IGs in building their offices also can be seen in table 8-7. For example, while his departure from the Commerce OIG may have precipitated a staff loss, Sherman Funk's arrival at State clearly resulted in staff growth. Although the State OIG remained relatively small, Funk's ability to recruit both dollars and staff is notable, if only because the department initially was unenthusiastic about the IG concept.

The same can be said of Joseph Sherrick and June Gibbs Brown at Defense, who, along with their deputy, Derek Vander Schaaf, produced a 60 percent overall increase, and, to a lesser extent, John Martin at EPA. Charles Dempsey was able to keep his staff complement from tumbling as HUD was cut across the board.

Of all the IGs, however, HHS IG Kusserow was easily the most successful in organizational development, nearly doubling the size of his total staff, while boosting investigation 243 percent. The very

Table 8-8. *Change in Total Staff Devoted to Investigation versus Audit, 1983–90*
Percent

Department or agency	Change in total staff
Investigation gained shares[a]	
HHS	18
State	17
Defense	15
NASA	10
Energy	7
Interior	7
Labor	3
Transportation	3
HUD	3
EPA	2
VA	2
GSA	1
No change	
Agriculture	0
Investigation lost shares	
Education	−11
AID	−9
Commerce	−5
SBA	−4

a. A share is calculated by taking the percentage of total staff (audit plus investigation) devoted to investigation in 1990 and subtracting the percentage devoted to investigation in 1983, yielding the total increase or decrease at the expense of audit.

activities that exposed him to great risks in the Diefenbach case also earned increased staff from OMB. At least in the 1980s, statistical accomplishments and visible fraud busting produced bigger staffs and budgets. With convictions a sure-fire method for generating visibility, IGs who wanted to build staff invested more heavily in investigations.

Broad differences existed among OIGs in the shift of shares between investigators and auditors (see table 8-8). Some IGs changed greatly, particularly the two largest OIGs—HHS and Defense. Others changed only slightly. Ten of the seventeen offices shifted less than five shares—that is, percent of total staff devoted to one or the other role—one way or the other. Nevertheless, the increase at HHS, the most visible of the domestic OIGs, sent a strong signal to the rest of government about the need to increase investigator share, as did the large increases at State and Defense.

The increase in the ratio of investigations to auditors reflects a number of trends, including OMB's desire for ever-increasing statistical achievement. However, many IGs also would argue that the investigatory function was understaffed from the beginning. One reason Representative L. H. Fountain was motivated to produce the 1976 HEW IG bill was that the department had only ten investigators. By 1983 HHS had expanded to 134 investigators. So noted, State was still operating with only 4, NASA, 13; Energy, 23; and AID, 26.

Furthermore, OIG investigatory duties increased during the Reagan administration. Under the False Claims Act Amendments of 1986, as implemented by the Civil Division of the Department of Justice, for example, the IGs were given informal responsibility to investigate citizen allegations of fraud, mostly in the form of suits against government contractors. Under these so-called qui tam complaints, individual citizens can reap enormous rewards—up to 30 percent of all damages or recoveries due the federal government.[8] The specific amount is largely dependent on whether the government lets the citizen proceed alone or takes action itself. The Civil Division, however, by statute had only sixty days to make the go or no-go decision on preempting the citizen action; hence the desire to get the IGs and their staffs involved to make the preliminary review. At HHS, the number of qui tam investigations, while relatively small in number, grew from two in 1987 to eight in 1988 and seventeen in 1989. As Kusserow explained to the House Judiciary Committee:

If you talk about having 17 cases, that is not very large, when you are talking about an organization such as ours that last year produced about 1,300 criminal convictions through the Department of Justice and another 800 civil administrative prosecutions. But the problem with the qui tam is that it is very time sensitive. Sixty days means that you have to set aside everything else you are doing and make sure that you meet that time deadline. Our experience has been that thus far we have been able to manage, but almost on a routine basis we are asking for extensions.[9]

To Investigate or Not to Investigate

Investigations have a positive impact on program effectiveness, if only because they plug one hole of what economist Arthur M. Okun once called the leaky bucket.[10] Whether IG investigations contribute to the long-term prevention of fraud, waste, and abuse in government is somewhat less clear. The deterrent effect of one successful prosecution, for example, may be as powerful as one hundred. And, if those extra ninety-nine convictions come at the cost of basic program operating capacity, therefore creating more exposure to fraud and abuse, they could be detrimental to overall management improvement.

The IGs are not the only investigators in government. The Department of Agriculture, for example, has nine investigatory units besides the OIG, including the Agricultural Marketing Service, Animal and Plant Health Inspection Service, Federal Crop Insurance Corporation, Food and Nutrition Service, and Meat and Poultry Inspection Operations, Food Safety and Inspection Service. What separates the IG investigators is that they are classified under a different civil service General Schedule (GS) code. Almost all IG investigators are hired as GS 1811s, while their counterparts are GS 1810s. The Office of Personnel Management lists their different qualifications as follows:

1810: Description of Work: Investigators plan and conduct investigations relating to the administration of, or compliance with, Federal laws and regulations. The duties performed typically include those such as the following: Collecting facts and obtaining information by observing conditions, examining records, and interviewing individuals; writing and securing affidavits; administering oaths; preparing investigative reports to be used as a basis for court or administrative action; testifying before administrative bodies, or serving as a witness for the Government. The work occasionally may involve criminal investigations.

1811: Description of Work: Criminal investigators plan and conduct investigations relating to alleged or suspected violations of Federal laws. The duties typically performed include those such as the following: obtaining physical and documentary evidence; interviewing witnesses; applying for and serving warrants for arrests, searches, and seizures; seizing contraband, equipment and vehicles; examining files and records; maintaining surveillance; performing undercover assignments; preparing investigative reports; testifying in hearings and trials; and assisting U.S. Attorneys in the prosecution of court cases. Most criminal investigators are required to carry firearms and to be proficient in their use.[11]

The 1811 series sets a minimum standard for criminal investigators, including a specific kind of training, skill, and experience. Although 1810s occasionally make criminal investigations, they do not have the same investigatory skills as 1811s. Besides the OIGs, few offices in the federal government have 1811s: Bureau of Export Administration (Commerce); Public Buildings Service (GSA); Drug Enforcement Administration, FBI, Immigration and Naturalization Service, and Marshals Service (Justice); Bureau of Indian Affairs and Bureau of Land Management (Interior); and Bureau of Alcohol, Tobacco, and Firearms, Customs Service, and Secret Service (Treasury).

The IGs might be tempted to feature criminal investigations for two reasons. The first is that most of the alternative 1811 investigation units are stretched to the breaking point. Noting that 90 percent of the FBI's fraud investigations were being worked in tandem with the IGs, FBI Assistant Director Floyd Clarke, in 1988 hearings before the House Government Operations Committee, offered the following rationale for IG involvement:

One of the problems that we encountered in 1982 was when the FBI was given concurrent responsibility for the enforcement of our Federal drug laws. We were given that responsibility with no enhanced resources. So within the existing programs we had to find resources to deal with that very serious problem.

In addition, in 1984, the Comprehensive Crime Control Act of 1984 was enacted, which again expanded the responsibilities of the Bureau—and once again we had to look internally. Each of these had its effect on our white-collar [crime] program, which is one of our priorities. And within the white-collar program, the governmental fraud subprogram is the top priority. But it caused us to have to take some of the resources that we were using in this area to address these other areas of responsibility.

So ours is one of constantly balancing the priorities across the board in many areas of responsibility.[12]

Responding to committee questions, Clarke acknowledged that the FBI would "really be kind of over the barrel" without IG help. Just as the Civil Division of Justice found the IGs ready to help on qui tam complaints, the FBI turned to the IGs as a safety valve on fraud.

The second is that many IGs believe that the 1810 units are neither motivated nor trained for the criminal job. As Funk once said of criminal investigations, "If we don't do it, ain't nobody else gonna do it."[13] According to acting Labor IG Ray Maria's 1990 testimony before the Senate Governmental Affairs Committee:

> Congress has to arrive at some kind of agreement and provide some kind of imprimatur that says, yes, criminal investigations are important. And I am not, you know, to the right of Genghis Khan or Attila the Hun. I risk sounding that way. But I think this must be factored into the enforcement strategy at the Department of Labor if there is going to be any credibility to the entire enforcement process. The question is, if you accept that, who will do it? Who is most qualified to do it? In this constricted budget environment, who is best equipped to do it?[14]

For Maria, the answer was the OIG, and not because Labor program offices did not do criminal cases; PWBA, for example, did twenty-five cases a year. Instead, not enough cases were handled to achieve a credible deterrent, and the officers in charge lacked the hunger for what Maria called the "visible odium that accrues to being indicted, convicted and jailed."[15] It was a quantity, not quality, argument.

Therein lies the problem. With each new staffer added to the investigations, the IGs, OMB, Congress, and the president were choosing not to add a new staffer elsewhere, either inside the IGship or not. Whether additional IG investigatory capacity is the best way to improve government management remains in doubt, particularly given the kind of concerns highlighted by Dwight Ink, former HUD assistant secretary for administration, about the Mod Rehab. "HUD illustrates the value of an independent investigative capacity by the inspector general," Ink argued, "but it also illustrates the folly of relying so heavily upon that kind of external review that the internal capacity of oversight erodes. After all, it is the manager who has the basic responsibility for oversight of those programs, and it is the manager, not the external review agencies, that can take quick, corrective action."[16]

Ink overstated when he defined the IG as external to the agency. Nevertheless, the controversy remains: Investing in IG investigatory staff means not investing in something else. IG staff deployment must reflect more than a hunch that criminal fraud is available to be found. And with IG staff growth slowing in the 1990s, internal staffing increasingly has become a zero-sum game between auditors and investigators.

No matter what, auditors and investigators must be able to work together closely if the IG concept is to succeed. A recent Supreme Court case raised double jeopardy concerns when the federal government seeks both criminal and civil penalties for the same statutory

violation, which shows the wisdom of early cooperation among investigatory personnel.[17] For government to maximize recovery and
deterrence, auditors and investigators must talk early and often,
developing their cases together, if possible, and in some priority.
However, the challenge may be surmounting the increasingly sophisticated, some say balkanized, organizations that have evolved in
support of the IGs.

CONCLUSION: PROTECTING IGs

The ultimate test in selecting IGs is less about having auditing
or investigating expertise and more about ensuring quality and
independence. If the IGs are to be free to monitor performance and
capacity as well as compliance, they must be able to report their
findings and make their recommendations without fear of retribu-
tion from both ends of Pennsylvania Avenue.

The IGs once addressed this issue by devising their own search
process. However, the White House not only reexerted control over
IG selections in 1989, but a hint of politicization also has crept into
the process. First, several former members of Bush's Secret Service
entourage were chosen for new small agency IGships, then A. Mary
Sterling was appointed IG at Transportation.

Sterling had limited experience in government: she served three
years as an assistant U.S. attorney in Missouri, one year with a
Department of Justice organized crime strike force in Kansas City,
one year as a White House Fellow, and one year as assistant secretary
for labor-management standards at Labor in 1989–90. She was the
prototypical presidential appointee—a former campaign worker who
progressed to a series of short-term appointments in government, a
Harvard graduate whose contact with government was from the top
down, not bottom up. Sterling was a clear break with the past and
a worrisome precedent to the IG community.

New blood is not anathema to the IG concept, and the IGs are
not the only ones who can successfully select their successors. But
how can the appointment of both independent and objective persons
be ensured?[18] Several recommendations can be made: a fixed term
of office, a new appointments mechanism, and the elimination of
the appearance of conflict of interest.

A Term of Office

Even before the 1981 firings, some in the IG community believed a
set term of office could provide needed protection against partisan-
ship. After the firings, sentiment in favor of a fixed term, whether

Representative Benjamin Rosenthal's ten-year proposal or a lesser span, increased dramatically. A term would have discouraged the 1981 firings and encouraged IGs to stay in office long enough to establish some institutional memory.[19]

Terms of office are not unique in government. Many independent regulatory commissioners and assorted board appointees operate under fixed terms of two to ten years. The government's chief auditor and chief investigator also serve prescribed tenures: The comptroller general of the United States occupies a fifteen-year term, and the director of the Federal Bureau of Investigation holds a ten-year appointment.

Having a fixed term of office does not mean the officeholder cannot be easily removed. However, the term sends a signal, albeit small, that the position is somehow less political than other presidential appointments.

The question arises whether providing this protection is worth the legislative cost. Some in the IG community argued that a term cannot supply courage where none exists. "Either the IG has the guts or he or she doesn't," Dempsey remarked. "And tenure's not going to make them do their jobs properly."[20] Others noted that a term does not guarantee freedom from interference on Capitol Hill or in the White House. For example, the four-year term of the head of the Office of Personnel Management, imposed under the 1978 civil service reforms, was used by the Senate to deny a second-term appointment to Reagan's director, Donald Devine.

The IGs, however, do not believe length of service is immaterial. Almost all of the IGs interviewed acknowledged the need to stay in one place and learn the job as a prerequisite for effectiveness. At the same time, most of the IGs appeared to be saying that nothing magical exists in a fixed term that alone would give an IG the integrity to succeed.

Acknowledging the limits, a term of office does offer at least three potential advantages in enhancing IG institutional memory. First, a term would quell any uncertainty during the change of administrations. Not only would the IGs and their incoming bosses be able to start building a working relationship immediately, but less potential also would exist for the kinds of crippling vacancies that occurred in 1989–90.

Second, a term would allow an IG to plan for a longer agenda. As Kusserow argued, "I think that becoming very familiar with the programs, having an institutional memory that allows you to make sure that you could outlast others, especially the politicos, and making sure the commitments are followed through on, are assets and not necessarily something that should be considered liabilities. I have sat through three department secretaries and their rotations of staff since I have been inspector general at HHS and there is not much continuity on that front."[21] Merely knowing that one is expected to be in a particular place for a long period may enhance the confidence to establish a long-term agenda.

Third, and most important, a term of office would send a strong message that IG appointments are to be handled differently from other appointments in the White House personnel process. As transition teams scurry to match jobs with their political allies, the IGs can stand aside.

A New Recruiting Path

Despite the advantages, a term of office does nothing to improve the overall quality of appointments. The White House personnel office still can give secretaries and administrators the final say over the IG, presidents still can fire en masse, and political hacks still can win appointments. For any reform to have weight, it must be wed to a high quality appointment.

Assuming that every president wants to make the best appointment for every job, the challenge is to identify a pool of strong candidates, assess the fit to the job, and make the recruitment. Unfortunately, as John F. Kennedy once remarked, "I must make the appointments now; a year hence I will know who I really want to appoint."[22] The onslaught of office seekers is enormous, the time to screen applicants nil, and the pressure to find jobs for friends of friends unyielding.

Presumably, the task of filling jobs would be easier when the sitting vice president becomes president, particularly when the president-elect is as seasoned a Washington insider as George Bush. However, as G. Calvin Mackenzie noted, the Bush transition was anything but smooth. New records for slowness were set; getting appointees confirmed took an average of 8.1 months, compared with 5.3 months for Reagan and 2.4 months for Kennedy. "Put another way," Mackenzie wrote, "the average Bush appointee did not take the oath of office and begin functioning until September 1989." Mackenzie described the impacts of the process as follows:

Agency after agency lumbered through the early months of this administration, waiting for new leadership. Three-quarters of the way through 1989, the Energy Department had only 4 of its 18 top officials confirmed and in place. On Oct. 1, 6 of the assistant secretary positions at the Department of Veterans Affairs lacked confirmed appointees, as did 6 of 11 assistant secretary slots at the Labor Department.[23]

The challenge to recruit IGs is complicated by two facts. One, IGs rarely are picked first. They have been an afterthought in past selection processes. Cabinet secretaries, under secretaries, and even assistant secretaries come before IGs, and rightly so given their role in developing the president's agenda. Two, picking a successful IG involves searching for specific skills.

This is where the IG search process developed under Harper and Wright in OMB paid high dividends. Notwithstanding a high degree of inbreeding among the IGs, the process resulted in the recruitment of candidates who met some minimal test of professionalism, even narrowly defined. The IG selection process also was fast because a list of names was available whenever an IG vacancy existed. As such, the process was not unlike the one used for selecting a comptroller general of the United States. Whenever an opening occurs, a search commission is formed to recommend names to the president. Although the president can select a different candidate, the process favors the commission recommendation.

A similar process could work for the IGs, albeit modified to prevent a new search for each vacancy among the sixty-plus IGships. The commission itself could be composed of some mix of the current PCIE members, the comptroller general, and other representatives from the professional accounting, evaluation, and investigation communities, thereby allowing for a broader field of potential candidates. The commission could also administer a new bonus system to eliminate the appearance of conflict of interest discussed below.

Ultimately, the value of a term of office and search commission rests in sending a signal to future presidents that the IGships are best seen as a source of institutional memory and honest advice, not as a political plum to be filled by campaign workers in need of a job. The duties of an IG must be taken seriously.

A Question of Appearance

One change is warranted immediately: No IG should be allowed to accept pay bonuses and cash awards determined by the secretary or administrator. Even though these bonuses and awards are legal under the Civil Service Reform Act and are to be based on merit and performance alone, the conflict of interest is palpable.

From 1987 to 1989, according to the Office of Personnel Management, at least nine IGs received bonuses or awards: Bill Colvin,

NASA, $33,730; John Martin, EPA, $23,463; Frank Sato, VA, $20,000; John Layton, Energy, $17,715, June Gibbs Brown, Defense, $16,000; James Thomas, Education, $15,796; Frank DeGeorge, Commerce, $14,475; William Doyle, Railroad Retirement Board, $7,000; and J. Brian Hyland, Labor, $3,875.[24] The amounts are not insignificant.

Under the 1978 Civil Service Reform Act, all members of the Senior Executive Service are eligible for cash bonuses (of up to $10,000 per year) or Presidential Rank Awards (of $10,000 for meritorious service or $20,000 for distinguished service), even if they occupy a presidential appointment. Moreover, almost all midlevel members of the civil service, including OIG employees, are eligible for pay for performance.

The IGs, however, are unlike other appointees. The appearance of conflict prompted almost half of the Carter and Reagan IGs to voluntarily remove themselves from review for bonuses and awards. Because IGs are under the supervision of secretaries and administrators who work for the president, bonuses and awards can influence investigations or audits that move too close to the top. In addition, IG staffs may appear compromised by their eligibility for department and agency-wide merit pay. As one IG argued, "No one should evaluate an IG but God." The point was echoed by SBA IG Charles Gillium before the House Government Operations Committee, "It is critical that an IG be free of any possible personal bias in making decisions about audits and investigations of agency programs and personnel. An IG whose performance is evaluated annually by an agency head, who is compared to and competes with other top agency officials for bonuses, and who is thus rewarded or punished, may find it difficult to dispel the perception that a bonus has no influence on his/her decisions."[25] Imagine, for example, the criticism and charges of cover-up that might have come had HUD IGs Dempsey and Adams not elected to remove themselves from the bonus and award system that Secretary Samuel Pierce oversaw.

There are two problems in banning IG bonuses outright, however. First, many of the IGs' employees receive awards. Defense Deputy IG Derek Vander Schaaf, for example, received $35,000 in presidential awards under Reagan, making him more highly paid than his boss for three years. Therefore, a ban from the system would have to involve all of the OIGs, not just those at the top. Second, as Gillium noted, the decision to opt out would deprive the IGs of a significant source of additional pay. Although federal pay increased in both 1989 and 1990, bonuses and presidential awards offer as much as a 20 percent augmentation in any given year.

Nevertheless, keeping a system that half the IGs find so objection-
able that they voluntarily withdraw from it does not strengthen the
IG concept. If the IGs and their OIG staffs are to receive bonuses
and awards for excellence—as they should—an entirely independent
system, one that raises no appearances of conflict, should be devised.
Although an independent appraisal system would further insulate
the IGs from the day-to-day realities of government, it may be a
small price to pay for the fullest freedom to audit and investigate.
IGs covered under the current bonus and award system cannot help
but be influenced, whether consciously or not.

The Organizational IGs

THE IGs had unprecedented freedom in organizing their offices. This freedom resided in Section 6 of the IG Act. Although the act required that each OIG have assistant IGs for audit and investigation, the rest of the organizational structure and operating system was left open. Each IG decided where to invest new staff, how to structure the hierarchy, and how hard to fight for independence within their own departments and agencies. Their definition of accountability is reflected in each decision.

At a logistical level, for example, Section 6 guaranteed "appropriate and adequate office space at central and field office locations . . . together with such equipment, office supplies, and communications facilities and services as may be necessary for the operation of such offices, and necessary maintenance services for such offices and the equipment and facilities located therein." This translates into all the paper, pencils, desks, chairs, and paper clips needed to get the job done, and the space and janitors to go with it. At an operational level, Section 6 also provided access to both internal and external information, whether through direct requests or document subpoenas, while prohibiting any interference with IG audits and investigations—in short, all the answers, data, and leverage to make a case.

Notwithstanding these protections, Section 6 is most important for permitting the IGs to structure their enterprises however they wanted. Under Section 6(a)(6), and subject to the civil service code, the IGs were given sole authority "to select, appoint, and employ such offices and employees as may be necessary for carrying out the functions, power, and duties of the Office." By using that authority to the fullest extent, the IGs would be minimally dependent upon close associations with the departments or agencies. With OMB largely guaranteeing staff and budget increases, the IGs needed little else to become semiautonomous.

Table 9-1. *Measures of Organizational Expansion, 1980–89*

Department or agency	1980 Units	1980 Phone numbers	1983 Units	1983 Phone numbers	1986 Units	1986 Phone numbers	1989 Units	1989 Phone numbers
Agriculture	4	23	5	31	4	27	3	28
AID	4	17	5	17	5	17	6	19
Commerce	3	14	4	15	6	21	5	22
Defense	⋯	⋯	7	40	7	44	8	44
Education	3	13	3	23	3	19	3	16
Energy	3	29	3	33	3	36	4	33
EPA	2	14	3	22	3	25	3	23
GSA	3	21	3	24	3	22	3	26
HHS	3	34	5	41	3	31	3	32
HUD	3	22	3	27	3	24	3	24
Interior	3	17	3	18	3	19	3	20
Labor	2	22	3	27	4	25	4	22
NASA	3	14	4	17	3	17	3	20
SBA	0	9	2	12	4	15	4	15
State	1[a]	9[a]	2	12	2	7	5	21
Transportation	3	21	3	19	3	17	3	14
Treasury	1[a]	8[a]	2[a]	16[a]	2[a]	19[a]	2	19
VA	2	15	3	20	3	21	3	19
Total	43	302	63	414	64	406	68	417

Source: *Federal Yellowbook* (Washington: Monitor Publishing, Winters, 1980, 1983, 1986, and 1989).
a. Nonstatutory.

AN ORGANIZATIONAL HISTORY OF THE OIGS

That the IGs sought a measure of independence is not surprising. At one level, the drive for organizational self-sufficiency was merely an operational convenience—the IGs complained that they could not get adequate service from their department or agency. Yet the IGs also wanted what every other federal manager wanted: freedom from the cumbersome rules and regulations governing the management of their units.

Measures of Expansion

What made the IGs different from other federal managers, however, was that they had the authority to create their own organizations. Under Section 6(a)(6), the IGs were free to hire their own people, which meant they could develop their own bureaucratic structures and break free from some of the internal squabbling that goes into the day-to-day management of government.

As the OIGs grew fatter with the new audit and investigation staff provided by OMB, they grew wider by creating new OIG units —evaluation, inspection—across the organizational span of control. The 1978 statute required only two units, one for audit and one for investigation. Thus, additional units can be seen as an expression of a given OIG's effort to define itself. Through ever-larger spans of control, the OIGs went from relatively flat organizations in the late 1970s to increasingly variegated operations, rising from a total of forty-three subunits in 1980 to sixty-three in 1983, sixty-four in 1986, and sixty-eight in 1989 (see table 9-1). Alongside this general thickening, the OIGs grew taller, creating new layers of management—deputies, special assistants, associate deputies—and coming to resemble more traditional government organizations.

Enormous variation existed within this trend. The oldest OIGs—Agriculture, HUD, and HHS—remained relatively constant in total number of units over the period, while the youngest—State and Treasury—grew rapidly. Labor and Commerce both increased. Defense started out wide and stayed that way, reaching eight units in 1989: Administration and Information Management, Analysis and Followup, Audit Policy and Oversight, Auditing, Criminal Investigations Policy and Oversight, Inspections, Investigations, and Special Programs.

The OIGs at the Departments of State and Treasury are particularly useful examples of the tendency toward wider spans of control.

At Treasury, the nonstatutory IG had a single Office of Audit in 1980 but added a nonstatutory Office of Investigation by 1983, six years before being brought under the IG Act. Position titles also changed—a deputy IG was added in 1986 and a general counsel and more directors of audit in 1989.

At State, a single office of audit and administration existed in 1980. After the department was brought under the IG Act, a separate office of investigations was created. During an IG vacancy in 1986, the staff shrunk, then reexpanded under the new IG, Sherman Funk, to five units and a tripling of phone listings by 1989.

The data in table 9-1 also show a pattern of growth in spans of control followed by consolidation. The older OIGs may have become so wide that they had to create a new layer of management to consolidate units. Or, more likely, the older OIGs may have entered a different phase of the organizational life cycle, becoming taller as small units were combined.

The HHS OIG shows these two effects. In 1980, the four-year-old HHS OIG operation had three major units—Administration, Investigations, and Audit and Systems—led by a presidentially appointed IG and a deputy IG. The office also had two assistant inspectors general, statutorily required; an executive assistant inspector general; a senior assistant inspector general; and an assistant inspector general for health care and system review.

By 1983, the office had expanded to five units—Administration, Audit, Health Financing Integrity, Investigations, and Program Inspections—still led by a presidentially appointed IG and statutory deputy IG, but now with four assistant inspectors general, and a new special assistant. And the OIG legislative liaison office was located in the executive suite, and out from underneath the director of administration where it had been located in 1980. HHS is one of the few OIGs with a position formally labeled as legislative liaison. Although several other OIGs have staff dedicated to congressional relations, they are called by titles such as "special projects assistant" or "analysis and external coordinator."[1]

In 1986, the HHS OIG appeared to be smaller—only three units and thirty-six phone numbers—but it actually had achieved a higher organizational plane. Numerous units were drawn into formally labeled offices and divisions that began to resemble small government agencies. The list of 1986 staff titles serves as an illustration of the increasing complexity of the organization (the positions in italics were required under the original HEW IG statute; the rest were created by subsequent IGs):

Inspector General
  Executive Officer
Deputy Inspector General
Assistant Inspector General, Office of Analysis and Inspections
  Deputy Assistant Inspector General
    Management Operations Division Director
    Program Inspections Division Director
Assistant Inspector General, Office of Audit
  Deputy Assistant Inspector General for Audit
    Audit Management Division Director
    Audit Operations Division Director
  Deputy Assistant Inspector General for General Grants and
  Information Systems
    EDP Audits Division Director
    Grants and Internal Systems Audits Director
  Deputy Assistant Inspector General for Health Care
  Financing and Audits
    Health Care Financing Audits Division Director
  Deputy Assistant Inspector General for Social Security Audits
    Social Security Audits Division Director
Assistant Inspector General, Office of Investigations
    Special Assistant
  Deputy Assistant Inspector General for Civil
  Administration Division
    Management Information Services Staff Director
    State Fraud Bureau Chief
  Deputy Assistant Inspector General for Criminal
  Investigations

Instead of retaining a wide span of control composed of many small operations such as legislative liaison, the 1986 HHS organization chart established a more elegant structure. Whereas only a half dozen layers existed in 1980 between the top of the OIG in Washington and the bottom in the field offices, at least ten were present six years later, most added at the headquarters level.

The movement toward a full-blown bureaucratic structure continued into 1989. By then, the executive officer was the "executive secretariat," the deputy assistant IG for health care financing covered separate Medicare and Medicaid audit divisions, and the newly created deputy assistant IG of investigations for headquarters operations gained the new "computer techniques staff director" and the old state fraud bureau chief.

Table 9-2. Measures of Organizational Independence, 1983, 1989

Department or agency	1983						1989					
	Deputy IG	General counsel	Personnel office	Line budget	Evaluation and inspection	Executive Level	Deputy IG	General counsel	Personnel office	Line budget	Evaluation and inspection	Executive Level
Agriculture	Y	Y	Y	Y	Y	Y	Y	Y	N	Y	N	Y
AID	N	N	N	N	Y	N	Y	Y	Y	Y	N	Y
Commerce	Y	Y	Y	N	Y	N	Y	Y	Y	Y	Y	Y
Defense	Y	N	N	N	Y	Y	Y	Y	Y	Y	Y	Y
Education	Y	N	N	N	Y	Y	N	N	N	Y	Y	Y
Energy	Y	Y	Y	Y	Y	Y	Y	N	Y	Y	Y	Y
EPA	Y	N	N	Y	Y	N	Y	N	N	Y	N	Y
GSA	Y	Y	Y	Y	Y	N	Y	Y	Y	Y	Y	Y
HHS	Y	N	N	Y	Y	Y	Y	N	Y	Y	Y	Y
HUD	Y	N	Y	N	N	Y	Y	N	Y	Y	N	Y
Interior	N	N	Y	N	N	N	Y	N	Y	Y	N	Y
Labor	N	N	N	Y	N	Y	Y	Y	Y	Y	Y	Y
NASA	Y	Y	Y	N	N	N	Y	N	Y	Y	N	Y
SBA	N	Y	N	N	N	N	Y	Y	Y	Y	N	Y
State	Y	N	N	Y	N	Y	Y	N	Y	Y	Y	Y
Transportation	N	N	Y	Y	N	Y	Y	Y	Y	Y	N	Y
Treasury[a]	..	..	..	..	..	..	Y	N	N	Y	N	Y
VA	N	N	N	Y	N	Y	Y	N	N	Y	Y	Y

Source: The 1983 data come from Veterans Administration, "Workload Assessment and Staffing Requirements Profile," April 20, 1983. The 1989 data are from a phone survey of all IG offices. Because of possible inconsistencies in the methodologies used to gather the data, they are best treated as suggestive, not determinative, of actual organizational structure.
a. Nonstatutory in 1983.

The entire OIG staff, having outgrown its quarters in the Hubert H. Humphrey Building, moved across the street to the former HHS headquarters. HHS IG Richard Kusserow's new personal office had been the secretary's suite in the pre-Humphrey building days. "At times," one HHS management officer noted, "we're not sure whether we don't have two Secretaries in the department."

Measures of Independence

The OIGs did not grow in a random, haphazard manner. They grew wider and taller by enhancing their independence through a series of specific organizational initiatives. Whether working on their own volition or through the 1988 IG Act Amendments, the OIGs expanded their organizational base in six key areas (see table 9-2).

Some OIGs moved closer to organizational independence during the 1983–89 period than others. Some, such as Labor, Interior, AID, SBA, and Defense made significant enhancements of their administrative infrastructure, adding new layers of protection against dependency. Others, such as Agriculture and Energy, lost ground.

Some OIGs had further to go than others. The AID OIG made a change in all six potential areas of expansion: It added a deputy IG, a general counsel, a personnel officer directly responsible for most OIG recruitment, and a line budget; moved up to Executive Level IV; and dropped the evaluation and inspection function. (Two of the changes were mandated by the 1988 IG Act Amendments.) Treasury gained in four of the six areas, half due to passage of the 1988 amendments, half as a result of its own action. State gained in three areas, largely because of Funk.

By comparison, HHS moved up in only one area by adding a personnel officer. However, in 1983 HHS already had a statutory deputy IG, a line budget, and an evaluation and inspection function, and the IG had been paid at Executive Level IV all along. Furthermore, although Kusserow received his legal advice from the department's general counsel under a memorandum of understanding, the attorneys who provided that advice were housed in the OIG office complex and were fully dedicated to the OIG mission.

Of the six possible areas of expansions, promotion to Executive Level IV and institution of a line appropriations account were the most popular (see table 9-3). Both, however, were required by the 1988 IG Act Amendments. The rest of the changes were ones made by choice.

DEPUTY IGS. The popularity of the deputy IGs is easy to explain.

Table 9-3. *Organizational Gains and Losses, 1983–89*

Possible area of expansion	OIGs that gained	OIGs that lost
Deputy IG	6	1
General counsel	4	2
Personnel office	7	1
Line budget	8	0
Evaluation and inspection function	3	3
Move to Executive Level IV	7	0
Total	35	7

Source: See table 9-2.

First, given the evolution of the IG selection process under Reagan, creating a deputy IGship provided greater training opportunities for future IGs and a source of potential candidates. Second, creating a deputy also helped the OIGs resemble a more traditional bureau or agency operation, contributing to the overall insulation of the OIG from outside influence. Finally, a deputy allowed the IGs to divide their responsibilities more effectively, particularly as the number of units increased.

Some, such as Kusserow, made an inside-outside split of duties, with the IG taking a more visible public stance and the deputy a more active operational role. Others, such as HUD IG Charles Dempsey, used the position to groom a successor. When Dempsey was called to take the EPA vacancy on an acting basis after the previous IG was forced out in 1983, his HUD deputy, Paul Adams, was ready to fill in.

By 1989, all but one of the OIGs, at Education, had established a deputy IGship. For the Education IG, James Thomas, however, the question was whether a deputy made sense in what was already a very tight operation. As Thomas explained, "It was the only way to keep our travel and audit budgets going, and was vacant to boot. We always had the line budget, but it didn't help a bit. It has always been nip and tuck in this office, and the deputy just didn't make sense in such a small shop."[2]

COUNSEL. Three years later, however, Thomas would begin the fight of his ten-year career just to hire a single attorney as an independent OIG legal counsel. His rationale was one shared by many IGs: The Department general counsel could not be trusted to provide timely, accurate advice. As one of his IG colleagues described a similar fight, "The Secretary's General Counsel was *his* lawyer, not

mine, and since an attorney cannot serve two clients on two potentially differing sides, I could not then be assured of independent legal
advice."

Thomas's decision to hire his own attorney was a direct response
to the Kmiec memo. Thomas no longer was sure that the legal staff
advising him on behalf of the department's general counsel had
the OIG's best interest at heart. Even though the Office of General
Counsel (OGC) offered to assign an attorney (Ellen Bass) to OIG
issues on a permanent basis, the proposed limitations on her were
intolerable:

- Ellen may not provide written legal advice under her signature, unless that advice is cleared through OGC;
- Absent clearance of her advice by OGC, the Office of the
  Inspector General (OIG) may not, in oral or written conver-
  sations with Department officials outside of OIG, indicate
  that it has obtained her advice or advice of counsel. This
  would include a bar on her representing OIG in discussions
  with other offices of the Department or outside the Department where OIG's position is inconsistent with that of
  OGC; and
- In the event OIG intends to take a position on a legal issue
  at odds with OGC's position, you will first contact us and
  try to resolve the issue.[3]

Presented with continuing resistance from the department's legal
counsel, Thomas took his case to the secretary, and then to Capitol
Hill and Senator John Glenn. Only then did Thomas get his wish
for his own attorney, hired by and reporting only to him.

However, the department's general counsel won a small victory
governing any legal opinion by the new IG attorney: "If an OIG
Counsel opinion to the IG or OIG staff is to be circulated outside
of OIG, the opinion shall contain the following statement at the
beginning of the opinion: This opinion is an OIG Counsel opinion
to the Inspector General and does not represent the legal position
of the Department of Education."[4]

Other IGs reported similar resistance. Yet many wondered how
they could afford not to have their own counsel, if only because they
might need a good lawyer to write a rebuttal to some future solicitor's
attack. "The problems which led to the Inspector General [J. Brian]
Hyland's decision to hire his own counsel remain," acting Labor IG
Ray Maria testified almost two years after Hyland first petitioned
the secretary for permission to transfer four attorneys to the OIG.

"Any first year law student knows an attorney cannot serve two masters with competing interests."[5]

PERSONNEL. If the driving force for establishment of separate OIG legal counsel was distrust, the push for separate personnel offices—either in addition to or in lieu of the department or agency process—was economy and efficiency. As the National Academy of Public Administration argued in 1983:

> The *Federal Personnel Manual* (FPM) has eight thousand eight hundred and fourteen pages. If regulations generated good personnel management, the Federal government would have the best personnel system in the world. But instead, when managers and personnel experts all over government were consulted, they simply reaffirmed what is common knowledge—the frustrations with the system are general and profound. Even experienced personnel officers admit that nobody really understands those 8,814 pages. They certainly are not understood by managers, nor do they describe a personnel system which works for them or for their employees in the workplace where a personnel system should really pay off. In sharp contrast to successful personnel systems elsewhere, Federal managers do not feel that the system is designed to meet their needs, but see it as just another set of obstacles they must overcome in doing their jobs.[6]

NAPA went on to argue:

> Executives and line managers feel almost totally divorced from what should be one of their most important systems. They regard themselves as being required to operate under a system which is imposed on them from outside their own agencies, and they feel that they play almost no role in the development of that system, either governmentwide or within their own agencies. . . . They recognize that 8,814 pages of FPM means that the system rests in the hands of the personnel specialists, many of whom have only a tenuous grip on their own processes."[7]

These views should not be surprising given the state of the federal personnel system during the 1980s. This system prompted the National Commission on the Public Service (Volcker Commission) to recommend deregulation of the hiring process: "Even when the public sector finds outstanding candidates, the complexity of the hiring process often drives all but the most dedicated away. Perceptions of the public service as a lackluster career are compounded by the belief among potential candidates that getting a government job is an exercise in frustration."[8]

Although the IGs wanted independent personnel authority to eliminate unnecessary delays in the process, many also saw the department or agency personnel system as dominated by inflexible bureaucrats who knew only how to say "no" or staffed by career civil servants who resented the IG expansion during a period of cutbacks, or both. Some IGs believed they had the right to go directly to the Office of Personnel Management if and when they had a problem. After all, they had a similar relationship on the budget with OMB.

The IGs merely wanted what every other government manager wanted: Out of the cumbersome, rule-bound personnel system; out of the endless paperwork; out of the inflexible regulations and oversight; out of the clutches of the classification analysts in their departments. They wanted to be trusted to do the right thing and had both Section 6(a)(6) and OMB protection. But by breaking free of the burdens that most managers faced and making their organizations more efficient, the IGs lost some measure of sympathy for those they oversaw because they became less sensitive to the colossal problems of managing in a tightly regulated environment and less understanding of the shortcuts some managers had to take to get their jobs done.

LOCATION. One potential measure of OIG independence that ended up not making any difference was physical location. Whether the IG and staff were housed in the same building as the secretary or several blocks away was neither detrimental nor advantageous.

Most IGs were just down the hall or around the corner from the department or agency head. Only VA, EPA, and Education were located in different buildings in 1980. The Defense OIG set up outside the Pentagon in 1982, and HHS moved out by 1986. They both, however, were so large that separate quarters were almost a necessity. For Defense, the move allowed for consolidation of OIG employees from a half-dozen locations; for HHS, Kusserow and his staff were permitted to occupy what had been premier HEW office space. The Defense IG also retained an office along the secretary's corridor at the Pentagon.

The EPA and Education OIGs, while relatively small, were in different locations because no room was available otherwise. EPA was spread across a campus in Southeast Washington built next to and on top of a Safeway grocery store, while Education was shoehorned into a building shared with NASA, across the street from the National Air and Space Museum. Being apart from the secretary or administrator was no indication of a lack of status, for a host of other offices were with the OIGs. The exception, however, was the VA OIG. Plenty of room existed in the huge VA headquarters building across the street from Lafayette Park and the White House, but the OIG was situated three blocks away. This was only one of several frustrations for the OIG. Another was that the IG had but 300 employees in an agency where almost 250,000 employees provided medical care and benefits to 3 million veterans a year.

Organizing for Influence

One reason the OIGs grew so predictably was that the IGs learned from each other. They had a common forum—what one detractor called a "trade union"—that met every month during the Reagan administration: the President's Council on Integrity and Efficiency.

The PCIE was not the first IG coordinating mechanism, however. Carter had created the Executive Group to Combat Fraud and Waste in Government by executive memorandum in May 1979. What made Reagan's approach more serious perhaps was its leadership. First, whereas the Carter group had been chaired by the deputy attorney general, the PCIE was chaired by the deputy director of OMB, with the vice chair reserved for a sitting IG. OMB was in the lead, not Justice.

Second, whereas the Carter group was created by memorandum, the PCIE was sanctioned by a formal executive order, suggesting its much more visible role in the Reagan war on waste. Short of enacting the PCIE by statute, it was the strongest signal possible of the president's commitment.

Justice was not completely out of the picture, however. At least one sentence in the relatively short executive order bore a heavy Justice imprint: "The Council will recognize the pre-eminent role of the Department of Justice in matters involving law enforcement and litigation."[9] Justice also insisted that the FBI's executive assistant director of investigations be a full PCIE member. Furthermore, the department won OMB's promise that any PCIE projects or committees dealing with law enforcement would involve either the deputy attorney general or the FBI, and the FBI was given permanent chairmanship of the PCIE standing committee on integrity and law enforcement.

These gestures to Justice notwithstanding, OMB has played the stronger role. As a result, some in Congress and the IG community worried about politicization of the IG concept. Looking back over the Reagan years in its ten-year review of the IG Act, the House Government Operations Committee noted what it saw as "subtle indications of attempts to direct the inspector general [*sic*] and to use the PCIE for partisan purposes" but offered only tepid examples of possible politicization.[10]

The PCIE did impose a burden on the IGs for joint projects. In 1987, for example, the five standing PCIE committees had thirty-two separate projects under way, including ones on deposits of payroll taxes by federal grantees and contractors (audit committee), computer system integrity (computer committee), legal analysis of IG subpoenas (inspectors and special reviews committee), characteristics of successful procurement and financial investigations (investigations and law enforcement committee), and feedback to whistleblowers (prevention committee). "The downside of the PCIE," one IG remarked in an interview conducted by House Government Operations staff, "is that some subcommittees promote work just to keep the subcommittees going. The IGs have too much that needs to be done to be involved in make-work projects. The tendency, however, is to try to get every one involved when some do not have a valid need or interest in a particular area."[11]

Whatever the costs, the PCIE was roundly endorsed as a tool for both enhancing the lobbying power of the IGs and building the informal networks that support organizational learning. "I'm not so sure it was the idea that they didn't want to kind of keep a closer eye on us," Kusserow once explained, "as much as really encouraging us to do our business. But the end result has been . . . it has permitted us to work together, and to come together."[12]

His view was echoed by other IGs. As EPA IG John Martin noted in 1988, for example, "The PCIE as an organization allows us the type of framework where we don't necessarily have to stand alone against an individual agency head; that we can rely on the cohesiveness of a Governmentwide system like that to give us support in times when perhaps our individual agencies may wish to see us disappear." As his colleague, Transportation IG John Melchner put it:

> The PCIE and the way it operates gives me an opportunity to check in with my colleagues from time to time and ask them—say I'm being confronted with thus and so, a particular issue; what do you think about it? . . . There are very few people who are in the unique position that inspectors general are. As my colleagues have said, you need to balance it with some understanding, some compassion; at the same time, you need to protect your independence. It is a valuable resource to me to

be able to go to that group and know them from dealing with them on a regular basis.[13]

Thus did the PCIE become much less a device to control the IGs than an opportunity for the IGs to insulate themselves from OMB and Congress. The PCIE not only was a vehicle for lobbying staff and budget increases but also a home for the IG selection process. In many ways, "it is nothing more than a trade union, a bargaining union, for the IGs," as one assistant secretary for management bitterly complained, "an opportunity to get together and figure out ways to grow."

The PCIE began to lose strength toward the end of the second Reagan administration. First, inevitable disruption occurred with the changes in leadership at OMB. Recall Wright's difficulty keeping associate directors for management. According to one OMB staffer, "The string of associate directors caused a loss in focus by 1984. Joe was important to the PCIE, but the associate director kept it going, made the train run on time, sent out the paperwork, that kind of thing. Once Joe decided to create an IG vice chair [for the PCIE], OMB was effectively out of it, and it became even less important to the associate directors."

Second, the expansion of the IG concept to other departments and agencies meant more players at the table. Getting together as a group of fifteen or eighteen in the early 1980s was one thing, convening a meeting of twenty-five or thirty in 1988 was another. More importantly, under Executive Order 12625, the PCIE in 1986 was expanded to include a "Coordinating Conference" covering all the small agency IGs. Although the PCIE still met separately, the Coordinating Conference was represented at the table and in specific PCIE projects.

Third, the Kmiec OLC memo deeply divided the PCIE. As vice chairman at the time, State IG Sherman Funk unsuccessfully took responsibility for negotiating a solution to the controversy. His efforts prompted the following response from Acting Labor IG Maria in testimony before the Senate Governmental Affairs Committee:

I and my staff are personally outraged as a result of it. I am not certain that all the—I am speaking only as the acting, all right. Many would interpret me as an interloper, so I can have perhaps the courage of my convictions, which others may not have. I perceive that all the Inspectors General are not marching to the same drum beat, they are all not singing from the same song sheet. Some have very vigorous, very credible programs, and I think others have very comfortable situations in which their investigative authority is really of little consequence to them.[14]

Finally, as the IG concept matured over the 1980s, the need for a strong PCIE lessened. The class of 1985—trained and selected under the informal IG recruiting committee—had less need for a networking device and the comraderie and empathy derived from talking to colleagues about the start-up frustrations in their departments and agencies.

THE ORGANIZATIONAL FUTURE

Entering the 1990s, the IGs showed no signs of backing off from growth. Not only did most press for new resources, but their hierarchies also continued to rise. However, growth could come on two basic paths: expanded law enforcement authorities or investment in evaluation and inspections. The first already was familiar to the IGs; it was the path of compliance monitoring. The second was more risky, but potentially more useful to government.

Ideally, the IGs would strengthen criminal investigations and evaluation at the same time. As Kusserow argued, evaluation can be particularly effective in setting targets for investigations and audits:

> Investigations are like the artillery because they use big guns against a given target; audits are like the infantry since they are more personnel intensive and have to systematically move from one provider, or group of providers, to the next; and inspections are like a cavalry that is smaller in number than the opposition but is sent out to scout the opponent's overall position in order to engage in a limited encounter or to report back and draw up a larger battle plan.[15]

However, even the IGs increasingly are bound by a zero-sum game that dictates hard choices. Thus, the IG organizational future has become less about what the IGs want and more about what the government needs.

The Case for a Blanket Enhancement

As summarized in H.R. 1361, introduced by Representative Harley O. Staggers, Jr. (D-W.V.), March 7, 1991, the case for blanket law enforcement authority is as follows:

The Congress finds that—

(1) the lack of full law enforcement authority for criminal investigators of the Offices of Inspector General has severely impacted recruitment, retention, and morale of such investigators;

(2) the Offices of Inspectors General in the Federal Government have lost at least 300 criminal investigators to agencies with full law enforcement authority;

(3) many investigators of the Offices of Inspector General are often at risk because they are in one-man posts of duty;

(4) deputization of such investigators to grant them full law enforcement powers may take as long as 6 months;

(5) such investigators are required to meet the same experience and training requirements as agents with full law authority; and

(6) the system of operating Offices of Inspectors General with investigators who may not exercise full law enforcement authority is inefficient.

The question never has been whether the approximately two thousand IG investigators need law enforcement authority, but where they would get it—from the Department of Justice on a case-by-case basis or from a blanket amendment to the IG Act. For the IGs, the answer supporting blanket authority is found in issues of equity, safety, and efficiency.

EQUITY. Either OIG 1811 investigators are responsible enough to carry a firearm or they are not. However, as of 1990, roughly half of OIG investigators had full law enforcement authority under statute, while the rest had to (1) ask Justice for permission to make an arrest or serve a warrant, or (2) ask the FBI or the U.S. Marshals Service to loan a fully deputized agent. Having statutory authority—such as the Agriculture investigators had under 7 U.S.C. 2270, Defense under 10 U.S.C. Section 1585, or GSA under 40 U.S.C. 318(d)—hardly justifies blanket authority for the rest of the IGs. One way to assure equity, for example, would be to place every OIG investigator under case-by-case Justice deputization.

SAFETY. According to the IGs, there were at least 650 cases in the late 1980s where the lack of law enforcement authority had jeopardized an investigation. They were summarized in a three-inch bound document presented to Congress in 1989.[16] Even in the most troublesome of the cases, however, it was not always clear how an armed OIG agent would have been any more successful in preventing an assault than an unarmed agent. Congressional Research Service specialist Fred Kaiser made just such an argument regarding an incident in which an OIG agent (unarmed) and a deputy U.S. marshal (armed) were taken hostage. Assume as Kaiser does that the IG agent would have been operating without a deputy marshal:

> Under these circumstances, an armed OIG investigator, compared to an unarmed agent accompanied by a Deputy Marshal, would not necessarily have been better able to prevent the hostage situation from arising in the first place or prevent it from escalating. This is because U.S. Marshals, who are responsible for Federal court security and protection of judges and witnesses, among others, receive special training in protective matters. They are taught, moreover, to take precautionary measures to minimize the prospect of a hostage situation and to prevent an escalation of violence surrounding it or harm to innocent bystanders. It is unlikely that OIG agents with full law enforcement powers would undergo the same kind and extent of training or develop the same expertise in personal security matters as Marshals.[17]

Despite the documentation the OIGs provided Congress and the inconvenience, hassles, and threats the IG investigators faced, the costs of blanket authority were higher. The point of limiting law enforcement authority was not to make life miserable for the IG criminal investigators, but to protect citizens from unnecessary harm and potential abuses of power. As the House Government Operations Committee concluded in its ten-year review of the IG Act:

> While a blanket grant of all law enforcement functions may be the most efficient way for IG's to obtain them, such an action by itself would not provide the due process and protection of individual rights inherent in the grand jury process, used when the inspectors general conduct investigations in cooperation with the U.S. attorney, nor would it provide the oversight inherent in the deputization process. Any proposal to extend law enforcement to inspectors general on other than a case-by-case basis without careful analysis and specific provision for the protection of individual rights would be unwise.[18]

Given that the report was released under the signature of Jack Brooks, who was about to become chairman of the Judiciary Committee, and that the Judiciary Committee would have some jurisdiction over blanket authority legislation, it seemed unlikely to become law.

EFFICIENCY. Ultimately, the argument for law enforcement authority boils down to one of efficiency. At least until the Department of Justice changed its process in the early 1990s, the IGs were enormously frustrated with the way Justice handled requests for case-by-case deputization. The IGs were not a priority; the thirteen-step process was extraordinarily complicated; and the procedure was prone to delay. During the late 1980s, the average wait for Defense Department requests was two to six months; EPA, four months; Interior, from two to six months; and Transportation, three months. For all the OIGs, according to Justice, the average deputization in 1989 took 48.5 days to process.[19]

Although the complaints about inefficiency and hopelessly confused procedures were legitimate, granting sweeping authority to such a large number of newly empowered police officers, whether called OIG agents or not, is questionable. Furthermore, implementing the change would not be inexpensive. Noting the substantial training costs that would be involved in giving law enforcement authority to all OIG investigators, Frederick Kaiser suggested that the net effect of the blanket approach might be a shift in OIG priorities from auditing to investigation, which already was well under way by the mid-1980s:

> There might be an incentive or bias to demonstrate that the new law enforcement authority was, indeed, a worthwhile investment. This could lead to pressure to use the new powers, possibly extensively, to justify their added costs, particularly as these authorities are expected to enhance OIG capabilities and effectiveness. This, conceivably, could result in favorable consideration and treatment for the criminal investigative activities and proposals, at the expense of other OIG activities and plans.[20]

The solution, then, to the bureaucratic delays lies not in blanket authorities, but in efficiency—in this case, a Justice commitment to respond in a timely fashion.[21]

Despite the generally negative outlook on blanket deputization, good reason exists to give the IGs another kind of law enforcement power: limited testimonial subpoena authority. Some federal contractors have become adept at defeating the IGs' existing document subpoena authority.

There is no doubt that Congress wanted the IGs to have enough authority to compel information from contractors and other recipients of federal funds, a point forcefully made in the Senate report on the 1978 IG Act,

> Subpoena power is absolutely essential to the discharge of the Inspector and Auditor General's functions. There are literally thousands of institutions in the country which are somehow involved in the receipt of funds from Federal programs. Without the power necessary to conduct a comprehensive audit of these entities, the Inspector and Auditor General could have no serious impact on the way federal funds are expended.[22]

Hence the 1978 provision gave IGs the right to subpoena "the production of all information, documents, reports, answers, records, accounts, paper, and other data and documentary evidence necessary."

The list was so broad that some IGs assumed it permitted testimonial subpoenas. The Energy IG, for example, in 1978 issued a subpoena *ad testificandum* against John Iannone, an employee of the American Petroleum Institute, compelling him to testify regarding the release of sensitive information on American petroleum reserves. The subpoena was issued under the Department of Energy Act, which established the Energy IGship when the department was created. The subpoena provision essentially was the same in the 1978 IG Act.

Ruling in *U.S.* v. *Iannone*, the U.S. District Court for the District of Columbia noted that while the Department of Energy Act did authorize the IG to subpoena "all information," the act mentioned only documentary evidence. "If Congress had intended to authorize the Inspector General to compel oral testimony under oath," the court concluded, "there is simple language by which it could have unequivocally expressed its intent. . . . The fact that Congress did not expressly include the power to issue subpoenas *ad testificandum* . . . while it has done so elsewhere weighs against reading [the IG Act] to authorize such subpoena power for the Inspector General."[23]

One argument for granting testimonial subpoena powers to IGs is that Congress has given the same authority to other federal investigators—at last count, at least seventy-three such grants existed.[24] However, the best case can be made solely on the grounds that the targets of IG investigations, particularly contractors, can easily frustrate an IG document subpoena. As contract law experts Herbert L. Fenster and Darryl J. Lee warned federal contractors:

> Although many organizations feel obliged to cooperate with federal auditors, experience has shown that such a stance often

leads to trouble. A company and its officials should do everything required under the contractual and statutory provisions
... but they have every right to stop at that point and offer no
further assistance in their own investigation. "Extreme Cau-
tion" should be the standard, and every responsible company
official should know the rules.[25]

Fraud often is hard to detect, particularly when either contracts
are so complex or records are so disorganized that an IG investigator
or auditor cannot understand the operating scheme or cull enough
evidence to convince a U.S. attorney to convene a grand jury to
compel testimony.[26] Properly circumscribed to protect individual
due process, limited testimonial subpoena power may be the kind
of organizational enhancement the IGs need to accomplish their
mission.[27] With its focus on making the case, not making the bust,
testimonial subpoena power is a law enforcement tool the IGs increasingly need.

The Case for Evaluation

In the final analysis, the problem with enhanced law enforcement
authority rests in the signal it sends to IGs about the proper balance
between their competing responsibilities to government. The IGs
would be more valuable to their agencies and Congress if they focused less on short-term statistical accomplishments, particularly
those involving investigations, and more on program design emerging from outcome-oriented evaluations and inspections.

As a result, the IGs might move away from the compliance model
of management improvement and toward the capacity-building approach. Instead of participating in program reviews on a post-hoc
basis, after the damage already has been done, capacity building
would require a more active role for the IGs at the beginning of the
legislative and regulatory process. They would be asked to address
workability at the key agenda-setting phase of the policy process.

The IGs have an ample mandate to make recommendations on
proposed legislation and regulations. That they have not taken the
initiative to do so is not surprising, given OMB's emphasis on short-
term statistical accomplishment. No doubt exists that they could
develop greater strength in program design, for at least one IG—Kusserow at HHS—did.

Nevertheless, building organizational capacity for evaluations and
inspections has been among the least popular of possible enhancements. Three OIGs added the function between 1983 and 1989; three

dropped it. The hope that IGs will become more actively engaged in evaluation remains appealing, however, if only because evaluation units outside the OIGs were deeply cut during the 1980s.[28]

According to a GAO study of the first four years of the Reagan administration, the number of federal evaluation units not only declined, but the kind of evaluations produced in those units also narrowed significantly.[29] In 1988 GAO warned the incoming Bush administration that "with few exceptions, we have found that both program evaluation and data collection capabilities have been gravely eroded in the executive branch."[30] As the warning continued,

The same work was not being done in 1984 or in 1988 as had been done in 1980. Work shifted from complex evaluations that give more precise measures of program effects to less complex studies and nontechnical reports.

In our 1988 sample of units, there was a greater reliance on external professionals. Unlike earlier years, when internal professionals performed small-scale, quick-turnaround studies, staff shortages appear to have reached a critical level, forcing evaluation units to contract out even small-scale studies. To make matters worse, one agency official suggested that this pool of qualified contractors is also shrinking.

Further, reports are increasingly produced at the request of program managers, and primarily for internal consumption. Evaluations for external consumption—for congressional oversight and public scrutiny—were limited in number [by 1988] and were primarily studies mandated by Congress, which set aside funds for this purpose.[31]

Furthermore, the government, throughout Reagan's second term, continued to disinvest in the data gathering needed for evaluation and policy analysis. Without basic information to evaluate programs, government is effectively blinded from the future. Efforts to prevent problems are undermined, and policy analysts and presidential appointees focus on what they can see best, the short-term.

WHY IG? Why look to the OIGs for a rebirth of program evaluation? The answer is twofold.

First, many of the evaluation staff lines cut by Reagan wound up under OIG control. Personnel was, and still is, a zero-sum game, particularly among department and agency staff units. Thus, gains in the OIGs often meant cuts in evaluation. "Contrasted with the reduced role of more traditional program evaluation in federal agencies," HHS evaluator William Moran argued, "it seems reasonable to suggest that the responsibility for evaluating federal programs is increasingly shifting to OIGs. "[32]

At HHS, the shift was real. The 150 positions cut from the Office of Planning and Evaluation moved virtually intact to the IG's rapidly expanding Office of Evaluation and Inspections. Similar transfers occurred across government, though in most instances the evaluation positions were reclassified, or converted, into audit or investigation or both.

Second, OIG-based evaluation offers some protection against the politics of analysis. Asked whether the IGs should expand their evaluation capacity, one non-OIG evaluation expert said, "Short answer: at least it's not auditing—not checking down a compliance list. It'd be good for the IGs. Long answer: the IG has much better defenses against pressure than most non-IG units can muster. Great problems now exist across government in the politicization of information and analysis. IGs could protect honest work."

The argument generally is supported by GAO's work on the need for honest reporting in federal evaluation: "Some of the problems with agency evaluations have included the failure to conduct necessary studies, nontechnical influence on draft reports that have concealed or distorted findings, technical flaws affecting study quality, the uncertain access of top managers to complete and unvarnished study findings, and the limited use of evaluations in making policy."[33]

Although OIG-based evaluation does not solve all these problems, enough operational independence would be available to give traditionalists the desired freedom to do their jobs in what has become a more politicized analytic environment. According to Moran,

> While traditional program evaluators may have to submit their results for review through the agency's chain of command, inspections staff know that their IG has the final say on the report that they publish. This does not mean that inspection results are not circulated for review outside OIGs for comment. What it does mean is that an IG can promulgate a report without concurrence from any other source within his or her agency. This authority becomes extremely important when dealing with sensitive or controversial subjects.[34]

Moreover, not only are IG reports public, but their authors also have the statutory freedom to audit and investigate where they wish. Whether traditional evaluators like it or not, the OIGs have the staff, the resources for contracting, and the backing of history to undertake a more aggressive evaluation role. Evaluation would move the IGs aggressively toward performance and capacity-based monitoring. Unlike criminal investigations, which can be characterized as the most backward looking of individualized compliance approaches, evaluation offers a forward-looking program and agency level alternative.

WHY NOT IG? The problems with IG-based evaluation also are twofold. First, some traditionalists do not accept the IG approach to evaluation. IGs often label evaluation as "inspections," which points to the clash of perspectives. Consider, for example, the following assessment of auditors as evaluators made by public administration scholar Dwight Davis:

> Auditors tend to emphasize variables related to "management control...." Auditors are more likely to address program impacts now than they used to be, but they are still less likely to do so than evaluation researchers.

> Auditors also tend to be more concerned with legal and procedural compliance issues than evaluation researchers. Auditors are obliged by the [Generally Accepted Government Accounting Standards] to examine such issues.

> The tendency of audits to focus on management control and compliance issues may result in program evaluations that are simply "nitpicking" or "bean counting." The emphasis on accountability may result in reports that are more critical in tone than necessary and, therefore, unbalanced or unfair.

> There are reasons for believing that auditing is less innovative and conceptually rich than evaluation research.[35]

Davis's outlook is favorable, however, when compared with public administration scholar Kathryn Newcomer's parody of the IG option as one of the ten best ways to kill evaluation: "Once evaluation has been transferred to the IG's office then one can simply let the IG staff finish off the job. The IG can convince any political appointee that auditing really is evaluation, and evaluation is really auditing, and auditing is actually auditing, and evaluation is actually nothing more to speak of."[36]

Even the OIGs are not sure what evaluation means. The OIG evaluation and inspection units are called different names, use different kinds of staffs, have different coverage—targeted being narrowly focused studies, systemic being broader in scope—and range in size from small (Commerce at 12) to large (Defense at 180 and HHS at 150) (see table 9-4).

Table 9-4. *OIG Evaluation and Inspection Units, 1989*

Department or agency	Unit name	Staff	Scope of inspection
HHS	Office of Evaluation and Inspections	Program	Systemic analyses
Energy	Office of Inspections and Analysis	Generalists, engineers	Targeted
Commerce	Office of Planning, Evaluation, and Inspections	Auditors, accountants, economists	Targeted
GSA	Office of Audit	Auditors	Targeted
Defense	Office of Inspections	Program analysts	Mixed
State	Office of Investigations, Office of Security Oversight	Generalists	Mixed

Source: Adapted from William Moran, "Evaluation within the Federal Offices of Inspector General," in M. Hendricks, M. Mangano, and W. Moran, *The Growth of Evaluations within the Federal Offices of Inspector General; New Directions for Program Evaluation,* no. 48 (San Francisco: Jossey-Bass, Winter 1990).

Evaluation and inspections is so broadly defined that virtually all of the OIGs could claim that they do evaluations of some kind. Of the nine OIGs with an inspection and evaluation function, only one—HHS—has something resembling traditional evaluation, and only one—HHS—labels its evaluation unit as such. The eight others use the term "inspections" loosely at best, applying it to everything from traditional audits (compliance reviews at Defense) to three-to-four week field visits (minimanagement audits at Commerce).

THE HHS APPROACH. The HHS Office of Evaluations and Inspections (OEI), was given its name in 1989 as a way to express a closer tie to the evaluation community, so announced Kusserow in a letter to every member of the American Evaluation Association.[37]

The name accurately described the unit's agenda, and reflected the special emphasis on time-sensitive inspections as a key component of the evaluative role. According to Michael Mangano, assistant HHS IG for evaluations and inspections, "We were originally created because there was a gap in the HHS evaluation capability. At the cabinet and subcabinet levels in Washington, events move quickly, and decisions are needed just as quickly. Traditional evaluations are often too slow to help—in the past, decisions were regularly being made before the results of traditional evaluations were available."[38]

The Kusserow-Mangano approach to evaluation puts maximum emphasis on speed, not ordinarily the overriding concern of traditional evaluation. "We recognize completely that if evaluations are to be useful," Mangano argued, "they must be available before decisions are made. We aim to complete each inspection within four to six months, and we are sometimes much faster."[39]

Nevertheless, the HHS model was particularly interested in the prevention of future problems. The OEI technical assistance guide on report writing—one of seven guides published by the HHS OIG—is explicit on this point, offering the following tips for effective recommendations:

—Consider all issues in your Inspection to be "fair game." Be alert to all possibilities for improvement.

—Consider the larger context into which the Inspection recommendations must fit. Remember that recommendations must make sense within an existing organizational setting.

—Show the future implications of recommendations, especially the benefits expected from each recommendation. If helpful, spell out the resources necessary to implement each recommendation.

—Make your recommendations easy to understand. Categorize recommendations in a meaningful way, and tie each one directly to the Inspection findings. If possible, convey recommendations to key audiences in a personal briefing as well as a written report.[40]

In the final analysis, evaluators may have little choice but to strike a bargain with the IGs: support for OIG-based evaluation in return for the protections the increasingly independent OIGs can provide. As GAO evaluation division director Eleanor Chelimsky argued, "Because of the carefully protected independence of audit offices, program evaluation can actually escape from politicization there. The fact is that, today, speaking truth to power is a pretty uncommon luxury in a government environment in which merely identifying a *problem* has become as hard as it used to be to agree on a solution."[41]

The best interests of the IG concept also would be served by the bargain, which Congress easily could encourage by creating a statutory assistant IG post for evaluation and inspections. By requiring a separate focus on evaluation, Congress would be reminding the IGs that monitoring toward performance and capacity building are part of the continuing mandate.

THE IGs AS INSTITUTIONAL MEMORY

An added attraction of evaluation is that it encourages the IGs to take on a more aggressive role within their agencies as a source of institutional memory on what works and does not work. With political appointees now assuming even the deputy assistant secretary levels of government, five levels down, and with traditional sources of policy analysis imperiled, the IGs and their career staffs may be the last, best hope for restoring and protecting the long-term memory of government.

The HUD scandal is an example of how compliance monitoring can eclipse a broader vision of accountability. As Dwight Ink argued from his vantage point as a former HUD assistant secretary for administration during the 1970s,

> I believe that one source of the HUD problems had its roots in the early 1970s when the department began to shift emphasis from prevention to investigation. More effective investigation would have been a positive move if it had not been at the expense of prevention. One of the most serious consequences was a gradual de-emphasizing of early warning systems which were so important in the early days of the department.[42]

As Ink remembered, the change was most pronounced in the timing of action. "Emphasis was on prevention of problems to the extent possible and the early detection of emerging problems before they became serious. When this approach began to be replaced with a heavy reliance on investigation by external oversight units, the Department lost much of its capacity to avoid abuse or to take immediate corrective action when lapses did occur."[43]

Persuading the IGs to embrace evaluation and policy analysis and, in doing so, invest some of their resources and independence in performance and capacity-based accountability would be no small accomplishment in restoring some of the long-term institutional memory of government. Nevertheless, creation of an IG who is well-buttressed against politicization, selected through a careful search process, given a fixed term of office, and tasked to help both Congress and the president examine the feasibility of programs before scandals occur is worth working toward.

Questions of Effectiveness

Measuring the Impact of IGs

THE test of any monitoring system, whether directed toward compliance, performance, or capacity building, is whether it improves the overall accountability of government. The question is one of effectiveness.

The first step in answering the question is defining "effectiveness." From an organizational perspective, for example, the IGs have been very effective. Their offices have become more independent. Their staffs have increased greatly.[1] They have reduced their dependence on their departments and agencies for basic resources and have gained a measure of certainty over their unstable political environment.

From a fraud, waste, and abuse perspective, the IGs have also been effective, if, that is, effectiveness is measured in purely statistical terms. The IGs have accumulated huge savings over the past decade, along with increasing amounts of that visible odium that comes from indictment and conviction of individual wrongdoers. To fully estimate IG effectiveness in the war on waste, however, it is also necessary to estimate the amount of waste to begin with.

If, for example, Reagan was correct in noting that one out of every five federal dollars is lost to waste, the IGs would have to recover $200 billion a year to break even. To date, they have not come close. In fact, as Steven Kelman argued, Reagan estimates were based on horror stories of waste that were "almost always gross exaggerations." As Kelman noted,

> People are too quick to conclude that programs are wasteful when they think the programs are not worthwhile. But if government delivers a worthless product, the condition should be directed at the decision to deliver the product, not vented in charges of incompetence and venality against those making the deliveries.[2]

Yet defining effectiveness in purely organizational or dollar terms is far too narrow. Effectiveness also rests in what is best for government. As Mark Moore and Margaret Gates noted, not only are the words "fraud," "waste," "abuse," "economy," and "efficiency" difficult to define, IGs can apply those terms in "forward-looking," "backward-looking," "cost-controlling," or "output-oriented" ways.[3] Thus whether IGs are effective depends on what one believes they should be doing and how they are doing it.

MEASURES OF EFFECTIVENESS

Using this broader definition of effectiveness prompts at least five questions of IG operations: (1) How professional are the offices? (2) How deep is the coverage? (3) How great are the savings? (4) How good are the cases? (5) How visible are the results? The first two questions deal with inputs into the process; the final three deal with outputs which in turn give at least some sense of the impacts on fraud, waste, and abuse. Although the issues raised are not exhaustive, they do offer a range of perspectives on how the IGs have done in their day-to-day work over the past decade or so.

Professionalism

One possible way to gauge effectiveness is to set minimum standards of performance against which to measure compliance; in short, monitoring the OIGs for professionalism. GAO's version of this approach, used in testing a half dozen OIGs over the past decade, is based on twenty-three highly detailed standards—twelve for audits, eleven for investigations—that every OIG must meet as a basic precondition of effectiveness.[4]

On audit independence, for example, an OIG must assure that its auditors are independent from their agency targets, free from "personal or external impairments to independence," and maintain an independent attitude about their work. On auditor qualifications, an OIG must also assure that all auditors meet the Office of Personnel Management's requirements for their jobs and take one or more training courses during the previous two years. GAO does not indicate, however, for example, which of these qualifications might be most important to an OIG's impact, or whether weaknesses in any one of the twenty-three standards might be more serious than others.

Consider the GAO's 1987 review of the General Services Administration OIG as an example of how this compliance checklisting is used.[5] Drawing on a sample of only twenty-six audits and investigations, each out of a universe of thousands, GAO discovered weaknesses in three areas: audit supervision, audit evidence, and investigation planning. The weaknesses resemble the same kind of "gotcha" findings that so often frustrate the targets of OIG audits and investigations. On the supervision standard, for example, GAO found that four of the twenty-six audits contained statements that were not properly supported by the work papers, while four contained work papers that needed further interpretation by the auditors. Most significantly, ten of the twenty-six sampled audits did not meet one or both of the elements of the supervision standard.

In 7 of the 10 audits with supervisory deficiencies, GAO found little or no written evidence that a supervisor monitored the subordinates' work. For example, GAO reviewed one audit where none of the regional offices' work papers and only 20 percent of the headquarters' work papers GAO sampled were signed by a supervisor to document supervisory review. In 4 other audits, GAO found factual inconsistencies between the reports and supporting work papers indicating that the supervisory review was inadequate.[6]

The problem with this kind of compliance test is that it reveals little about an OIG's effectiveness. The fact that GSA met the minimums on twenty out of twenty-three standards does not mean it is more effective than Agriculture and HHS, both of which met eighteen, or Transportation, which met nineteen. Nor does the fact that VA scored a perfect twenty-three out of twenty-three mean it is the best of the lot. An OIG could be 100 percent in compliance and still be of absolutely no value to the department or agency. In compliance testing, whether it is done by the GAO of the OIGs or the OIGs of their own departments and agencies, a passing grade depends entirely on the checklist. Hence in this case being professional does not mean being useful.

Coverage

That the IGs did very well in building their staffs under Ronald Reagan is clear; their offices grew faster or shrunk less than their agencies or departments. The question is whether that growth assured adequate coverage. Two ratios can be offered as partial answers: (1) total IG staff to total department or agency employees and (2)

Table 10-1. *Ratios of OIG Coverage, 1989*
Outlays in millions of dollars

Department or agency	Ratio of IG staff to total agency employees	Ratio of IG staff to total agency budget outlays	Department or agency	Ratio of IG staff to total agency employees	Ratio of IG staff to total agency budget outlays
Agriculture	1:134	1:60			
AID	1:19	1:9	Interior	1:247	1:18
Commerce	1:192	1:12	Labor	1:35	1:43
Defense	1:669	1:203	NASA[b]	1:158	1:75
Education	1:14	1:66	SBA	1:31	1:3[a]
Energy	1:69	1:47	RRB	1:18	1:6
EPA	1:45	1:16	State[b]	1:98	1:14
GSA	1:46	1:0.5[a]	Transportation	1:135	1:57
HHS	1:89	1:304	USIA	1:175	1:18
HUD[b]	1:27	1:40	VA[b]	1:546	1:77

Source: *Budget of the United States Government, Fiscal Year 1991.*
a. GSA figures are based on budget authority, not outlays.
b. 1990 estimates.

total IG staff to total department or agency budget outlays (see table 10-1).

According to the employment data, for example, the Railroad Retirement Board (RRB), SBA, AID, Education, and GSA provide the deepest coverage. The RRB is at the top of the list, even though it is the second smallest OIG in government (72 staff). It also is one of the smallest agencies in government (1,265 full-time positions), so ends up with one IG staffer for approximately every eighteen agency employees. In contrast, Defense, with the largest OIG (1,572 staff) covering more than 1 million civilian employees, comes in last. Penultimate on the list is the VA—one of the smallest OIGs (389 staff) in one of the largest agencies (212,200 FTE).

In the ratio of IG staff to budget outlays, SBA, GSA, and AID again are on top. At SBA, for example, there is one IG staffer for every $3 million in outlays; at AID, one for every $9 million. Defense takes the next-to-last spot, with a large OIG responsible for a very large budget of $318 billion. HHS is at the bottom, stretching 1,300 OIG staffers over its $400 billion in Social Security, Medicare, and human services accounts.

The ratios come with three qualifiers. First, the Defense numbers were figured without counting the roughly 4,000 additional employees at the Defense Contract Audit Agency (DCAA) whose work liberates the Defense IG to focus on bigger questions. Adding in the

DCAA employees lowers the ratios to one IG staffer for every 194 civilian employees and $59 million.

Second, the ratios do not count either the number of clients an agency handles or the number of contractors. The Defense IG's work may be simplified, for example, because much of the department's procurement is handled by a relatively small number of contractors, while the HHS IG's work may be complicated because each of the 36 million Social Security recipients could be viewed as a source of potential fraud.

Third, the ratios imply that the IGs have maximum flexibility to use their staff as they wish, but many have significant statutory responsibilities to concentrate on specific programs. At SBA, for example, the IG staff is so busy conducting mandated audits of the approximately 500 Small Business Investment Companies (SBIC) funded by the federal government that little time remains to do much else. Prior to 1988, all SBICs were audited annually; after 1988, every other year. Meanwhile, as SBA IG Charles Gillium testified in 1989, the statutorily required audits consumed almost 70 percent of staff resources, but less than 40 percent of the work produced findings of any major significance.

Despite the caveats, comparing similar agencies can reveal important disparities. As of 1988, for example, the VA had one of the smallest OIGs in government, but was one of the largest and most decentralized departments. Given the agency's relatively high exposure to fraud in its $15 billion-per-year income security program, its OIG appeared understaffed. Congress as a result authorized forty new OIG positions as part of the legislation elevating VA to cabinet status. The Senate Governmental Affairs Committee had pressed for an increase of 165 positions, arguing for an IG staff-to-agency workforce ratio of 1:365 as a minimum staffing floor.

The challenge, however, in setting OIG staff floors rests in making credible estimates of need. Staffing need could be less a function of ratio than guaranteeing some absolute minimum number in audit, investigation, or clerical positions. Perhaps the smallest agency must have a certain number of auditors and investigators to be effective, while a large agency needs only that number plus a ratio-based amount. Determining staff need has proven exceedingly difficult, if not impossible.

The need for a staffing floor is particularly acute at the smallest agencies covered under the 1988 IG amendments. These one- or two-person OIGs must contend with the dual problems of expertise and dependence. Responsible for both audit and investigations, these

Table 10-2. Relative OIG Savings, April 1 – September 30, 1989
Dollars

Department or agency	Funds put to better use	Total investigative recoveries	Total savings	Savings per OIG employee	Total agency outlays (billions)	Ratio of total savings to agency outlays
Agriculture	256,833,000	36,100,000	293,933,000	361,987	48.3	1:164
AID	142,882,000	182,946	149,279,000	621,996	2.1	1:14
Commerce	120,514,000	472,000	125,334,000	599,684	2.6	1:21
Defense	858,790,000	65,957,520	926,903,520	589,663	318.3	1:343
Education	240,248,000	5,529,024	374,915,024	1,153,585	21.6	1:58
Energy[a]	425,500,000	1,441,443	447,000,000	1,862,500	11.4	1:26
EPA	31,708,000	1,347,114	49,826,114	160,729	4.9	1:98
GSA	118,594,428	1,359,718	125,759,859	300,143	0.2[b]	1:1.6
HHS	5,787,143,000	5,500,000	5,915,696,000	4,491,797	399.7	1:68
HUD	23,669,000	4,339,978	59,279,978	120,488	19.7	1:332
Interior	620,600,000	6,673,760	628,637,078	2,175,215	5.2	1:8
Labor	33,800,000	1,341,727	107,841,727	206,198	22.7	1:211
NASA	55,900,000	3,000,000	59,870,525	410,072	11.0	1:184
SBA	1,592,000	360,998	1,991,998	15,206	0.4[b]	1:201
RRB	100,385,000	900,290	101,285,290	1,406,740	0.4	1:4
State	24,100,000	98,092	24,198,092	93,429	3.7	1:153
Transportation	68,746,000	7,100,000	183,745,000	393,458	26.6	1:145
USIA	560,879	2,121	659,000	13,180	0.9	1:1,366
VA	113,000,000	2,674,000	116,674,000	299,933	30.0	1:257

Source: Semiannual reports for the period April 1 – September 30, 1989. Portions of table were compiled by the Department of Health and Human Services, Office of Inspector General.
a. Energy figures were drawn from the October 1, 1989 – March 31, 1990, semiannual report.
b. GSA figures are based on budget authority, not outlays.

OIGs rely on the agency not only for legal advice, but also for every drop of operating support—from clerical to printing.

Some on Capitol Hill, including Lorraine Lewis, general counsel of the Senate Governmental Affairs Committee, recommend a five-person minimum for OIGs—the IG, a secretary, an auditor, an investigator, and a lawyer. The suggestion sounds reasonable for the Interstate Commerce Commission, for example, which could use more than a one-person OIG given its total staff of 701. However, the case becomes less persuasive when the agency has only nine employees, such as the Board for International Broadcasting, or sixty-nine, such as the Appalachian Regional Development Commission.

Amount of Savings

Once beyond inputs into the OIG process—professionalism and coverage ratios—the question of effectiveness turns to outputs. On the audit side of OIG effectiveness, success is usually measured in dollars. During the Reagan administration, for example, the tally of dollars saved or dollars put to better use reached $100 billion. According to the data in table 10-2, great differences existed among the IGs in both the absolute level of savings and savings per employee. Furthermore, the "funds put to better use" category always was the most significant source of savings.

What, if anything, do the data reveal about IG effectiveness? Not surprisingly, given its size and programs, which have a high vulnerability to fraud and abuse, HHS comes in first with $4.5 million in savings per OIG employee. SBA and the U.S. Information Agency (USIA), among the strongest OIGs in staff ratios, show the lowest savings at $15,206 and $13,180, respectively. Since a single IG staff position costs in the neighborhood of $150,000 in salary, supplies, expenses, and clerical support, four IGs fall below the cost-benefit cutoff—HUD, State, SBA, and USIA—with EPA barely above the line.

The data, however, cannot support an assertion that HHS is the most effective OIG. The figures do not measure fraud deterred or waste prevented. Furthermore, conclusions cannot be drawn about how much fraud exists. The HHS OIG may be capturing only a fraction of total fraud, waste, and abuse, while other OIGs may be getting it all. Or, an argument could be made that the HHS total reveals a breakdown in the department's prevention program. How could so much be slipping through?

Neither HHS IG Richard Kusserow nor any of the other IGs have been misleading Congress, however. The HHS OIG undoubtedly saved real money. According to the data in table 10-2, the OIG reclaimed $1 for every $68 in outlays; VA, for every $257; HUD, for every $332; Defense, for every $343; and USIA, for every $1,366.

Such comparisons are fraught with risk, nevertheless. At VA, for example, most of the agency costs reside in fixed personnel accounts. A certain amount of money is necessary to keep VA doctors on the payroll. Thus VA fraud exposure may have been less than HHS.[7]

Furthermore, most of the HHS savings fall in the category labeled "funds put to better use." The phrase is not meaningless, but considerable confusion remains over just what the figures mean. According to an initial survey of the "lessons learned" from implementation of the new reporting requirements passed in 1988, the IGs were clearly worried that "Congress may interpret the savings estimated in 'Funds Put to Better Use' exhibit too literally and as direct, potential budget savings." As the survey of nine large and small agency IGs suggested:

> A number of agencies have difficulty placing a dollar value on "Funds Put to Better Use." To quote one IG, these recommendations "do not result in *real* reductions in outlays or deobligation of funds. These are more *cost avoidances*." A realistic estimate is often not available until the recommendation is implemented, and it is difficult to account for offsetting costs. The computations must be based upon assumptions of conditions which either do not now exist or will exist within the audited entity. The computations also depend upon assumptions as to the course of action the audited entity will take to implement the recommendation. Changes to these assumptions occurring after the report is issued will impact the funds actually realized. Consequently, there can be a significant difference between projected and realized benefits.[8]

Congress and the president likely would have interpreted the "funds put to better use" category as budget savings, particularly in a tough budget environment. Nevertheless, the choice of the word "savings" to label the bottom line may be misleading, allowing Congress and the president to believe whatever each wants about the totals.

Quality

Turning to outputs of OIG investigations, the raw indictment and conviction rates do not require qualifiers and are not open to interpretation. A conviction is a conviction, plain and simple. However, the IGs varied widely in their investigatory success (see table 10-3).

Table 10-3. *IG Policing Rates, 1989*

Department or agency	Total indictments	Total convictions	Department or agency	Total indictments	Total convictions
Agriculture	466	289			
AID	0	5	Interior	51	20
Commerce	25	8	Labor	775	741
Defense	300	249	NASA	11	12
Education	97	114	SBA	22	24
Energy [a]	8	11	RRB	24	39
EPA	10	21	State	45	3
GSA	29	27	Transportation	70	41
HHS	787	584	USIA	0	0
HUD	161	135	VA	135	105

Source: Semiannual reports for the period April 1 – September 30, 1989. Table compiled by the Department of Health and Human Services, Office of Inspector General.

a. Energy figures were drawn from the October 1, 1989 – March 31, 1990, semiannual report.

Agriculture, Defense, HHS, and Labor are on top for one or a combination of three reasons: they have large numbers of clients, large numbers of employees, or large numbers of contractors. According to a PCIE study of every investigative case closed in an unidentified single month in 1988, half of the cases involved a benefit or entitlement program, 11 percent a loan or loan guarantee, 11 percent a federal employee problem—for example, time, attendance, travel, and pay—and 10 percent contracts or purchasing.[9] The PCIE estimated that benefit recipients constituted 32 percent of the case targets; contractors and subcontractors, 16 percent; and federal employees, 15 percent. Agriculture, Defense, HHS, and Labor simply have more of the kind of business that leads to investigative cases.[10] Equally important, these four departments have the largest absolute number of investigators, giving them more resources to look for and develop cases.

However, the volume of IG investigative activity may reveal little about the long-term impact of IG cases. For example, 64 percent of the PCIE cases resulted in fines of less than $1,000, while 56 percent produced restitutions in similar amounts.[11] Thus, just as the drive for ever-greater savings may narrow the range of audit targets to the quick and easy cases, so, too, can the search for convictions create a production mentality that weakens the quality of IG cases.

Indeed, the IGs have a mixed record of success on the number of cases pursued to successful closure. While some cases involved more than one outcome, according to the PCIE study, 28 percent resulted in a criminal conviction, 14 percent involved an administrative recovery or settlement, 21 percent were declined for prosecution by the

Department of Justice, and 34 percent were closed without further action. In short, half of the investigations succeeded, half failed. Of the 473 cases referred to Justice for criminal prosecution, 283 were accepted for action, of which 255 resulted in a conviction.[12] Once the IGs get into court, they do very well.

Conviction and prosecution rates varied significantly among the different sources of leads. Looking just at conviction rates, for example, cases referred from the DCAA, the GAO hotline, the IG hotline, and IG audits had the highest rates of failure, while cases referred from nonfederal sources and U.S. attorneys had the highest rates of success. According to the PCIE analysis, "cases from the IG hotline were successfully prosecuted only 3 percent of the time, and 57 percent of IG hotline cases were closed without any action."[13] Thus, if the goal is the "visible odium" associated with aggressive prosecution and ultimate conviction, the IGs might be better off restricting themselves to nonfederal sources and U.S. attorneys, while hanging up the hotlines.

Justice Department declination rates provide another measure of quality. Cases produced through IG proactive work fared the worst, with 50 percent rejected, while U.S. attorney cases did much better, with 61 percent successfully prosecuted.[14] Of the cases refused by Justice, 17 percent fell below the minimum dollar threshold required for prosecution in a particular district. Another 40 percent of the Justice declinations reflected a judgment that civil, administrative, or state action would produce quicker results or larger returns, 10 percent involved weak or insufficient evidence, 9 percent a lack of criminal intent, 8 percent no federal offense, and 3 percent statute of limitations problems. Many of these cases never should have been presented in the first place.[15]

Nevertheless, the risks for the IG who abandons quantity in pursuit of some abstract notion of quality are considerable. Neither Congress nor the president may be tolerant. In 1990, the House Energy and Commerce Committee, headed by chairman John Dingell (D-Mich.), held a hearing on EPA based on one statistic: In spite of a 26 percent increase in OIG investigative staff between 1987 and 1990, IG-initiated prosecutions had fallen 76 percent.

More remarkable than the committee's single-minded focus on statistical accomplishment was its failure to listen to its own witnesses, particularly Deidre Tanaka, a former IG investigator. For Tanaka, the problem at EPA was not the low number of indictments and convictions. The staff was under such tremendous pressure to produce immediate results that they could not work the bigger cases.

Dingell picked up on the point, but not on the broader impact of the hearing itself as another source of prosecutorial demand:

> Mr. DINGELL. You're saying you were under considerable pressure. That was to proceed more rapidly?
>
> Ms. TANAKA. Yes, to close cases within a year and to meet your indictment quota for the year, and to open a certain number of cases per agent and close certain cases per agent. The size really didn't matter. I mean, it was just opening and closing, you know, real attention to administrative detail.
>
> Mr. DINGELL. What you're saying is a case like this has its own rhythm and its own time demands and its own complexities, and that it requires individual treatment rather than being according to some formula mandated by somebody else, is that right?
>
> Ms. TANAKA. That's correct.[16]

Despite Dingell's concern regarding investigatory coverage of the multi-billion-dollar Superfund program, the hearing sent a different message: produce volume or else.

Whether the IGs have enough control over the volume or quality of cases to make a reasonable test of success is not clear. At Labor, for example, the number of convictions soared from 174 in 1983 to 775 six years later, not because the IG suddenly had become extraordinarily effective but because the FBI abandoned unemployment insurance fraud, leaving those investigations to the Labor IG. Having investigated just 33 such cases in 1983, the Labor OIG handled 504 in 1985.[17]

Before turning to the final output measure, visibility, it is useful to note that the PCIE sample of IG cases produces only lukewarm support for enhancing IG law enforcement authority. According to the data in table 10-4, most IG investigations do not involve high-risk operations, but the more mundane work of sifting through files, interviewing potential witnesses, and sorting through computer runs.

Even if blanket deputization would increase efficiency, the data do not definitively determine whether full law enforcement powers would improve overall IG success rates. The PCIE cases involving deputization were small in number and of no value for raising the IG conviction rates.

The data, however, do reinforce the potential value of testimonial subpoena power. Testimonial subpoenas would not only expand the range of investigatory options prior to the grand jury stage but also

Table 10-4. *Characteristics of Successful Investigations*
Percent

Technique	Cases using technique	Results		
		Convictions	Declinations	Closed
Computer analysis	16	33	39	15
Confidential funds to buy information	2	28	6	50
Confidential informant	8	24	12	44
Consensual monitoring	6	27	11	43
Crime lab exam	1	60	30	0
Deputization	*	0	0	0
Drug testing	*	25	0	25
Grand jury subpoena	8	60	27	6
Handwriting analysis	6	50	19	19
IG subpoena	2	13	47	20
Interview	78	33	19	29
Lab authentication of documentation	4	44	14	28
Polygraph	*	75	0	0
Search of financial records	47	34	20	25
Search of nonfinancial records	73	31	25	27
Search warrant	2	71	18	0
Specifications standards testing	1	33	11	33
Surveillance	11	32	14	36
Undercover	7	36	9	46

Source: President's Council on Integrity and Efficiency, Committee on Integrity and Law Enforcement, *Characteristics of Inspector-General Investigations* (July 1989), p. 26, table 26.
* Less than 1 percent.

would enhance techniques—interviews and document searches—that the IGs already use in much of their work.

Visibility

Visibility is critical to IG effectiveness for two reasons. First, deterrence is based on having potential offenders understand the consequences of their choices and believe they will get caught. Second, Congress and administrators cannot act on IG recommendations if they or their staffs never read the reports.

However, visibility is not completely under the control of the IGs. Although reports have grown shorter, dropping from an average length of one hundred pages in 1981 to seventy-six in 1989, members of Congress and their staffs do not have the time to read the executive summaries of even the most engaging semiannual report. Nor do

Table 10-5. *Rankings of OIG Activity, 1978–89*

Department or agency	Congressional appearances[a]		Media citations	
	Number	Points	Number	Points
Agriculture	33	16	30	12
AID	7	2	6	1
Commerce	16	8 (tie)	20	11
Defense	23	13	54	16
Education	20	12	10	3 (tie)
Energy	18	10	17	9 (tie)
EPA	11	5 (tie)	45	15
GSA	27	15	33	13
HHS	68	17	157	17
HUD	10	4	34	14
Interior	16	8	17	9
Labor	19	11	10	3
NASA	4	1	8	2
SBA	12	7	12	7
State	9	3	10	3
Transportation	26	14	14	8
VA	11	5	10	3

Sources: Semiannual IG reports, *Congressional Information Service,* and *New York Times* and *Washington Post* indexes.

a. Total does not add to 339 because Railroad Retirement Board and Community Service Administration are not included.

cabinet secretaries, administrators, senior managers, or OMB associate directors. The onslaught of competing information is too great, and the twice-yearly IG reports still are too long for a quick skimming. Many IGs use the same cover page from year to year, merely changing the dates from the previous jacket. Arriving on schedule and without fanfare, the report easily can be overlooked by senior policy makers.

Only two ways exist to lead policy makers to take on additional reading. One would be to have a finding so compelling, so dramatic, that the report could not be ignored, either by Congress or the *Washington Post.* The other would be to convince congressional staff, most likely subcommittee staff, that the report, or a specific finding, would make a decent oversight hearing. The data in table 10-5 suggest, however, that most IGs have not fared well with either approach, if they even tried.

Some OIGs, such as NASA, AID, SBA, and VA, hardly received any attention—few stories, fewer hearings. Others, such as those at Agriculture, Energy, and HUD, have been in the news off and on over the years—never a deluge, but a steady stream. Still others, including the Defense and HHS IGs, have been highly visible, accounting for more than half the total media citations and congressional appearances.

QUALITY AND QUANTITY. Visibility data does not always equal impact. Some newspaper stories in the data were directly related to IG scandals—for example, the 1983 EPA scandal and an ongoing fight between the GSA IG and a highly visible agency whistleblower. Others were the product of a single story that played out over a long period of time—for example, defense cost overruns and the HUD scandal. Still others focused on individual appointees snagged in a conflict of interest or misdeed; a vice admiral and his subordinates who brought automatic rifles home following the U.S. military incursion into Grenada, and a HUD assistant secretary who used his personal secretary to type a book manuscript. In short, the mix of stories was generally heavy on highly individualized cases of fraud, waste, and abuse, and light on substantive government findings.

Not all of the congressional hearings were about IG findings, either. Of the 339 IG congressional appearances in 1978–89, 46 were nomination hearings in the Senate, 109 were appropriations hearings on OIG budgets, 66 were oversight hearings on the operation or expansion of the IG concept, and 118 involved specific testimony on department or agency programs. And, as with the media citations, many of the appearances were related to individualized scandals and highly focused audits.

If any IG broke this general mold, it was Kusserow, perhaps because he had so many chances to diversify. Of the IGs, none was more visible during the 1980s. He appeared in more congressional hearings and was cited in a greater number of *Washington Post* and *New York Times* articles than most of his peers combined. Although some of this visibility was the product of an effective public relations staff—for example, three mentions of Kusserow in the *New York Times* were in "Washington Talk"—page news briefs—many of his citations centered on significant reports and controversies, with occasional references to highly visible fraud cases.

Not all the news coverage was about government failure, however. For example, one story was about how well the Social Security Administration was doing in delivering its checks to eligible persons. In "A Reason to Sleep Better," the *Times* reported that "remarkably, everything seemed to be going just right."[18]

Kusserow's congressional testimony covered an eclectic range of subjects, reflecting both his flair for matching IG product to congressional need and member interest in the largest agency of government. However, what made Kusserow's testimony particularly interesting was the unusually heavy focus it had on setting the congressional agenda.

Of his twenty-one appearances in 1990, two dealt with the OIG appropriation; four with oversight of the IG concept; seven with traditional issues of fraud, waste, and abuse; four with the performance of specific HHS programs; and six with program design and agenda setting. Like his peers, Kusserow's testimony was clearly most valuable at the subcommittee level. Of his twenty-three appearances, sixteen were before subcommittees, almost evenly divided between the House and Senate.

GETTING NOTICED. Thus the key question is whether visibility is a true indicator of effectiveness or a mere product of luck and timing. According to the data in table 10-6, which compares IG visibility rank by several different measures of staffing and deployment, visibility was strongly related to three specific measures:

1. The absolute size of the department or agency budget, a likely surrogate for overall public and congressional interest.

2. The absolute number of investigators on the OIG staff, a likely indicator of the IG's ability to deploy staff across the widest range of topics.

3. The absolute number of auditors, a surrogate for the number of high savings reports.

Agencies with larger budgets and OIG staffs do well in terms of visibility. Bigger agencies with deeper IG staffs produce more and better stories for newspapers and hearings, better stories being defined as those with a potentially wide readership and constituent interest. The large IGs have come to understand the value of volume in achieving notice.

The two variables that did not make a difference in visibility were the relative growth in investigatory staff as a proportion of total staffing and the average length of the semiannual reports. Visibility appeared more tightly related to the size of the investigating staff and not overwhelming the audience.

If report length does not have a bearing on visibility, formats may. The OIGs with larger staffs tend to organize their reports by program area instead of under the audit or investigation heading. Because readers do not have to search through a list of audits for those related

Table 10-6. *Determinants of OIG Visibility*

Visibility rank[a]	1989 budget outlays (billions of dollars)	1990 investigators as percentage of total staff	1983–90 percentage change in investigation versus audit staff	1990 absolute number of investigation staff	1990 absolute number of audit staff	Average length in pages of semiannual reports
Less than 10 points						
1. AID (tie)	2.1	13	-9	32	208	41
NASA	11.0	38	10	39	64	54
3. State	3.7	30	17	34	79	35
4. VA	30.0	25	2	82	246	38
Average	11.7	27	5	47	149	42
10–19 points						
5. Labor (tie)	22.7	50	3	193	196	115
SBA	0.1	43	-4	49	51	49
7. Education	21.6	33	-11	80	166	61
8. Interior	5.2	20	7	58	292	70
9. HUD	19.7	24	3	80	252	82
10. Commerce (tie)	2.6	20	-5	25	100	74
Energy	11.4	29	7	53	127	48
Average	11.9	31	0	77	169	71
More than 19 points						
12. EPA	4.9	24	2	60	194	44
13. Transportation	26.6	19	3	75	321	65
14. Agriculture (tie)	48.3	40	0	265	398	44
GSA	0.3	34	1	89	159	47
16. Defense	318.4	39	15	388	597	94
17. HHS	400.0	38	18	460	766	89
Average	133.1	32	7	223	406	64

a. Visibility rank is calculated by adding the rankings of congressional appearances and media citations listed in table 10-5.

to a topic of interest, the high-volume reports are more easily accessible. Reporters working a specific beat can turn quickly to their pet topics; congressional staff can skip everything outside their areas.

So what is a smaller OIG to do? One way any OIG, large or small, might generate visibility is through the seven-day letter. Created under Section 5(d) of the 1978 act, the letter is to be used to notify Congress of any "serious or flagrant problems, abuses, or deficiencies relating to the administration of programs" in an IG's department or agency. However, although the IGs call the seven-day letter a "holstered weapon," it has become, for all intents and purposes, a holstered pop-gun, used under mostly trivial circumstances, if at all.

Between 1978 and 1990, only eleven letters were issued. According to a review by the Senate Subcommittee on Oversight of Government Management, chaired by Carl Levin (D-Mich.), five of the nine letters not classified "secret" did not purport to address serious or flagrant issues: Three opposed pending legislation, and two issued last-minute requests to secure additional OIG funding. In a letter to OMB, Levin noted,

> This means that the 16 IGs have issued only four unclassified Section 5(d) letters addressing substantive management problems in a period of 12 years. These four letters, according to the IGs, addressed: (1) the propriety of assistance provided to a construction project by the Department of the Interior; (2) the use of FY 1982 appropriations by the Department of Agriculture to contract for assistance in FY 1983; (3) the objections of the Interior IG to the Government of Guam's tax policy; and (4) access to the criminal investigative files of the Pension Welfare Benefits Administration by the Labor IG.[19]

The problem with the seven-day letter, as with any IG report, is one of congressional reaction. The IGs worry that Congress will weaken their credibility if they issue a seven-day letter that is subsequently ignored, a concern expressed by Charles Dempsey, Paul Adams, and other IGs during the Senate HUD hearings. As Sherman Funk noted,

> In a number of cases, 7-day letters have been written by IG's and they have disappeared into a void here on Capitol Hill, sir, and that does not give us much confidence. When you say, well, if I get into a bad scene, I am going to slip them a 7-day letter and then you do it and you have no hold card left, at that point you are very naked, sir, you are very naked indeed. So, you have to be careful, if you pull a gun, there damn well better be ammunition in it, and that is one problem.[20]

Yet, to date, the IGs have been aiming the seven-day letter at relatively small targets. The reason some letters were ignored was that they were not of sufficient importance to warrant attention.

CONCLUSION: QUESTIONS OF PERFORMANCE

In the final analysis, an IG's effectiveness involves much more than professionalism, coverage, size of savings, strength of cases, and visibility. Reading the 1978 mandate in the broadest terms, an IG also must focus on department or agency performance. It is simply not enough to catch bad guys. The long-run success of the IG concept can be measured only by the quality of life produced by government. This value can be inferred by four simple, if imperfect, questions regarding interest, trust, vulnerability, and value added.

IS ANYONE LISTENING? The answer is likely "no." First, many IG audits and investigations deal with very small problems, often ignoring the larger systemic issues that produce the same small problems over and over. Second, the IGs have shown uneven success even when recommending resolution of the small problems.

On the audit side, the IGs continue to have problems securing action, whether inside the agency or on Capitol Hill. In theory, for example, every audit finding must be answered—either the money has to be put back, the system fixed, or the finding refuted. In practice, audit resolution still is a weakness in most OIGs. The best most IGs can do is threaten to expose management noncompliance in one of several appendixes now required in every semiannual report.

On the investigative side, the track record is hardly better. Of all the cases studied by PCIE, only 4 percent resulted in a recommendation for management improvement. Recommendation is not the goal, and most IGs do little to develop broader recommendations. Some, however, like Kusserow, make it a priority. The HHS OIG each year publishes the *Orange Book*, which summarizes program and management improvement recommendations. Divided into chapters on each HHS unit, the book contains concise summaries of major findings, resulting recommendations, management action, and current status. The problem then becomes one of gaining readership. If the *Orange Book* is not read, it can have little impact.

IS THE PUBLIC MORE TRUSTING? Here, the answer is "yes, then

no." Public trust in government increased during the early to mid-1980s, rising from its all-time low in 1974 following Nixon's resignation. Whether measured by traditional questions regarding government's ability to do what is right or by perceptions regarding the level of government waste, trust increased under Reagan. According to political scientists Jack Citrin, Donald Green, and Beth Reingold, "Ronald Reagan came to Washington to bury government rather than to praise it. Ironically he wound up presiding over a resurgence of trust in the country's political institutions. 'America is back,' exulted the President at the end of his first term, and the polls showed that an optimistic public agreed."[21]

Other measures of trust also moved up, often dramatically. Those who saw the government as being run "for the benefit of all people" gained 25 percentage points from the view that "a few big interests" rule. Furthermore, in a survey of how much of the taxpayers' money people believe the government wastes, the category "a lot" lost 30 percentage points to "some" and "not very much."[22]

However, just as the rise is unmistakable, so, too, is the more recent decline. Public trust began falling during the Iran-contra scandal, and continued to fall under Bush.[23] The numbers who said government wastes a lot of money and cannot be trusted to do what is right most of the time both returned to their 1980 levels. The public may have been reacting to any number of events—the savings and loan failures, the House Speaker's problems, the Senate scandal surrounding Charles Keating, Wall Street insider trading, or the recession that began in 1990. Thus, neither the gains nor the declines in trust are attributable to what the IGs did.

IS THE GOVERNMENT LESS VULNERABLE TO FRAUD, WASTE, AND ABUSE? Here, the answer appears to be "yes, but." Asked about the amount of waste they saw in government both before and after their service, roughly half the IGs interviewed saw no change; one-quarter, an increase; and one-quarter, a decrease.

Some evidence of success exists, however. Although the IG savings totals could be discounted by some margin—from, say, the 8 percent of the 1987 HHS total that GAO could not validate in its assessment of the OIG's performance—savings still were made, and they probably exceeded the cost of getting them.[24] Stated differently, even if Kusserow's claim of almost $6 billion in April–September 1989 savings is ten times too high, a substantial amount of money had to have been saved.

The government seemed better equipped in 1989 to catch wrongdoing, albeit after the fact, than in 1978. However, saving money and putting bad guys in jail does not mean reduced vulnerability. Unless the underlying problems are fixed, the vulnerability remains.

Here is where the "but" comes into play. Too many IGs stop work when the audit is filed and the wrongdoer jailed or fined. "One of the areas where we have had some degree of concern," a GAO officer noted in the House hearings on the ten-year review of the IGs, "is that the IG's just accept management's word that a problem has been corrected. Instead, we believe that IG's should, on some kind of a test basis, go back out and look to see whether corrective action has taken place; and whether it has in fact resulted in a change in the agency operations to make it better."[25]

This concern for closure prompted the 1988 reporting mandate for detailed summaries of unresolved issues, thereby making more visible management's progress. Whether Congress will pay any more attention to the long appendixes that have resulted is still questionable.

Moreover, according to the internal assessments required under the Federal Managers' Financial Integrity Act of 1982, the federal government still had numerous weaknesses by the end of the decade. Of the eighteen largest entities, ten had problems in procurement, seven in credit management, four in eligibility and entitlement determinations, eight in cash management, thirteen in automated data processing, ten in property management, seventeen in financial management and accounting systems, and ten in personnel and organizational management.[26]

The IGs, however, cannot fix all the shortcomings in government without help. They cannot force the president to appoint good people, the Senate to take the confirmation process seriously, and Congress to exercise more systematic oversight. The IGs also cannot redesign programs; nor can the IGs create capacity where little exists.

IS THE GOVERNMENT PRODUCING OUTCOMES OF GREATER PUBLIC VALUE? Here, the answer is "yes and no."[27]

To the extent that the IGs discover fraud, for example, they plug a hole in the leaky bucket of federal programs. To the extent that they close even the smallest investigations successfully, whether through convictions, restitutions, or administrative sanctions such as debarment or suspension, the IGs make government more efficient. And to the extent that they recommend improvements in programs through evaluation, policy analysis, or program design, they contribute to government's future effectiveness. All IGs do something to increase public value, and some, like Kusserow, do a great deal. All is to the good.

However, if Congress and the president allow IG growth at the expense of basic program delivery capacity, a greater potential for errors is created. The hole is filled even as a large number of small holes are being drilled. If, for example, Congress and the president use the IGs as an excuse for increasing the burdens of government without supplying additional administrative support—arguing that internal oversight is an acceptable substitute for programmatic capacity—then the IG concept would not contribute to effectiveness as much as it could. If, for example, Congress and the president remain willing to fund increases in IG staffing and pull back from committing to new financial management systems, competitive pay, adequate training, and more aggressive recruitment, the IGs will continue to set yearly records in both savings and convictions.

As Donald Kettl argued, the result of micromanagement in general, and IG monitoring by implication, "is not so much paralysis as administrative sluggishness. Checking and cross-checking slow down the administrative process. Administrators become more circumspect in making decisions, less likely to take chances that could improve production or save money, and more likely to avoid making decisions at all if they can be avoided."[28] By increasing the ratio of reviewers to doers, Congress and the president work against the accountability they seek, causing an impact never imagined by the IG founders. As the IG numbers go up, effectiveness may go down.

CHAPTER 11

The Future of the IG Concept

AFTER all the statistical accomplishments are totaled and all the staff and budget increases reviewed, government appears no more accountable today than before the IG Act. The IG savings and conviction totals continue to rise year by year with no decline in sight. The IGs have not done their job poorly, but they may be doing the wrong job—putting too much emphasis on compliance and not enough on performance and capacity building.

The pressure to produce short-term results was not created by the IGs, however. The incentives to focus on compliance monitoring existed before the first IG went to work. Compliance monitoring not only produces the kinds of findings Congress and the president appear to value most—high volume, high visibility, easy measurement, and high credit-claiming yield—it generates more acceptable recommendations—less costly, less divisive, more convenient, and faster.

The IGs also were taught important lessons in the legislative history of the IG Act. Although Congress gave the IGs a broad mandate, passage of the 1978 statute had much less to do with improving government performance or rebuilding administrative capacity than with responding to the real politics of fraud busting and the rising demand for information. Behind the rhetoric of fraud, waste, and abuse was a much deeper concern for fueling the rising tide of oversight. Although concerns for government effectiveness—what some called a thirst for accountability—were part of the debate, Congress also needed access to executive detail, which was lost in the 1950s when GAO stopped maintaining the government's accounts.

The lessons of compliance monitoring were further reinforced during the implementation of the IG Act. The IGs were heavily rewarded for producing the dollars and the convictions that even now may lull Congress and the president into false confidence about government's vulnerability to future scandals. Starting with the early fight to establish their offices against the continued opposition of their departments and agencies, and immediately reminded of their vulnerability by the 1981 firings, the IGs were ready for an alliance with OMB, an alliance driven almost exclusively by the ability to generate victories in the Reagan war on waste.

As new records were set yearly by the IGs, Congress and the president were encouraged to promote the idea that the war was being won. And as long as the totals went up, the IGs could do no wrong. Their budgets were given special director's review to assure proper staffing, and their offices secured a remarkable amount of self-determination. First, the IGs won the right to investigate wayward colleagues, then they were given an unprecedented role in selecting their successors. Even in the backlash that followed these glory days, the IGs could find support for compliance monitoring. They always were on the safest ground when producing high volumes of findings and low cost recommendations.

Thus, by the late 1980s, few of the IGs could respond to White House interest in evaluation. Many had invested too heavily in investigatory capacity because of Reagan administrative incentives. With the shift in staffing shares—which moved the ratio of auditors to investigators from 3:1 to 2:1—the OIGs signaled their growing capacity for the most narrow form of compliance monitoring, criminal investigation. In addition, the IGs moved further away from the departments and agencies in which they worked through a series of organizational changes. Six IGs added a deputy IG; four, a general counsel; and seven, an office of personnel. With Congress's help, nine IGs received their own line in the budget, and nine moved up to level four of the executive pay schedule, reaching parity with the assistant secretaries and administrators in their establishments.

Although an element of added independence came with each change, the net effect may have been to isolate the IGs from contact with the real world of government management. This, in turn, may have led them away from systemic explanations for the fraud, waste, and abuse they uncovered, thereby reinforcing the compliance philosophy of accountability.

THE IG ACT INNOVATIONS

The IGs, however, are here to stay. They have proven remarkably durable organizational entrepreneurs and likely will survive the recent backlash intact. Thus, the question is less "if" the IGs will stay, and more "what" they should be doing. The place to start looking for answers is with the eight innovations included in the 1978 statute that offer lessons on IG reform.

Dual Reporting

The dual reporting proviso was, and still is, the most intensely debated feature of the IG Act. Those who subscribe to clear-cut separation of powers find the requirement particularly offensive; those who view the Constitution as a blueprint for separate institutions sharing power are more comfortable. Moreover, despite the vehement opposition of the Department of Justice, and worries across government about divided loyalties, the dual reporting innovation has barely affected IG operations. The greater problem has been a lack of interest in IG reports at both ends of Pennsylvania Avenue. As a result, the most visible IGs are those who use informal channels of access to Congress, which generally are available to any executive branch official and were a source of presidential consternation long before 1978.

Nonpartisan Appointments

Under statute, the IGs were to be selected "without regard to political affiliation and solely on the basis of integrity and demonstrated ability." The appointees mostly have been both able and nonpartisan, but in large part because they came from professions that set minimum qualifications for entry, were historically nonpartisan, and maintained career-long barriers to politics. For example, GAO's *Standards for Audit* explicitly requires that government auditors be free from organizational impairments to independence; that is, "organizational structures and reporting relationships that require the auditor to be subject to policy direction from superiors who are involved in policy affecting the audit staff or who are undergoing the audit."[1] During the Reagan administration, the IG selection process was clearly nonpartisan, thereby rendering the statutory prohibition moot. Moreover, both political affiliation and demonstrated ability are in the eye of the beholder, as amply demonstrated in the appointment of Transportation IG Mary Sterling. Thus, even with the IG selection process now defunct, the statutory provision may still be moot.

Removal

Although Carter had only passing interest in the IG Act, he insisted that the IGs be removable at his discretion, noting at one point in a brief cabinet conversation that the IGs were "good if under my control." In 1981, Reagan used that power to fire all of the Carter appointees en masse. In 1989, Bush failed to act one way or the other, leaving the IG community in limbo for the better part of the year. Although asserting that the removal clause has compromised IG independence is difficult, it has affected IG operations. The ease with which Reagan dismissed the Carter IGs sent a signal of vulnerability that continues to this day.

Integration of Audit and Investigation

Of all the changes in the IG Act, perhaps none was as important as the effort to combine audit and investigation into one operation. Audit long had been part of the management function in departments, while investigation generally was housed in small, highly independent units near the top of their establishments. The hope was that the two professions would reinforce each other, and that both would benefit from pooled resources and independence.

In reality, the two remain separate and rarely work together on cases. According to a PCIE study, only 10 percent of the IG investigatory cases had any kind of audit assistance, whether defined as a separate audit, direct work on a case, or information provided to open an investigation.[2] Investigators are more likely to work with the Department of Justice or the FBI than the auditors within their own OIGs, while the auditors continue to express some resentment about the special pay and status accorded investigative staff. What the IG Act put together, the two professional cultures appear capable of keeping apart.

Organizational Freedom

Using the freedom afforded them in Section 6 of the 1978 act, the IGs made impressive progress in building distinctive organizations. Learning from each other in the PCIE, the OIGs went through two rough phases in organizational development that can be tracked through an analysis of federal phone books. The first involved an augmentation of the OIGs through the creation of fragmented units—for deputy IGs, personnel, legal counsel. The second phase involved consolidation of those increasingly disparate units into a more orderly hierarchy. Older OIGs such as Agriculture, HHS, and Commerce, for example, expanded the number of units between 1980 and 1986, then reduced them by 1988, a path that newer OIGs such as Defense and State likely will follow. The tendency of the

OIGs is to become more like traditional government bureaus, although the OIGs increasingly are exempt from some of the more onerous internal regulations that other government managers face.

Detailed Reporting

Left to their own decisions in reporting information to Congress under the 1978 act, each IG seemed to have a different definition of savings. As a result, Congress acted in 1988 to tighten up the reporting requirements. The result has been a much greater volume of information, including standardized definitions and a set of new appendixes summarizing IG findings and recommendations.

If the changes were designed to rebuild lagging congressional readership, they have made little difference. No evidence is available that members of Congress or congressional staffs have found the IG semiannual reports more compelling. What has happened, however, is that departments and agencies have become more interested in fighting with the IGs over the new appendixes. They imply that management is to blame for the failure to implement IG findings and recommendations, even though inaction may indicate disagreement or irrelevance. Before the 1988 amendments, management could easily ignore such conflicts, merely relegating the IG reports to a dusty shelf. Thus, if any impact has been felt because of the reporting changes, it has been to make IG reports required reading in the departments and agencies, engendering legitimate, and likely helpful, debates over what the IGs do.[3]

Seven-Day Letters

The IGs rarely have used their seven-day-letter authority. In the HUD case, however, this reluctance was widely interpreted as positive proof of the IG's failure to warn Congress. "While the Office of the HUD Inspector General performed admirably in detecting problems in the administration of many housing programs," the House investigating committee noted, "the watchdog did not bark loud enough. Instead of shouting these warnings to Congress, they were whispered."[4] In many ways, the seven-day provision represents the greatest tension in the separation of powers. Issuance of the letter expresses the IG's belief that Congress, not the president, is responsible for resolving an immediate crisis. Not surprisingly, most letters have dealt with routine problems in either the administration of the OIGs or appropriations, both seen as legitimate interests of Congress.

Access to Information

One of the greatest fears about the 1978 IG Act was that it would create a statutorily protected class of moles free to dig up information on the executive branch. As a result, the Justice Department objected to the removal provisions, and Carter expressed concern about loyalty. The IGs, however, never have come close to adopting a muckraking mentality. Their auditors have done their work in relative quiet, and their investigators have focused most of their energies outside the government's corridors on either contractors or benefit recipients. Congress still gets most of its information on the executive branch the old-fashioned ways—through the media, indirect contacts with whistleblowers, staff investigations, and letters from constituents.

A REPRISE ON REFORM

Looking back over implementation of the IG Act, little cause for worry existed in 1978. Most IGs have proven content to focus on compliance work, booking annual increases in savings and convictions, but rarely startling Congress or the president with sweeping recommendations for new performance approaches or capacity building.

The IGs have not faded into the background, though. A host of IG reform proposals still are floating around Washington. Some involve wholesale changes, including the "super-IG" proposed by Democratic Tennessee Senator Jim Sasser's staff as a way to provide greater whistleblower protection. Some are more conventional, including further tightening of the IG semiannual reports, elevation of the small agency IGs to presidential appointee status, creation of a Federal Bureau of Investigation IG, clarifying the relationship of the presidentially appointed Defense IG with the individual service IGs, and strengthening the IGs' role in financial management reform.[5]

While these reform proposals provoke debates on the continuing evolution of the IG concept, they must be measured against three questions regarding the future of IGs: (1) What is the best way to improve government accountability? (2) What kinds of monitoring are most useful in the effort to improve government accountability? (3) What is the best way to assure objectivity whatever the IG role?

IMPROVING ACCOUNTABILITY. The first question may be the most difficult because the answer depends on who is asked. Supporters of merit pay and full funding of civil service reform may single out performance incentives or capacity building as the keys to improvement, while former FBI investigators may prefer the deterrent effects of compliance monitoring. Moreover, the question creates a false competition among the forms of accountability.

Nevertheless, compliance accountability may bring about perverse consequences. Not only does compliance accountability often reward short-term gains instead of long-term capacity building, but it also may distract Congress and the president from addressing the hard questions about how to design institutions and programs to work better from the beginning. They may assume that workability can be "inspected-in" after the fact.

Furthermore, the more statistical accomplishment the IGs produce, the more Congress and the president may be tempted to enact more rules. A proliferation of regulations could produce more fraud, waste, and abuse, as employees and beneficiaries seek informal redress for increasing levels of paperwork and micromanagement. Federal procurement regulations now are the fourth most burdensome source of paperwork in the federal government and provide no increased assurance of lower cost or greater accountability, which suggests that other forms of accountability may produce greater returns. And, although scholars have yet to calculate the cost of mistrust in the federal government, the maintenance of compliance systems is expensive. The record years of statistical accomplishment did not come without a price, one exacted in staff and resources expended in the battle as well as the lost productivity of government managers and employees who had to spend time and energy preparing to be audited and investigated.

IMPROVING MONITORING. Given the unintended effects of compliance accountability, the second question attempts to determine what the most useful kind of IG monitoring is. Recall again that monitoring is all that the IGs are allowed to do. They can neither order change within their departments and agencies nor suspend programs. They provide the findings and recommendations that might lead others to act.

Considering how the IGs might be most useful leads away from the most extreme form of compliance monitoring—investigations—and toward evaluation. The IGs are capable of supplying much of the missing evaluation and analysis to Congress and the president, and they have the organizational independence to protect that evaluation and analysis from the kinds of politicization that dominated the Reagan administration.

An enormous need exists for more evaluation and analysis in government, particularly given the evisceration that occurred during the Reagan years. As political scientist Walter Williams wrote of the "anti-analytical presidency,"

Ronald Reagan launched an eight year war on policy information and analysis and more broadly on the institutional capacity of the executive branch; he won. The most ideological president in memory, certain of the rightness of his policies without needing facts and figures, became the first modern anti-analytic president. His unconcern with or distaste for expert policy information, analysis and advice led to the destruction of much of the institutional analytic capacity built up in the executive branch in the postwar period as Reagan cut deeply into the personnel, budgets, and influence of analytic and evaluation units.[6]

The push toward evaluation and analysis is not without risks, however. The evaluation community has serious reservations about OIG-based evaluation. However, as the HHS experience amply demonstrates, evaluation can allow an IG to fully engage in the kinds of research that produces program reform.

ENHANCING OBJECTIVITY. Objectivity is key whatever the chosen IG role. The IGs ranked the possible reforms as follows:

1. Restrict the president's removal power.
2. Create a fixed term of office.
3. Establish the President's Council on Integrity and Efficiency through statute.
4. Require simultaneous budget transmission to Congress and the president.
5. Establish a search commission for selecting IGs.
6. Create a permanent PCIE staff.

IG opinions on reform depended in large measure on which administration they served (see table 11-1).

The Carter IGs were much more likely to support simultaneous budget transmission, no doubt because of their experiences getting set up in the late 1970s, and to support a fixed term of office, because of their mass firing during the Reagan transition. The class of 1985, which served in Reagan's second term, was much less supportive of strengthening the PCIE through permanent staff, confirming the

Table 11-1. *Support for IG Reform, by Class*
Percent

Variable	Class of 1979[a]	Class of 1981[a]	Class of 1985[a]
Create a new appointments process[b]			
Do not support	80	65	86
Support	20	35	14
Require simultaneous budget transmission[c]			
Do not support	50	87	86
Support	50	13	14
Create a fixed term of office[c]			
1 (Greatly strengthen IG)	36	29	14
2	27	21	43
3	27	14	14
4	0	14	14
5 (Not greatly strengthen IG)	9	21	14
Provide removal only for cause[d]			
1 (Greatly strengthen IG)	54	47	57
2	27	13	0
3	9	13	43
4	0	7	0
5 (Not greatly strengthen IG)	9	20	0
Create a permanent staff for PCIE[e]			
1 (Greatly strengthen IG)	13	7	0
2	25	27	29
3	13	7	29
4	25	33	0
5 (Not greatly strengthen IG)	25	27	43
Establish the PCIE through statute[e]			
1 (Greatly strengthen IG)	13	0	0
2	25	7	14
3	13	27	43
4	13	47	14
5 (Not greatly strengthen IG)	38	20	29

a. Data are based on responses from 12 Carter and 28 Reagan (first- and second-term) appointees. Some respondents did not answer every question. Totals may not add to 100 because of rounding.
b. $N = 31$.
c. $N = 32$.
d. $N = 33$.
e. $N = 30$.

declining impact of the PCIE as both the level of staff and absolute number of IGs grew.

Together, however, the numbers confirm the IGs' support for greater political protection—the majority of IGs support a fixed term of office and removal only for cause. Although simpler solutions are available to ensure smooth transitions between administrations—for example, by amending the Vacancies Act to establish a presumption in favor of continued IG service in the absence of presidential action—the term of office may hold merit in signaling future administrations that the IGs are to be considered long-term appointees.

Removal only for cause is a more difficult reform because it would sever completely the IGs and their audit and evaluation capacity from their departments. It also would be enormously difficult to enact into law. Thus, accepting the political realities of continued congressional support for the more flexible removal power under the 1978 act, and in spite of partial IG opposition, a search commission coupled with a fixed term of office would be the best way to address the need for job security among the IGs as administrations come and go and for the selection of professionally qualified individuals as IGs.

Beyond such questions of protection, the IGs should be removed from the senior executive bonus and awards system. The current two-class system, in which some IGs voluntarily exempt themselves from the awards process while their colleagues prosper from it, neither serves the goal of objectivity nor protects the IGs from undue influence. As one IG explained, "How can an IG be truly independent who is willing to accept a large cash award for performance . . . when the award must be recommended by the individual to whom the IG reports? This question arises inevitably in such a situation. When it does, the perceived credibility of the IG—perhaps his or her most important asset—is undercut. The game is simply not worth the candle, even a $20,000 candle."[7]

Under a fixed term and a quasi-independent search process, the IG concept would move a step or two back toward the original Rosenthal alternative. A fixed term would create a presumption in favor of long-term service and, perhaps, long-term thinking and analysis. A search commission recruiting process would place a greater weight on integrity and demonstrated ability, which may have been eroding in recent selections. Although neither of these changes would turn the IG concept from strong right arm into Rosenthal's lone wolf, they would place a greater emphasis on the IG's role as a source of long-term perspective on government.

A SAFE HARBOR FOR ANALYSIS

Taking the long view involves great risk. Speaking truth to power—as the IGs will have to do as they dig through issues of institutional design, program workability, and evaluation—demands a commitment that is impossible to encode in statute. The safer route politically is to remain firmly focused on post-hoc audit and investigation, where the crooks are easy to identify and the sanctions obvious. The more difficult path demands forward-looking evaluation and analysis of the mistakes that are made in the White House, on Capitol Hill, and by interest groups.

Yet this may be where the IG concept promises its greatest payoff. With a presidency dominated by short-term political appointees, buffeted by a short-term political culture, and with limited access to the long-term thinking once available on Capitol Hill and in the career civil service, the IGs are one of the last, best hopes for rebuilding government's institutional memory on management, while countering the pressures that characterize the presidential policy-making process. As the Senate HUD investigation strongly suggested, that balance is not likely to emerge from OMB:

> Given the mismanagement and abuse of certain HUD programs during the 1980s, it is important to inquire why OMB oversight of HUD management failed to uncover or prevent it. The answer has been evident since OMB's creation in 1970. OMB's management efforts have been largely unable to compete for resources or attention with the high-priority budget process, and have therefore been minimal. Even when certain management oversight strategies have received attention and resources from OMB, their effects have been adversely influenced by the short-term budget mindset and highly politicized nature of that organization.[8]

Whether the IGs will rise to the need depends in part on their ability to resist the pressures so evident in the OMB demand for statistical accomplishment. Nevertheless, the OIGs are one of the very few places left in government where politicization remains at bay and a strong civil service ethic and career path remains in place.

While the IGs are not the only source of institutional memory, they too often are ignored as a source of political protection and leadership as government gnaws at the basic management questions that will drive improvement. As much as some see the creation of an Office of Federal Management, carved out of the management side of OMB, as the solution to the continuing lack of presidential management leadership, the IGs may have to do in the immediate future.[9] Whether Congress and the president will let the IGs answer the call of OMB and move into the more qualitative realm of evaluation, which produces few statistical accomplishments but has great potential value, still is in doubt.

Interview Contacts

FOLLOWING is a list of those who participated, between late 1990 and early 1991, in face-to-face or telephone interviews for this book. Most of these interviews were quite detailed; however some were brief. Unless otherwise indicated, titles refer to the position held at the time of the interview.

Paul Adams, IG, HUD

Melissa Allen, former deputy associate director, OMB

Richard Allen, assistant general counsel, Consumer Product Safety Commission

Robert Ashbaugh, deputy IG, Justice

Richard Barnes, staff director, Subcommittee on Legislation and National Security, House Government Operations (chaired by Jack Brooks)

JoAnne Barnhart, former minority staff director, Senate Governmental Affairs (chaired by William Roth)

Herbert Beckington, IG, AID

Joyce Blalock, former IG, Government Printing Office

Ralph Bledsoe, former executive secretary to the Domestic Policy Council (during the Reagan administration)

Marsha Boals, assistant director, Accounting and Financial Management Division (AFMD), GAO

Celia Boddington, majority staff member, Subcommittee on Employment and Housing, House Government Operations (chaired by Tom Lantos)

June Gibbs Brown, former IG, Interior, NASA, and Defense

Hale Champion, former under secretary, HHS

Eleanor Chelimsky, assistant comptroller general, director, Program Evaluation and Measurement Division, GAO

David Clark, associate director, AFMD, GAO

Morton Cohen, former director, Internal Audit, NASA; former chief financial officer, National Academy of Public Administration (NAPA)

James Colvaard, former deputy director, OPM

Doc Cooke, director of administration and management, Defense

Alan Dean, former assistant secretary, Transportation

Charles Dempsey, former IG, HUD and EPA

Gene Dodaro, director of operations, AFMD, GAO

Marvin Doyal, professional staff member, Senate Governmental Affairs (minority staff directed by William Roth)

Stuart Eizenstat, former director, Domestic Policy Staff (during the Carter administration)

Robert Fairman, former assistant secretary, Transportation

William Fischer, former special assistant to the secretary, Energy

Richard Fogel, assistant comptroller general, director, General Government Division, GAO

John Franke, former assistant secretary, Agriculture

Harley Frankel, deputy director, Office of Presidential Personnel (during the Carter administration)

Orville Freeman, former secretary of agriculture

Sherman Funk, former IG, Commerce; current IG, State

Susan Gaffney, acting division chief, OMB

Charles Gillium, former deputy IG, GSA; former IG, SBA; current deputy IG, Agriculture

Paul Gottlober, deputy regional IG for evaluation and inspections (San Francisco), HHS

Linda Gustitus, majority staff director, Subcommittee on Government Oversight, Senate Governmental Affairs (chaired by Carl Levin)

Tom Haggenstadt, director of legislative relations, GAO

Edwin Harper, former deputy director, OMB (during the Reagan administration)

Robert Harris, deputy majority staff director, Senate Governmental Affairs (chaired by John Glenn)

Frank Hodsoll, associate deputy director, OMB (during the Bush administration)

J. Brian Hyland, former IG, Labor

Stewart Huey, executive director, Association of Federal Investigators

William Jones, former majority staff director, House Government Operations (chaired by Jack Brooks); staff director, House Judiciary Committee

Frederick M. Kaiser, specialist, Congressional Research Service, Library of Congress

Rosalyn Kleeman, senior associate director, General Government Division, GAO

Ray Kline, former deputy administrator, GSA; president, NAPA

Elliott Kramer, regional IG for investigation (San Francisco), HHS

Richard Kusserow, IG, HHS

John Layton, IG, Energy

Peter Levine, majority counsel, Subcommittee on Government Oversight, Senate Governmental Affairs (chaired by Carl Levin)

Lorraine Lewis, counsel, Senate Governmental Affairs (chaired by John Glenn)

William Lilly, former comptroller, NASA

Margaret Colgate Love, associate deputy attorney general

Michael Mangano, assistant IG for evaluation and inspections, HHS

John Martin, IG, EPA

Thomas McBride, former IG, Agriculture and Labor

John McGinnis, deputy assistant attorney general, Office of Legal Counsel

Cynthia Meadow, former professional staff member, Subcommittee on Legislation and National Security, House Government Operations (chaired by Jack Brooks); professional staff member, House Judiciary (chaired by Jack Brooks)

John Melchner, former IG, Transportation

Howard Messner, former assistant administrator, EPA; associate deputy director, OMB

Arnold Miller, former director, Office of Presidential Personnel (during the Carter administration)

Walter Mondale, former vice president of the United States

Thomas Morris, former IG, HEW

Karen Morrisette, deputy chief, Fraud Section, Criminal Division, Justice

James Naughton, former majority counsel, Subcommittee on Intergovernmental Relations and Human Resources, House Government Operations (chaired by L. H. Fountain)

Janet Norwood, commissioner, Bureau of Labor Statistics, Labor

James Pitrizzi, professional staff, Subcommittee on Education and Housing, House Government Operations (chaired by Tom Lantos)

Elsa Porter, former assistant secretary, Commerce

Anthony Principi, former staff director, Senate Veterans Affairs Committee (chaired by Frank Murkowski); deputy secretary, VA

James Richards, IG, Interior

Elliot Richardson, former secretary of HEW and Defense; former attorney general

Steven Ryan, former counsel, Senate Governmental Affairs (chaired by John Glenn)

Frank Sato, former IG, Commerce and VA

John Seymour, assistant secretary, Transportation

Ira Shapiro, former counsel, Senate Governmental Affairs (chaired by Abraham Ribicoff, then Thomas Eagleton)

Rexford Simmons, associate director, AFMD, GAO

Lewis Small, IG, GPO

Richard Sonnichsen, deputy assistant director, Inspection Division, FBI, Justice

Elmer Staats, former comptroller general of the United States

Hal Steinberg, former associate deputy director, OMB (during the Reagan administration)

Jeffrey Steinhoff, group director, AFMD, GAO

James Thomas, IG, Education

Jerry Toner, deputy assistant attorney general, Criminal Division, Justice

Warren Underwood, assistant director, AFMD, GAO

Derek Vander Schaaf, deputy IG, Defense

Gerald Riso, former assistant secretary, Commerce; former associate deputy director, OMB (during the Reagan administration)

Richard Wegman, former staff director, Senate Governmental Affairs (chaired by Abraham Ribicoff)

Len Weiss, staff director, Senate Governmental Affairs (chaired by John Glenn)

Herbert Witt, regional IG for audit (San Francisco), HHS

Don Wortman, former acting administrator, Social Rehabilitation Service; former acting administrator, Health Care Financing Administration; current special assistant to the president, NAPA

Joseph Wright, former director, OMB (during the Reagan administration)

Wendy Zenker, acting branch chief, Financial Integrity Branch, OMB

Al Zuck, former assistant secretary, Labor

NOTES

INTRODUCTION

1. Nancy Traver, "The Housing Hustle," *Time*, June 26, 1989, p. 19.
2. *Abuses, Favoritism, and Mismanagement in HUD Programs*, Hearings before the Subcommittee on Employment and Housing of the House Government Operations Committee, 101 Cong. 1 sess. (Government Printing Office, 1989), pt. 1, p. 499.
3. The survey excluded the two IGs who briefly served at the Community Services Administration before the agency was abolished in 1981, as well as any IG who held only an acting post.
4. See G. Calvin Mackenzie, ed., *The In-and-Outers: Presidential Appointees and Transient Government in Washington* (Johns Hopkins University Press, 1987), for a summary of the project.
5. Telephone interviews are a viable alternative to face-to-face contacts. See Paul C. Light, "Interviewing the President's Staff: A Comparison of Telephone and Face-to-Face Techniques," *Presidential Studies Quarterly*, vol. 12 (Summer 1982), pp. 428–33.

CHAPTER 1

1. I have elected not to give the statutory location or public law number for every statute mentioned. Such notations would be distracting for most readers, and they are not necessary except in the rare case when the information is crucial for confirming my conclusions.
2. See James L. Sundquist, *The Decline and Resurgence of Congress* (Brookings, 1981). See also James W. Fesler and Donald F. Kettl, *The Politics of the Administrative Process* (Chatham, N.J.: Chatham House, 1991), pp. 270–89, for an analysis of the micromanagement issue.
3. For a list of how the last set of devices has been applied in environmental policy, see Gary Bryner, *Bureaucratic Discretion: Law and Policy in Federal Regulatory Agencies* (Pergammon, 1987).
4. Francis E. Rourke, "Bureaucratic Autonomy and the Public Interest," in Carol H. Weiss and Allen H. Barton, eds., *Making Bureaucracies Work* (Beverly Hills: Sage Publications, 1979, 1980), p. 103.
5. Dennis Palumbo and Steven Maynard-Moody, *Contemporary Public Administration* (Longman, 1991), p. 255. For a similar list and approach, see B. Guy Peters, *The Politics of Bureaucracy*, 3rd ed. (Longman, 1989).
6. Frederick C. Mosher, "Comment by Frederick C. Mosher," in Bruce L.

R. Smith and James D. Carroll, eds., *Improving the Accountability and Performance of Government* (Brookings, 1982), p. 72.

7. Fesler and Kettl, *The Politics of the Administrative Process*, p. 317.

8. Ibid., p. 335. See also Donald F. Kettl, "Micromanagement: Congressional Control and Bureaucratic Risk," in Patricia W. Ingraham and Donald F. Kettl, eds., *Agenda for Excellence: Public Service in America* (Chatham, N.J.: Chatham House, 1992), pp. 94–112.

9. Janet Weiss, "Making Public Managers More Receptive to New Ideas," paper prepared for the University of California, Berkeley, conference on innovations, May 1992, p. 13. According to Weiss, "Measuring performance against the performance of other agencies facing similar problems, and especially against those regarded as leaders in the field, provides a demanding standard of accomplishment."

10. For a discussion of the conflict between democratic values and efficiency, see Douglas Yates, *Bureaucratic Democracy: The Search for Democracy and Efficiency in American Government* (Cambridge University Press, 1982).

11. Mary Walton, *The Deming Management Method* (Perigee Books, 1986), pp. 34–35.

12. Ibid., p. 36.

13. Anthony Downs, *Inside Bureaucracy* (Little, Brown, 1967), p. 30.

14. Michael Barzelay with Babak Armajani, *Breaking through Bureaucracy: A New Vision for Managing in Government* (University of California Press, 1992), p. 5.

15. See Max Weber, "Bureaucracy," in H. H. Gerth and C. Wright Mills, eds., *Max Weber: Essays in Sociology* (Oxford University Press, 1946). See also Frederick W. Taylor, *The Principles of Scientific Management* (Harper and Brothers, 1911).

16. Barzelay with Armajani, *Breaking through Bureaucracy*, p. 6.

17. See Samuel Krislov and David H. Rosenbloom, *Representative Bureaucracy and the American Political System* (Praeger, 1981).

18. National Academy of Public Administration, *Revitalizing Federal Management: Managers and Their Overburdened Systems* (November 1983), p. 3.

CHAPTER 2

1. See Kurt W. Muellenberg and Harvey Volzer, "Inspector General Act of 1978," *Temple Law Quarterly*, vol. 53 (1980), pp. 1049–66, for a general introduction to the IG concept.

2. For those still in doubt about the IG mandate, the negotiations between the House and Senate on the Inspector General Act reveal further insights into the hoped-for impact of the legislation. Of greatest interest was the Senate's definition of the IG audit function, which was designed

to ensure that auditing had a strong role in the new offices. The definition was dropped because conferees saw it, and its companion definition of investigations, as unduly narrow. The audit function would have included but would not have been limited to

1. the traditional examinations of financial transactions normally expected in an audit unit,

2. broader reviews of the "management, utilization, and conservation of resources," including "procedures, whether officially prescribed or informally established, which are ineffective or more costly than justified"; "the performance of work which serves little or no useful purposes"; "inefficient or uneconomical use of equipment"; "overstaffing in relation to the amount of work to be done"; and "wasteful use of resources"; and

3. even broader reviews of program results, asking whether "the program or activity is meeting the objectives established by the Congress of the establishment": and whether "the establishment has considered alternatives to achieve desired results at a lower cost"; and reviewing "the relevance and validity of the criteria used . . . to judge effectiveness in achieving program results"; "the appropriateness of the methods followed by the entity to evaluate effectiveness in achieving program results"; the "accuracy of the data accumulated; and the reliability of the results obtained."

3. See Margaret Gates and Marjorie Fine Knowles, "The Inspector General Act in the Federal Government: A New Approach to Accountability," *Alabama Law Review*, vol. 36 (Winter 1985), pp. 473–513.

4. Ibid., p. 475.

5. For an excellent history of the IG concept, see Mark Moore and Margaret Jane Gates, *Inspectors-General: Junkyard Dog or Man's Best Friend?* (Russell Sage Foundation, 1986).

6. Noted in John Adair and Rex Simmons, "From Voucher Auditing to Junkyard Dogs: The Evolution of Federal Inspectors General," *Public Budgeting and Finance*, vol. 8 (Summer 1988), p. 91. Adair and Simmons were the two key GAO officers responsible for most of the agencies' oversight of the IG concept. In 1989, both resigned to join the new IGship at the Resolution Trust Corporation.

7. Adair and Simmons, "From Voucher Auditing to Junkyard Dogs," p. 93.

8. Frederick C. Mosher, *A Tale of Two Agencies: A Comparative Analysis of the General Accounting Office and the Office of Management and Budget* (Louisiana State University Press, 1984), p. 21.

9. Load figures are drawn from Frederick C. Mosher, *The GAO: The Quest for Accountability in American Government* (Boulder, Colo.: Westview Press, 1979), p. 103. Staffing figures are from Norman J. Ornstein, Thomas E. Mann, and Michael J. Malbin, *Vital Statistics on Congress 1991–1992* (Congressional Quarterly Press, 1992).

10. P.L. 87-195, Sec. 624 (E)(7).

11. Quoted in Thomas W. Novotny, "The IGs—A Random Walk," *The Bureaucrat*, vol. 12 (Fall 1983), p. 35.

12. P.L. 87-195, Sec. 624 (E)(7).
13. Novotny, "The IGs—A Random Walk," p. 35.
14. According to Novotny, the IGA was a victim of both politicization and apathy. "Initially, IGA was led by former Hill staffers, allegedly under the protection of powerful congressional figures, working in administrations friendly to the foreign assistance programs and to the Hill powers," wrote Novotny. "As soon as this equation changed IGA/Hill relationships started downhill. Eventually a Senate appropriations subcommittee, was the only one exercising regular oversight authority over IG." See Novotny, "The IGs—A Random Walk," p. 38.
15. For an exception, see Stanley Anderson, "Inspectors General in Federal Agencies," draft report prepared for the Administrative Conference of the United States, August 1979.
16. Although it hardly matters which IG came first, the Agriculture IG was never encoded in statute and the 1976 HEW IG closely paralleled the 1961 inspector general, foreign assistance.
17. *Operations of Billie Sol Estes*, H. Rept. 89-196, 89 Cong. 1 sess. (Government Printing Office, March 22, 1965), p. 23.
18. Ibid., p. 22.
19. Six days after Carter signed the Inspector General Act of 1978, Estes pleaded guilty to another charge of conspiracy to defraud the government.
20. *Operations of Billie Sol Estes*, Hearings before House Committee on Government Operations, 88 Cong. 2 sess. (Government Printing Office, 1964) p. 1401.
21. Cited by House Government Operations Committee, "Authoritative Statements [by Chairman Jack Brooks] on Scope and Location of the Internal Audit Function," memoranda (undated), p. 11.
22. Quoted in Robert P. Doherty, "Shaping the Inspector General Law," *Government Accountants Journal*, vol. 28 (Spring 1979), pp. 1–2.
23. Walter Gellhorn, *When Americans Complain: Governmental Grievance Procedures* (Harvard University Press, 1966), p. 121.
24. Gellhorn, *When Americans Complain*, pp. 120–21.
25. Stanley Andersen, *Inspectors General in Federal Agencies*, draft report prepared for the Administrative Conference of the United States, August 1979, p. 13, author's emphasis added.
26. Ibid., pp. 12–13, author's emphasis.
27. Interview with author, June 12, 1990.
28. A nonstatutory IGship also was created at ACTION in 1975 but was abandoned in 1978. A new IGship was not established until 1988.
29. Commission on CIA Activities within the United States, *Report to the President by the Commission on CIA Activities within the United States* (1975), pp. 88–89.
30. Funk may have felt the sting after deciding to publicize allegations that the Israelis sold Patriot missiles to China in the wake of the 1991 Persian Gulf War.

CHAPTER 3

1. For an excellent list of the various reforms of the period, see Charles O. Jones, *The United States Congress: People, Place, and Policy* (Homewood, Ill.: Dorsey Press, 1982), p. 429.

2. See Robert A. Katzmann, ed., *Judges and Legislators: Toward Institutional Comity* (Brookings, 1988), for a discussion of the problems inherent in discerning legislative intent.

3. Suzanne Garment, *Scandal: The Crisis of Mistrust in American Politics* (Times Books, 1991), p. 6.

4. Mark Moore and Margaret Jane Gates, *Inspectors-General: Junkyard Dog or Man's Best Friend?* (Russell Sage Foundation, 1986), p. 1.

5. Department of Health, Education, and Welfare, *Prevention and Detection of Fraud and Program Abuse,* H. Rept. 94-786, 94 Cong. 2 sess. (Government Printing Office, January 26, 1976).

6. Quoted in *Congressional Quarterly Almanac,* vol. 32 (Washington: Congressional Quarterly, 1976), p. 562.

7. *Establishment of an Office of Inspector General in the Department of Health, Education, and Welfare,* Hearings before the Subcommittee on Intergovernmental Relations and Human Resources of the House Government Operations Committee, 94 Cong. 2 sess. (GPO, 1976), p. 1.

8. *Inspector General Act of 1978,* S. Rept. 95-1071, 95 Cong. 2 sess. (GPO, August 8, 1978), pp. 4–5.

9. General Accounting Office, *Greater Audit Coverage of Internal Financial Operations Is Needed,* FGMSD-77-3 (November 19, 1976).

10. General Accounting Office, *An Overview of Federal Internal Audit,* FGMSD-76-50 (November 29, 1976).

11. General Accounting Office, *Financial Audits in Federal Executive Branch Agencies,* FGMSD-78-36 (June 6, 1978).

12. Ibid.

13. Ibid.

14. Ibid.

15. Mathew D. McCubbins and Thomas Schwartz, "Congressional Oversight Overlooked: Police Patrols versus Fire Alarms," *American Journal of Political Science,* vol. 28 (February 1984), pp. 165–77.

16. Ibid., p. 168.

17. *Inspector General in the Department of Health, Education, and Welfare,* Hearings, p. 31.

18. Garment, *Scandal,* pp. 142–43.

19. Burdett Loomis, *The New American Politician: Ambition, Entrepreneurship, and the Changing Face of Political Life* (Basic Books, 1988), p. 233.

20. Kusserow testified on Medicare Part B claims processing, crack babies, tobacco control, and regulation of medical devices, the last three gaining national press publicity. As Loomis argued, "Waxman demonstrates the potential that a well-staffed subcommittee offers an activist chair," a

point that could not be lost on other entrepreneurial members of Congress. Loomis, *The New American Politician*, p. 163.

21. Loomis, *The New American Politician*, p. 163.
22. Joel D. Aberbach, *Keeping a Watchful Eye: The Politics of Congressional Oversight* (Brookings, 1990), p. 47.
23. Ibid., p. 101.
24. These data are recorded in Seymour Martin Lipset and William Schneider, *The Confidence Gap: Business, Labor, and Government in the Public Mind* (The Free Press, 1983), p. 17.
25. Robert Behn, "Innovation and Public Values: Mistakes, Flexibility, Purpose, Equity, Cost Control, and Trust," paper prepared for the Conference on the Fundamental Questions of Innovation, Duke University, May 3–4, 1991, p. 23.
26. Marver Bernstein, "The Presidency and Management Improvement," *Law and Contemporary Problems*, vol. 35 (Summer 1970), pp. 515–16.
27. General Accounting Office, *Selected Government-wide Management Improvement Efforts—1970–80*, GAO/GGD-83-69 (August 8, 1983), p. 8.
28. See General Accounting Office, *Managing the Government: Revised Approach Could Improve OMB's Effectiveness*, GAO/GGD-89-65 (May 4, 1989), p. 3.
29. *Establishment of Offices of Inspector General*, Hearings before the Subcommittee on Intergovernmental Relations and Human Resources of the House Government Operations Committee, 95 Cong. 1 sess. (GPO, 1977), p. 165.
30. A number of excellent histories of these issues predate the Watergate crisis. On executive privilege, see Raoul Berger, "Executive Privilege versus Congressional Inquiry," *UCLA Law Review*, vol. 12 (Winter 1965), pp. 1044–1119, and vol. 12 (Spring 1965), pp. 1288–1364; and on congressional inquiry, see Telford Taylor, *Grand Inquest: The Story of Congressional Investigations* (Simon and Schuster, 1955); James Hamilton, *The Power to Probe: A Study of Congressional Investigations*, (Random House, 1976); and Arthur M. Schlesinger, Jr., and Roger Bruns, eds., *Congress Investigates: A Documented History, 1792–1974*, five volumes (Chelsea House, 1975).
31. See Berger, "Executive Privilege versus Congressional Inquiry," p. 1061. Berger also explains why Congress did not create a similar reporting requirement in the bills establishing the departments of War and Foreign Affairs. A similar explanation of the events surrounding Treasury can be found in Gerhard Casper, "An Essay in Separation of Powers: Some Early Versions and Practices," *William and Mary Law Review*, vol. 30 (Winter 1989), pp. 211–61.
32. 273 U.S. 135 (1927).
33. 418 U.S. 683 (1974).
34. Peter Shane, *Negotiating for Knowledge: Administrative Responses to Congressional Demands for Information*, preliminary draft report for the Administrative Conference of the United States, July 1, 1990, p. 17.

Shane's report contains an excellent introduction to the terms of the struggle.

35. Ibid., p. 33.
36. No certainty exists that the bill would have made a difference. Congress had tried before to force access, with limited success. A half century earlier, for example, the predecessor of Government Operations had required every executive department and independent establishment to "furnish any information requested of it relating to any matter within the jurisdiction of [the] committee." The provision survives, with minor modification, in Title 5, *United States Code*, Section 2954.
37. H.R. 2819, emphasis added.
38. Aberbach, *Keeping a Watchful Eye*, p. 35.
39. Donald Kettl, "Micromanagement: Congressional Control and Bureaucratic Risk," in Patricia Ingraham and Donald F. Kettl, eds., *Agenda for Excellence: Public Service in America* (Chatham, N.J.: Chatham House, 1992), p. 101.
40. These totals do not include personal office and home district staff, which also increased dramatically. In 1950, the average House member had a staff of 4 full-time employees; by 1986, 18. In 1950, the average senator had a staff of 6; by 1986, 38.
41. These staffing figures were drawn from Steven S. Smith and Christopher J. Deering, *Committees in Congress* (Washington: CQ Press, 1984), p. 282.
42. Garment, *Scandal*, p. 143.
43. Aberbach, *Keeping a Watchful Eye*, pp. 105–29.
44. Department of Health and Human Services, Office of Inspector General, *Semiannual Report; April 1, 1990–September 30, 1990*, appendix C.
45. Moore and Gates illustrate a number of other possible unintended side effects, arguing, for example, that "The mechanisms through which the OIGs could harm government performance and credibility are less obvious, but perhaps no less likely. It is possible, for example, that the motivations and capabilities of government managers to control fraud, waste, and abuse are already strong, and that the OIGs add little to the nexus of institutions already devoted to this goal. In this case, the OIGs would *reduce* government efficiency because they would add costs to government operations, but produce no significant improvements." See Moore and Gates, *Inspectors General*, p. 4.

CHAPTER 4

1. "Benjamin Rosenthal," and "L. H. Fountain," in Alan Ehrenhalt, ed., *Politics in America* (Washington: Congressional Quarterly, 1981), p. 816 and p. 897, respectively.
2. All of these provisions are drawn from H.R. 5302 as recorded in *Establishment of an Office of Inspector General in the Department of Health,*

Education, and Welfare, Hearings before the Subcommittee on Intergovernmental Relations and Human Resources of the House Government Operations Committee, 94 Cong. 2 sess. (Government Printing Office, 1976), pp. 3–5.

3. Ibid., pp. 17–18.
4. Ibid., p. 10.
5. Ibid., pp. 12–13.
6. Ibid.
7. These notes come from Eizenstat's files and are dated November 7, 1977. My thanks for the access and insights.
8. *Establishment of Offices of Inspector General,* Hearings before the Subcommittee on Intergovernmental Relations and Human Resources of the House Government Operations Committee, 95 Cong. 1 sess. (GPO, 1977, pp. 23, 122).
9. Elsa Porter, untitled speech, December 1, 1980, p. 3.
10. Department of Justice, *Memorandum on Constitutional Issues Presented by H.R. 2819,* reprinted in *Establishment of Offices of Inspector General,* Hearings, pp. 831–49.
11. Ibid., p. 844.
12. Ibid., pp. 848–49.
13. *Establishment of Offices of Inspector General,* Hearings, pp. 468–69.
14. Emphasis added.
15. 28 U.S.C. 596(a)(1).
16. 28 U.S.C. 596(a)(3).
17. 108 S.Ct. 2597 (1988). For various interpretations of the decision, see Earl C. Dudley, Jr., "*Morrison* v. *Olson*: A Modest Assessment," *American University Law Review,* vol. 38 (Winter 1989), pp. 255–74; Eric Glitzenstein and Alan B. Morrison, "The Supreme Court's Decision in *Morrison* v. *Olson*: A Common Sense Application of the Constitution to a Practical Problem," *American University Law Review,* vol. 38 (Winter 1989), pp. 359–82; Morton Rosenberg, "Congress's Prerogative over Agencies and Agency Decision Makers: The Rise and Demise of the Reagan Administration's Theory of the Unitary Executive," *George Washington Law Review,* vol. 57 (January 1989), pp. 627–703.
18. See Fountain's statement explaining changes in the bill, *Congressional Record,* April 18, 1978, p. 10403.
19. General Accounting Office, *Impact of Administrative Budget Procedures on Independence of Offices of Inspector General,* GAO/AFMD-84-78 (September 26, 1984).
20. *Inspector General Act of 1978,* S. Rept. 95-1071, 95th Cong. 2 sess. (GPO, August 8, 1978), p. 9.
21. *Serious Management Problems in the U.S. Government,* Hearings before the Senate Committee on Governmental Affairs, 101 Cong. 1 sess. (GPO, 1989), p. 55.
22. The recommendation was made on the basis of what the IG called a "strong perception of impropriety" and was implemented immediately

by HUD Secretary Jack Kemp upon assuming office during the Bush administration.

23. *Serious Management Problems in the U.S. Government*, Hearings, p. 209; emphasis added.

24. *Abuses, Favoritism and Mismanagement in HUD Programs*, Report to the House Committee on Government Operations, 101 Cong. 1 sess. (GPO, 1989), p. 67.

25. *Abuse and Mismanagement at HUD*, H. Rept. 101-977, p. 6.

26. *The Abuse and Mismanagement of HUD*, Hearings before the Subcommittee on HUD/Mod Rehab Investigation of the Senate Banking, Housing, and Urban Affairs Committee, 101 Cong. 2 sess. (GPO, 1990), vol. 2, p. 479.

27. *Final Report and Recommendations*, Committee Print, Senate Committee on Banking, Housing, and Urban Affairs, 101 Cong. 2 sess. (GPO, 1990), p. 218.

28. *Hud Inspector General Report*, Hearings before the Subcommittee on Housing and Community Development of the House Committee on Banking, Finance, and Urban Affairs, 99 Cong. 2 sess. (GPO, 1986), p. 70.

29. Ibid., p. 80.

30. *Abuse and Mismanagement at HUD*, H. Rept. 101-977, p. 3.

31. *Final Report and Recommendations*, Committee Print, pp. 218–19.

32. In 1988, the HUD IG recommended that the authority to suspend programs be granted. In 1989, HUD secretary Kemp adopted the recommendation.

33. See Paul C. Light, *Vice Presidential Power: Advice and Influence in the White House* (Johns Hopkins University Press, 1984).

34. This lack of sustained interest in Congress and the presidency resulted in a call from the National Academy of Public Administration for the establishment of a separate Office of Federal Management (OFM), partitioned off from OMB. The idea was endorsed by Representative Leon Panetta (D-Calif.) as the only way to "(1) advise and assist the president in carrying out the responsibilities of the president as Chief Executive *Officer* of the Government"; and "(2) provide overall leadership in the development and implementation of federal management policies and in the coordination of programs to improve the quality and performance of management personnel."

35. *Final Report and Recommendations*, Committee Print, p. 180.

36. *Abuses, Favoritism and Mismanagement in HUD Programs*, Report, p. 68.

37. *Abuse and Mismanagement at HUD*, H. Rept. 101-977.

CHAPTER 5

1. These figures were taken from George C. Edwards III with Alec M. Gallup, *Presidential Approval: A Sourcebook* (Johns Hopkins University Press, 1990) pp. 75–83.

2. For an excellent summary of Carter's problems with Congress, see Charles O. Jones, *The Trusteeship Presidency: Jimmy Carter and the United States Congress* (Louisiana State University Press, 1988).

3. See Paul C. Light, *The President's Agenda: Domestic Policy Choice from Kennedy to Reagan*, rev. ed. (Johns Hopkins University Press, 1992).

4. *Public Papers of the Presidents of the United States: Jimmy Carter, Book II, June 30 to December 31, 1978* (Government Printing Office, 1979), p. 1755.

5. The class of 1979 includes all of the Carter IGs, plus the two IGs nominated and confirmed before 1979—Thomas Morris at HEW and Kenneth Mansfield at Energy.

6. Judy Kopff, "The Inspectors General—On-the-Spot Watchdogs," *GAO Review*, vol. 15 (Spring 1980), p. 56.

7. See G. Calvin Mackenzie, ed., *The In-and-Outers: Presidential Appointees and Transient Government in Washington* (Johns Hopkins University Press, 1987), p. 9.

8. Ibid., p. 15.

9. *Inspector General Act Amendments of 1988*, Hearings before the Subcommittee on Legislation and National Security of the House Government Operations Committee, 100 Cong. 2 sess. (GPO, 1988), p. 123.

10. See October 29, 1989, letter from House Government Operations Committee chairman John Conyers (D-Mich.) to Bush.

11. Orville Freeman, diaries, December 1962.

12. This problem was clarified in the Inspector General Act Amendments of 1988.

13. *Statutory Offices of Inspector General: Leadership and Resources*, H. Rept. 97-211, 97 Cong. 1 sess (GPO, 1981), p. 17.

14. These reports are summarized in *Oversight of Offices of Inspector General*, Hearings before the Subcommittee on Intergovernmental Relations and Human Resources of the House Government Operations Committee, 97 Cong. 1 sess. (GPO, 1981), pp. 161–64.

15. The notion that the Community Services Administration IG was complaining about having to set strict priorities must have struck the non-IG CSA staff as mildly ironic, given that the office already was slated for elimination under the proposed fiscal year 1982 budget.

16. Mackenzie, *The In-and-Outers*, p. 137.

17. Ibid., p. 185.

18. The discussion was drawn from the second case study prepared for Mark Moore and Margaret Jane Gates, *Inspectors-General: Junkyard Dog or Man's Best Friend?* (Russell Sage Foundation, 1986); "Fraud, Waste, and Abuse at HEW," case 14-80-337 (Harvard University, John F. Kennedy School of Government, 1980).

19. "Fraud, Waste, and Abuse at HEW," p. 9.

20. Ibid., pp. 13–14.

21. Ibid., p. 16.

22. These figures were drawn from the respective IG reports; unless the reports are quoted extensively, they are not expressly noted.

CHAPTER 6

1. A party identification question in the pre-test for the IG survey elicited such negative response that it was dropped for fear of undermining the entire effort. Therefore, no concrete conclusions could be drawn about the political sympathies of the IGs.
2. These campaign references were drawn from *Statutory Offices of Inspector General: Leadership and Resources*, H. Rept. 97-211, 97 Cong. 1 sess. (Government Printing Office, 1981), p. 18.
3. *Weekly Compilation of Presidential Documents*, vol. 17 (January 26, 1981), pp. 27–28.
4. Quoted in Charles R. Babcock and Patrick Tyler, "Fired US Waste-Fighter Bears Government Followups," *Washington Post*, February 2, 1981, pp. A1, A8.
5. *The Inspectors General: A Ten-Year Review*, Hearings before the Subcommittee on Legislation and National Security of the House Government Operations Committee, 101 Cong. 2 sess. (GPO, 1989), p. 113.
6. *Oversight of Offices of Inspector General*, Hearings before the Subcommittee on Intergovernmental Relations and Human Resources of the House Government Operations Committee, 97 Cong. 1 sess. (GPO, 1981), p. 22.
7. Letter to Senator Max Baucus (D-Mont.), *Congressional Record*, February 6, 1981, p. S1215.
8. House 1981 IG Report, p. 22.
9. "Program for Economic Recovery," text of President Reagan's speech, *Weekly Compilation of Presidential Documents*, vol. 17 (February 23, 1981), p. 134.
10. G. Calvin Mackenzie, "Appointing Mr. (or Ms.) Right," *Government Executive*, vol. 22 (April 1990), p. 30.
11. *The Inspectors General*, Hearings, p. 11.
12. Ibid., p. 111.
13. Department of Justice, "Policy Statement of the Department of Justice on Its Relationship and Coordination with the Statutory Inspectors General of the Various Departments and Agencies of the United States," June 3, 1981 (revised), pp. 6–7.
14. *Statutory Offices of Inspector General*, H. Rept. 97-211, p. 24.
15. *The Inspectors General*, Hearings, p. 89.
16. Terry M. Moe, "The Politicized Presidency," in John E. Chubb and Paul E. Peterson, *The New Directions in American Politics* (Brookings, 1985), p. 235.

17. See National Commission on the Public Service, *Leadership for America* (Lexington, Mass.: Lexington Books, 1989). I wrote the draft of the final report.
18. *Statutory Offices of Inspector General*, H. Rept. 97-211, p. 8.
19. These government-wide staffing figures were drawn from the General Accounting Office, *Federal Employees: Trends in Career and Noncareer Employee Appointments in the Executive Branch*, GAO/GGD-87-96FS (July 1987).
20. *The Inspector General Act of 1978: A Ten-Year Review*, H. Rept. 100-1027, 100 Cong. 2 sess. (GPO, 1988), p. 38.
21. General Accounting Office, *Managing the Government: Revised Approach Could Improve OMB's Effectiveness*, GAO/GGD-89-65 (May 1989), p. 56.
22. Ronald C. Moe, "Traditional Organizational Principles and the Managerial Presidency: From Phoenix to Ashes," *Public Administration Review*, vol. 50 (March/April 1990), p. 134.
23. *The Inspectors General*, Hearings, p. 57.
24. Ibid.
25. *Waste, Fraud, and Abuse*, Hearings before the Senate Committee on Governmental Affairs, 100 Cong. 1 sess. (GPO, 1987) pt. 2, p. 12.
26. Ibid., p. 13.
27. *The Inspectors General*, Hearings, p. 116.
28. General Accounting Office, *State Department's Office of Inspector General Should Be More Independent and Effective*, GAO/AFMD-83-56 (June 2, 1982), p. ii.
29. One of the hotline cases involved an allegation that an EPA official had falsified information on his Personal Qualifications Statement prior to employment at the agency; a second involved an allegation that an EPA regional administrator had misused funds by redecorating his office unnecessarily; and a third centered on an allegation that an EPA assistant administrator had received entertainment favors from industries affected by his branch.
30. General Accounting Office, *Improvements Needed in EPA's Inspector General Operations*, GAO/AFMD-84-13 (October 21, 1983), p. ii.
31. General Accounting Office, *Deficiencies in the Department of the Interior OIG Investigation of the Powder River Basin Coal Lease Sale*, GAO/RCED-84-167 (June 11, 1984), p. ii.

CHAPTER 7

1. President's Council on Integrity and Efficiency, *Major Impacts of the Federal Offices of Inspector General, 1981–86: The First Five Years* (January 1987), pp. 9–12.
2. Under a hold, a single member of the Senate can delay a bill indefinitely,

particularly because much of the Senate's business is conducted by unanimous consent.

3. *Inspector General Act Amendments of 1988*, H. Rept. 100-771, 100 Cong. 2 sess. (Government Printing Office, July 13, 1988), p. 7.

4. *Staff Study of Allegations Pertaining to the Department of Justice's Handling of a Contract with INSLAW Inc.*, Committee Print, Subcommittee on Investigations of the Senate Governmental Affairs Committee, 101 Cong. 1 sess. (GPO, 1989), p. 53.

5. Costs were to be listed as questioned if they occurred because of (a) an alleged violation of law, regulation, contract, and so on (b) a finding that such cost is not supported by adequate documentation, or (c) a finding that the expenditure is unnecessary or unreasonable. Costs were unsupported only if they could not be backed up with adequate documents. Thus, unsupported costs would nest within questioned costs and might reflect more of a problem getting the vouchers in and paperwork done than outright fraud, waste, or abuse.

6. See table 2-1.

7. The survey was conducted by the Coordinating Conference, a small agency council under the sponsorship of the PCIE.

8. Letter from Robert Houk to the Speaker of the House and president of the Senate, May 18, 1990.

9. By this time, the onus was on Senator Glenn to look after the IGs because Jack Brooks had left House Government Operation to take over the chairmanship of the House Judiciary Committee.

10. *Serious Management Problems in the U.S. Government*, Hearings before the Senate Committee on Governmental Affairs, 101 Cong. 1 sess. (GPO, 1989), p. 48.

11. Ibid., p. 9.

12. In the same vein, the IG committee also rejected George Murphy for the post at the U.S. Information Agency, only to see the nomination survive through confirmation.

13. Memorandum from Dennis M. Kass, assistant secretary for pension and welfare benefits, to George R. Salem, Labor Department solicitor, and J. Brian Hyland, January 6, 1987, p. 1.

14. Letter from George R. Salem, Labor Department solicitor, to Douglas Kmiec, December 5, 1988, p. 1.

15. *Oversight of the Operation of Inspector General Offices*, Hearings before the Senate Committee on Governmental Affairs, 101 Cong. 2 sess. (GPO, 1990), p. 5.

16. Department of Justice, Office of Legal Counsel, *Authority of the State Department Office of Security to Investigate Passport and Visa Fraud*, memorandum, August 17, 1984. The memorandum argued that the IG could investigate only passport and visa fraud directly connected to the department, which only involved State Department employees.

17. The March 9 opinion was not Kmiec's only contribution to the IG debate, however. The OLC issued a second Kmiec memorandum two weeks later dealing with congressional requests for information. Again,

it was an opinion without a specific case, responding instead to a request from the PCIE regarding congressional demands for information on open criminal investigations.

According to the opinion, the IGs were not to provide such information in the absence of extraordinary circumstances: "Long-established executive branch policy and practice, based on consideration of both Congress' oversight authority and principles of executive privilege, require that in the absence of extraordinary circumstances an IG must decline to provide confidential information about an open criminal investigation in response to a request pursuant to Congress' oversight authority." (See Department of Justice, Office of Legal Counsel, *Congressional Requests for Information from Inspectors General Concerning Open Criminal Investigations*, memorandum, March 24, 1989, p. 12.)

Despite its sweeping implications and reopening of the executive privilege debate, the second Kmiec memo did not merit much of a reaction on Capitol Hill, in part because Congress barely noticed and in part because the IGs generally agreed with the thrust. The only response was a message from the House general counsel to Jack Brooks, chairman of the Judiciary Committee, that portrayed the memo as "a legally meritless invitation to stonewall Congressional oversight of waste and fraud." (See House of Representatives, Office of the Clerk, *Justice Department Memorandum Directing the Withholding from Congress of Inspector General Information*, memorandum May 2, 1989.) Absent a controversy, however, it was the kind of memo that was best ignored.

18. Department of Justice, Office of Legal Counsel, *Authority of the Inspector General to Conduct Regulatory Investigations*, memorandum, March 9, 1989, pp. 1–2.
19. Ibid., p. 8.
20. James R. Naughton, "Report on Authority of Inspectors General to Conduct Criminal Investigations Relating to Regulatory Programs," June 11, 1990, p. 5. The report was commissioned by the Senate Governmental Affairs Committee.
21. Ibid., p. N-6.
22. Department of Labor, Office of the Inspector General, *Semiannual Report: October 1, 1988–March 31, 1989* (1989), p. 1.
23. *Oversight of the Operation of Inspector General Offices*, Hearings, pp. 13–14.
24. Ibid., p. 8.
25. *Naked Reverse: Secretary Sullivan's Rescission of His Delegation of Investigative Authority to the Inspector General*, Committee Prints, Subcommittee on Oversight and Investigations of the House Energy and Commerce Committee, 101 Cong. 2 sess. (GPO, 1990), pp. 1, III.
26. Letter from Acting Deputy Attorney General William Barr to William Diefenderfer, deputy director of OMB, July 17, 1990, pp. 2–3.
27. The OLC opinion was not forgotten, however. In 1991, for example,

Representative John Dingell (D-Mich.) and forty-one cosponsors introduced H.R. 2454, giving the HHS IG full authority to investigate as needed any allegations of "fraud, false claims, waste, or abuse relating to programs or operations administered, carried out, financed, or conducted by the Food and Drug Administration." The bill also contained the following provision regarding delegations of authority of the kind overturned in the generic drug case: "In making determinations regarding any delegation of authority, the Secretary shall consider the expertise and resources available in the Office of Inspector General and the Food and Drug Administration." In short, the legislation reversed the "naked reversal." As of June 1, 1992, the bill had not advanced out of committee.

28. "Watching the Watchdogs," *Washington Post*, September 15, 1990, p. A22.
29. *Investigative Report: The Inspector General System*, draft report, Subcommittee on General Services, Federalism, and the District of Columbia of the Senate Governmental Affairs Committee (July 1990), p. 22.
30. For a discussion about how issues play out in the agenda-setting process, see John W. Kingdon, *Agendas, Alternatives, and Public Policy* (Boston: Little, Brown, 1984).
31. *Budget of the United States Government, Fiscal Year 1992*, pp. 2–342.

CHAPTER 8

1. The auditors follow the "Yellow Book" standards drafted by the General Accounting Office, *Government Auditing Standards*, rev. ed.(1988).
2. James R. Richards and William S. Fields, "The Inspector General Act: Are Its Investigative Provisions Adequate to Meet Current Needs?" *George Mason University Law Review*, vol. 12 (Winter and Spring 1990), p. 247.
3. "Bounty Hunters," ABC's "Primetime Live," transcript, September 20, 1990, p. 2.
4. Ibid., p. 4.
5. Letter from James Todd, American Medical Association, to Louis W. Sullivan, November 27, 1990, p. 1.
6. These differences may flow in part from decisions made in college regarding undergraduate major. Note the following relationships drawn from the IG mail survey:
    Political science majors had the least difficulty mastering departmental procedures and fared well with the media. They were less likely than either finance or humanities majors to experience difficulty with the short-term orientation in Washington politics or get frustrated with either the slow pace of decisions in their agencies or statistical measures of success. They had more than average difficulty in mastering office staffing and organization. However, they did express significant frustration, as did finance and law enforcement majors, with the resistance

of their agencies to change and were remarkably flappable regarding congressional interference.

Law enforcement majors were the least likely to have difficulty dealing with the media and had somewhat less trouble mastering program details. They felt the least frustration with the slow pace of decisions, perhaps because of contact with the judicial process, but had the greatest problem dealing with both the short-term orientation in Washington and office staffing and organization. Along with finance and accounting majors, law enforcement experienced the least frustration dealing with OMB and the media, and, like all of the majors, had little trouble with White House interference.

Accounting and finance majors had less trouble than the other majors with budget, office staffing, and organization and reported little frustration with either a lack of time to plan or a lack of resources. They did get frustrated with agency resistance to change and had difficulties dealing with the media and Congress. They had less trouble than political science and law enforcement majors with turnover among political leadership. They reported the greatest difficulties with department procedures, more so than any other undergraduate major, and had significant difficulty with program details. In many ways, they fit the stereotype of the beancounter—that is, they had deep knowledge of the finance and accounting process, but little else.

Finally, humanities majors emerged as the IGs with the greatest patience and fewest frustrations, although whether the patience was born of confidence or naiveté is not clear. They had more than average difficulties with departmental procedures, but almost none with the budget process; they had difficulties with program details, as did all the IGs to an extent, but had absolutely no difficulty dealing with the White House and OMB; and, most surprisingly perhaps, only 37 percent had a problem with Congress, compared with 79 percent of finance, 75 percent of political science, and 57 percent of law enforcement majors. Finally, they were exceedingly difficult to frustrate, with few mentioning the media, congressional interference, or agency resistance as a source of irritation. Just about the only place they felt frustrated was with lack of resources, where they were more than twice as likely as finance and political science majors to react, and the slow pace of decisions, where they were by far the most frustrated.

7. *Legislation to Establish Offices of Inspector General—H.R. 8588,* Hearings before the Subcommittee on Governmental Efficiency of the Senate Governmental Affairs Committee, 95 Cong. 2 sess. (Government Printing Office, 1978), p. 82.

8. The term "qui tam" is taken from the Latin "qui tam pro domino rege quam pro se ipso in hac pate sequitur," which means "who brings the action for the King as well as for himself."

9. *False Claims Act Implementation,* Hearings before the Subcommittee on Administrative Law and Governmental Relations of the House Judiciary Committee, 101 Cong. 2 sess. (GPO, 1990), p. 30.

10. See Arthur M. Okun, *Equality and Efficiency: The Big Tradeoff* (Brookings, 1975); see in particular pp. 91–95.
11. Office of Personnel Management, *Qualification Standards* (December 1968), p. 1.
12. *The Inspectors General: A Ten-Year Review*, Hearings before the Subcommittee on Legislation and National Security of the House Government Operations Committee, 101 Cong. 2 sess. (GPO, 1988), p. 86.
13. Quoted in Ruth Marcus, "Agency Inspectors General Feeling Justice Department's Leash," *Washington Post*, September 18, 1989, p. A17.
14. *Serious Management Problems in the U.S. Government*, Hearings before the Senate Committee on Governmental Affairs, 101 Cong. 1 sess. (GPO, 1989), p. 91.
15. Ibid., p. 84.
16. *Final Report and Recommendations*, Committee Print, Senate Committee on Banking, Housing, and Urban Affairs, 101 Cong. 2 sess. (GPO, 1990), p. 75.
17. 109 S. Ct. 1982 (1989).
18. For a discussion of the independence question as it relates to Defense Department military IGs, who are not governed by the 1978 IG Act or any of its amendments, see Stewart Harris, "In the Watchdog House," *Government Executive*, vol. 22 (October 1990), pp. 60–64, 74.
19. For Rosenthal, however, a term of office was not quite enough. He also advocated that no IG was to be eligible for reappointment to a second term. Even self-interest was to be curbed.
20. *The Abuse and Mismanagement of HUD*, Hearings before the Subcommittee on HUD/Mod Rehab Investigation of the Senate Banking, Housing, and Urban Affairs Committee, 101 Cong. 2 sess. (GPO, 1990), p. 490.
21. *Inspector General Act Amendments of 1988*, Hearings before the Subcommittee on Legislation and National Security of the House Government Operations Committee, 100 Cong. 2 sess. (GPO, 1988), p. 123.
22. Quoted in Carl M. Brauer, *Presidential Transitions: Eisenhower through Reagan* (Oxford University Press, 1986), p. 263.
23. G. Calvin Mackenzie, "Appointing Mr. (or Ms.) Right," *Government Executive*, vol. 22 (April 1990), p. 31.
24. Office of Personnel Management, fact sheet, August 1990.
25. *The Inspectors General*, Hearings, p. 335.

CHAPTER 9

1. Speaking from personal experience as a Senate staffer from 1987 to 1988, I can attest that the HHS legislative liaison operation was unabashedly pro-Congress and extremely effective in keeping members and staff informed of ongoing work. Calls from the OIG offering help were frequent, and requests were answered overnight. Moreover, the HHS OIG

would launch special projects for Congress, promising faster turn-
arounds than any other congressional agency, including GAO.

    Members and staff took advantage of HHS IG Richard Kusserow's
willingness to assist them. "During the year 1987," Kusserow explained,
"we received approximately 111 letters from Members of Congress requesting our assistance. Many of these requests required us to do full-
scale investigations or audits, often leading to hearings. . . . We also
forward, based on standing requests from various committee and subcommittee chairmen, draft audits and inspection reports pertaining to
subjects of interest to the Members." *The Inspector General: A Ten-
Year Review,* Hearings before the Subcommittee on Legislation and
National Security of the House Government Operations Committee,
101 Cong. 2 sess. (Government Printing Office, 1988), p. 174.

2. Interview with author, October 26, 1990.
3. Memo from Edward C. Stringer, general counsel, to James B. Thomas,
   December 12, 1989, p. 1.
4. *Department of Education Memorandum of Understanding between
   the Office of Inspector General and the Office of the General Counsel,*
   July 7, 1990, p. 2.
5. *Serious Management Problems in the U.S. Government,* Hearings before the Senate Committee on Governmental Affairs, 101 Cong. 1 sess.
   (GPO, 1989), p. 86.
6. National Academy of Public Administration, *Revitalizing Federal Management: Managers and their Overburdened Systems* (Washington, November 1983), p. 37.
7. Ibid.
8. National Commission on the Public Service, *Leadership for America*
   (Lexington, Mass.: Lexington Books, 1989), p. 28.
9. *Weekly Compilation of Presidential Documents,* vol. 17, no. 13, March
   30, 1981, p. 347.
10. *The Inspector General Act of 1978: A Ten-Year Review,* H. Rept. 100-
    1027, 100 Cong. 2 sess. (GPO, 1988), pp. 25–26.
11. This quote comes from a transcript of an IG interview conducted
    as part of the House ten-year review of the 1978 IG Act and is to
    be found in the House Government Operations Committee archived
    materials. I am grateful to Richard Barnes, former staff director of
    the Subcommittee on Legislative and National Security, for his help
    in retrieving the files from the National Archives. Under the ground
    rules established, the interview materials could be used only on a
    not-for-attribution basis.
12. *The Inspector General: A Ten-Year Review,* Hearings before the Sub-
    committee on Legislation and National Security of the House Govern-
    ment Operations Committee, 101 Cong. 2 sess. (GPO, 1988), p. 181.
13. Both quotes are from *The Inspectors General,* Hearings, p. 233.
14. *Serious Management Programs in the U.S. Government,* Hearings, p. 96.
15. Paraphrased by William Moran, "Evaluation within the Federal Offices
    of Inspector General," in Michael Hendricks, Michael Mangano, and

William Moran, eds., *Inspectors General: A New Direction in Evaluation*, no. 48 (San Francisco: Jossey-Bass, Winter 1990), p. 13. As FBI evaluation expert Richard Sonnichsen argued, Kusserow's analogies "hardly conjure up visions of evaluators and program managers cooperatively striving to understand each other's contributions to organizational effectiveness." See Richard C. Sonnichsen, "Another View of Program Inspections by the Offices of Inspectors General," in Hendricks, Mangano, and Moran, eds., *Inspectors General: A New Direction in Evaluation*, p. 81.

16. Offices of Investigations of the Statutory Offices of Inspectors General in Federal Government, *The Need for Full Law Enforcement Authorities*, compendium of cases, March 1989.

17. Frederick M. Kaiser, "Issues and Concerns Relating to Proposed New Law Enforcement Authority for Inspectors General," memorandum (Congressional Research Service, June 29, 1990), p. 10.

18. *The Inspector General Act of 1978*, H. Rept. 100-1027, p. 28.

19. Letter from the Office of Legislative Affairs to Senator John Glenn, March 22, 1990, p. 7.

20. Kaiser, "Issues and Concerns Relating to Proposed New Law Enforcement Authority for Inspectors General," p. 19.

21. In 1990, the deputy attorney general promised Glenn a seven-day turnaround on all IG requests. Interview with author, November 10, 1990.

22. *Inspector General Act of 1978*, S. Rept. 95-1071, 95 Cong. 2 sess. (GPO, August 8, 1978), p. 34.

23. *U.S. v. Iannone*, 458 F. Supp. 42–43.

24. Memorandum from Congressional Research Service, American Law Division, to House Committee on Government Operations, "Comments on Pending Proposals for Enlarging the Powers and Jurisdiction of the Inspectors General," July 6, 1990, p. 6.

25. Herbert L. Fenster and Darryl J. Lee, "The Expanding Audit and Investigative Powers of the Federal Government," *Public Contract Law Journal*, vol. 12 (March 1982), p. 220.

26. See Raymond McCann, "Procurement Fraud Investigative Techniques: The Need for Congressional Expansion of the Inspector General Subpoena Power to Include the Power to Compel Testimony," *Public Contract Law Journal*, vol. 16 (May 1987), pp. 502–03.

27. See, for example, the procedures used by the Securities and Exchange Commission. IG testimonial subpoenas also would be governed by the standards established by the Supreme Court in *U.S. v. Powell*, 379 U.S. 48 (1964).

28. This discussion is based on materials first presented in Paul C. Light, *The President's Agenda: Domestic Policy Choice from Kennedy to Reagan*, rev. ed. (Johns Hopkins University Press, 1991).

29. General Accounting Office, *Federal Evaluation: Few United, Reduced Resources, Different Studies from 1980*, GAO/PEMD-87-9 (January 1987), p. 2.

30. See General Accounting Office, *Program Evaluation Issues*, Transition

Series, GAO/OCG-89-8TR (November 1988), p. 1. The report is part of a series of documents produced for the transition of the next president into office.

31. Ibid., pp. 10–11.
32. Moran, "Evaluation within the Federal Offices of Inspector General," p. 16.
33. General Accounting Office, *Program Evaluation Issues*, p. 21.
34. Moran, "Evaluation within the Federal Offices of Inspector General," p. 15.
35. Dwight F. Davis, "Do You Want a Performance Audit or a Program Evaluation?" *Public Administration Review*, vol. 50 (January/February 1990), pp. 37, 39.
36. Kathryn E. Newcomer, "Ten Ways to Kill Evaluation," *The Bureaucrat*, vol. 18 (Fall 1989), p. 60.
37. Quoted in Sonnichsen, "Another View of Program Inspectors by the Offices of Inspectors General," p. 83; Sonnichsen reported that Kusserow originally intended to make the announcement at the association's annual meeting, scheduled to take place in San Francisco, but that an earthquake necessitated another avenue.
38. Hendricks, Mangano, and Moran, ed., *The Growth of Evaluations within the Federal Offices of Inspector General*, p. 26.
39. Michael F. Mangano, "Evaluation Within the U.S. Department of Health and Human Services Office of Inspector General," in Hendricks, Mangano, and Moran, ed., *Inspectors General: A New Direction in Evaluation*, p. 35.
40. Department of Health and Human Services, Office of Inspector General, Office of Evaluation and Inspections, *Special Steps for Writing an Inspection Report*, Technical Assistance Guide 6 (1990), p. 11.
41. Eleanor Chelminsky, "The Role of Program Evaluation at the General Accounting Office," remarks before the annual conference of the National Legislative Program Evaluation Society, Minneapolis, May 8, 1992, p. 16.
42. *The Abuse and Mismanagement of HUD*, Hearings before the Senate Committee on Banking, Housing and Urban Affairs, 101 Cong. 2 sess. (GPO, 1990), vol. II, p. 82.
43. Ibid., p. 86.

CHAPTER 10

1. An analysis by John Mingus, my lead research assistant for this book, suggested that, from the IG perspective, the most important resource is staff size. In that regard, "it would appear that the Departments of Defense, Interior, and Health and Human Services were the most effective OIGs and the Departments of Transportation, Agriculture and Veterans Affairs were the least effective in the period from fiscal 1981

through fiscal 1988." See John Mingus, "The Inspectors General: A Case Study in Organizational Effectiveness," paper submitted in partial fulfillment of the requirements for a master's degree, Hubert H. Humphrey Institute of Public Affairs, University of Minnesota, April 1990, p. 31.

2. Steven Kelman, "The Grace Commission: How Much Waste in Government," *Public Interest*, vol. 78 (1985), p. 63; see also Steven Kelman, *Procurement and Public Management: The Fear of Discretion and the Quality of Government Performance* (Washington: American Enterprise Institute, 1990).

3. Mark Moore and Margaret Jane Gates, *Inspectors-General: Junkyard Dog or Man's Best Friend?* (Russell Sage Foundation, 1986).

4. The minimums emerge from the comptroller general's *Standards for Audit of Government Organizations, Programs, Activities, and Functions (1988 revision)*—referred to as the "Yellow Book."

5. General Accounting Office, *Inspectors General: Compliance with Professional Standards by the GSA Inspector General*, GAO/AFMD-87-22 (July 1987).

6. Ibid., pp. 3–4.

7. State IG Sherman Funk referred to fraud exposure as "discretionary dollars," as opposed to funds that automatically were committed to personnel, heat, lights, maintenance, and the like. "By the time I left Commerce, we were returning $5 for each dollar appropriated," he noted during the House hearings on the ten-year review of the IGs. "I hope soon to reach the same level at State, although the discretionary budget is considerably smaller."

8. President's Council on Integrity and Efficiency, Council Coordinating Group, "Lessons Learned: Reporting under the 1988 Amendments to the Inspector General Act," survey, pp. 1, 5–6.

9. President's Council on Integrity and Efficiency, Committee on Integrity and Law Enforcement, *Characteristics of Inspector General Investigations* (July 1989), p. 17.

10. Ibid., p. 23.

11. Ibid., p. 5.

12. Ibid., p. 14.

13. Ibid., p. 14.

14. Ibid., p. 7.

15. Ibid., p. 7.

16. *Activities of the Environmental Protection Agency's Inspector General*, Hearings before the Subcommittee on Oversight and Investigations of the House Energy and Commerce Committee, 101 Cong. 2 sess. (GPO, 1991), p. 95.

17. See General Accounting Office, *Fraud: Characteristics, Sanctions, and Prevention at Agriculture, Labor, and GSA*, GAO/AFMD-88-34BR (June, 1988), pp. 24–29.

18. Phil Gailey and Warren Weaver, Jr., "A Reason to Sleep Better," *New York Times*, March 14, 1983, p. B6.

19. Letter from Senator Carl Levin to William Diefenderfer III, Chairman, President's Council on Integrity and Efficiency, March 5, 1990, p. 2.
20. *Final Report and Recommendations*, Committee Print, Senate Committee on Banking, Housing, and Urban Affairs, 101 Cong. 2 sess. (GPO, 1990), p. 217.
21. Jack Citrin, Donald Green, and Beth Reingold, "The Soundness of Our Structure: Confidence in the Reagan Years," *Public Opinion*, vol. 10 (November/December 1987), p. 18.
22. Ibid.
23. See Dan Balz and Richard Morin, "A Tide of Pessimism and Political Powerlessness Rises," *Washington Post*, November 3, 1991, pp. A1, A16–17.
24. General Accounting Office, *Compliance with Professional Standards by the HHS Inspector General*, GAO/AFMD-88-36 (September 1988), p. 33.
25. *The Inspectors General: A Ten-Year Review*, Hearings before the Subcommittee on Legislation and National Security of the House Government Operations Committee, 101 Cong. 2 sess. (GPO, 1988), pp. 35–36.
26. General Accounting Office, *Facing Facts: 1989 Annual Report* (1989), p. 12.
27. My thanks to Mark Moore for helping me understand this argument more clearly.
28. Donald Kettl, "Micromanagement: Congressional Control and Bureaucratic Risk," in Patricia W. Ingraham and Donald F. Kettl, eds., *Agenda for Excellence: Public Service in America* (Chatham, N.J.: Chatham House, 1992), p. 103.

CHAPTER 11

1. This summary of the GAO standard is by Cornelius E. Tierney, *Government Auditing* (Washington: Commerce Clearing House, 1979) p. 99.
2. President's Council on Integrity and Efficiency, Committee on Integrity and Law Enforcement, *Characteristics of Inspector General Investigations* (July 1989), p. 30.
3. For a summary of the implementation of the 1988 changes, see Council Coordinating Group, *Lessons Learned: Reporting Under the 1988 Amendments to the Inspector General Act*, survey, September 1990.
4. *Abuse and Mismanagement at HUD*, H. Rept. 101-977, 101 Cong. 2 sess. (Government Printing Office, 1990), p. 6.
5. For a list of possible reform areas, see Frederick M. Kaiser and Diane Duffy, "Issues Affecting Statutory Inspectors General," memorandum (Congressional Research Service, January 28, 1992).

6. Walter Williams, *Mismanaging America: The Rise of the Anti-Analytic Presidency* (University of Kansas, 1990), p. x.
7. This response came from a survey of all IGs by the Senate Governmental Affairs Committee.
8. *Final Report and Recommendations*, Committee Print, Senate Committee on Banking, Housing, and Urban Affairs, 101 Cong. 2 sess. (GPO, 1990), p. 194.
9. See Ronald C. Moe, "The HUD Scandal and the Case for an Office of Federal Management," *Public Administration Review*, vol. 51 (July/August 1991), pp. 298–307.

Aberbach, Joel, 45, 51, 53
Accountability in government:
bureaucratic paradigm, 20; command-and-control approach,
12–13; comparison of methods,
14–16, 18–20; conflicts created
by, 13; congressional initiatives
of 1960s and 1970s, 11; definitions of, 3–4, 12–14; ethical behavior and, 13; monitoring and,
16–21; post-bureaucratic paradigm, proposed, 21. See also
Capacity-based accountability;
Compliance accountability;
Performance accountability
Adair, John, 25
Adams, Paul, 1–2, 73–74, 75, 86,
182, 219
Agency for International Development (AID), 31, 181
Agriculture, U.S. Department of,
101; creation of own IGship,
31–35; IG staffing problems, 92,
94; investigatory units, 166; law
enforcement authority for IG investigators, 190; successful investigations by IG, 211
American Hospital Association,
154
American Medical Association
(AMA), 154–55
Anderson, Jack, 104
Armajani, Babak, 20, 21
Assistant secretaries for management: IGs and, 90, 91, 98; OMB
and, 112–14
Auditors as IGs, 122–24, 149–50,
227; audience for reports, 150,

155; demographic profile, 150; internal orientation, 156–57; introspective nature, 158; investigators, relations with, 160–61,
168–69; job satisfaction, sources
of, 157–58; reform of IG system,
view of, 158, 159; staffing and,
158–59, 160, 162, 163–65, 168

Barr, William, 143
Barton, William, 118
Barzelay, Michael, 20, 21
Bass, Ellen, 183
Bass, Mary, 83
Behn, Robert, 47
Bell, Griffin, 62
Bergland, Bob, 35
Bernstein, Marver, 47
Beuley, Robert, 86
Board for International Broadcast-
ing, 131
Bonus and awards system, 172–74,
233
Boucher, Paul, 83
Brady, James, 102
Brooks, Jack, 49, 50, 65, 103, 144,
191
Brown, June Gibbs, 82, 83, 86, 100,
105, 117, 122–23, 134, 163, 173
Budget and Accounting Act of
1921, 27
Bureaucratic paradigm of account-
ability, 20
Bush administration, 56; appoint-
ments, delays in, 171–72; IGs' ex-
periences during, 131–45; pro-
gram evaluation, focus on, 145
Butz, Earl, 33–34

Califano, Joseph, 63–64, 81, 99
Capacity-based accountability, 3;
    comparison with other account-
    ability methods, 14–16, 18–20;
    complexity of, 16; durability of,
    16; evaluation by IGs and, 194;
    management and oversight in,
    15–16; mechanisms for achiev-
    ing change, 15; monitoring and,
    18–20; reform of IG system and,
    230; sanctions, role of, 15
Career executives, 91
Carter, Jimmy, 39, 62, 99, 226–27
Carter administration: coordina-
    tion of IG offices, 186; IGs' expe-
    riences during, 90–101; Inspector
    General Act of 1978, 62–64, 67;
    popularity problems, 81; recruit-
    ment of IG candidates, 82–90
Central Intelligence Agency (CIA),
    35
Chelimsky, Eleanor, 199
Chief Financial Officers Act, 22
Chiles, Lawton, 90
Citrin, Jack, 221
Civil Service Reform Act of 1978,
    11–12, 13–14, 64, 172, 173
Clarke, Floyd, 167
Colvin, Bill, 86, 172–73
Command-and-control accountabil-
    ity, 12–13
Commerce, U.S. Department of,
    101
Compliance accountability, 3–4;
    bureaucratic paradigm and, 20;
    comparison with other account-
    ability methods, 14–16, 18–20;
    complexity of, 16; durability of,
    16; government officials' prefer-
    ence for, 3–4, 19–20, 22, 56–57,
    224–25; management and over-
    sight in, 15–16; mechanisms for
    achieving change, 15; monitoring
    and, 18–20; perverse conse-
    quences, 230; Reagan administra-
    tion's focus on, 102–03; sanc-
    tions, role of, 15

Comprehensive Crime Control Act
    of 1984, 167
Condon, Lester, 32–33, 35
Confirmation of IG nominees,
    88–90
Congress, U.S.: access to informa-
    tion through IGs, 28–29, 30, 56;
    accountability initiatives of
    1960s and 1970s, 11; compliance
    accountability, preference for,
    56–57; congressional-IG activity,
    patterns in, 53–56; GAO and,
    27–28; Health, Education, and
    Welfare IG Act of 1976, 40, 50,
    58–61; HUD scandal and, 75–76;
    IGs' loyalty to, 95, 96; Inspector
    General Act Amendments of
    1988, 128–31; law enforcement
    authority for IG investigators,
    190–91; oversight activity, expan-
    sion of, 51; small agency IGs
    and, 133; staffing of IG offices,
    110–11; staff trends in, 51–53.
    See also House of Representa-
    tives, U.S.; Inspector General
    Act of 1978; Senate, U.S.
Continental Congress, 25
Contracting-out initiative, 113
Conyers, John, 144
Coordinating Conference, 188
Coordinating mechanism for all IG
    offices, 186–89
Coverage capacity of IGs, 205–07,
    209

Davis, Dwight, 197
Defense, U.S. Department of: cover-
    age of activities by IG, 206–07;
    law enforcement authority for IG
    investigators, 190, 192; location
    of IG office, 185; staffing of IG of-
    fice, 163, 164, 165; successful in-
    vestigations by IG, 211
Defense Contract Audit Agency
    (DCAA), 206–07
Deficit problem, 114–15
DeGeorge, Frank, 86, 173

Deming, W. Edwards, 17
Dempsey, Charles, 71, 75, 86, 100, 103, 105–06, 116–17, 119, 122, 163, 170, 182, 219
Department of Energy Act, 193
Deputy IGs, 181–82
Devine, Donald, 170
Diefenbach, William, 152–53
Diefenderfer, William, III, 135
Dingell, John, 212–13
Downs, Anthony, 19
Doyle, William, 173

Eagleton, Thomas, 42, 67
Education, U.S. Department of, 2; deputy IGs, 182; legal counsel for IG, 183; location of IG office, 185; staffing of IG office, 94
Effectiveness of IGs, 203; coverage of agency activities, 205–07, 209; definition of *effectiveness*, 203–04; performance of departments and agencies, 220–23; professionalism issue, 204–05; savings as measure of, 101, 115, 121, 208, 209–210; successful investigations, 210–14; visibility of results, 214–20
Eizenstat, Stuart, 62, 67
Employment Standards Administration, 136
Energy, U.S. Department of, 2, 61; subpoena authority for IG investigators, 193
Environmental Protection Agency (EPA): law enforcement authority for IG investigators, 192; location of IG office, 185; problems with IGship, 118–19; staffing of IG office, 94, 163; successful investigations by IG, 212–13; visibility of IG results, 216
Estes, Billie Sol, 31, 32
Ethics in Government Act of *1978*, 11, 12, 14, 65
Evaluation and analysis by IGs, 145, 189, 230–31, 234–35; capac-

ity-based accountability and, 194; decline of, 194–95, 200; HHS approach, 198–99; negative aspects, 197–98; recommendations resulting from evaluation, 199; value of, 195–96
Executive Group to Combat Fraud and Waste in Government, 186
Executive privilege, 48–51

False Claims Act Amendments of *1986*, 22, 165
Federal Bureau of Investigation (FBI), 106, 167, 170, 186, 213
Federal Election Commission, 131
Federal Managers' Financial Integrity Act of *1982*, 222
Federal Maritime Commission, 131
Fenster, Herbert L., 193
Fesler, James, 13
"Fire-alarm" oversight, 42–43
Firing of IGs (*1981*), 102–04, 105–06
Food and Drug Administration (FDA), 141–42
Ford administration, 51
Foreign Assistance Act of *1961*, 29–30
Fountain, L. H., 31, 32, 39, 40, 48, 49–50, 58, 60, 61, 64, 67, 68, 103, 121, 139, 165
Freeman, Orville, 31–32, 90
"Funds put to better use" issue, 210
Funk, Sherman, 35, 69, 86, 134, 138, 141, 163, 167–68, 178, 188, 219

Garment, Suzanne, 39, 44, 53
Gates, Margaret, 24–25, 39–40, 204
Gellhorn, Walter, 33
General Accounting Office (GAO): accounting and auditing roles, conflict between, 27–28; on auditors and investigators as IGs, 161; budgets of IGs and, 67; contracting-out initiative, 113; EPA,

criticism of, 119; establishment
of, 27; on evaluation and analysis by IGs, 194–95, 196, 199; Inspector General Act of 1978,
41–42; Interior, criticism of, 119;
on OMB management initiatives,
47–48; on professionalism of
IGs, 204–05
General Services Administration
(GSA): law enforcement authority for IG investigators, 190; professionalism of IG, 205
Gillium, Charles, 86, 173, 207
Glenn, John, 56, 129, 133, 138,
141, 142, 144, 183
Gonzalez, Henry, 74
Gorsuch, Anne Burford, 118
Government Energy Efficiency Act
of 1991, 46
Government Printing Office (GPO),
132–33
Graziano, John, 116
Green, Donald, 221

Harper, Edwin, 103, 104, 105,
106–08, 110, 116
Health, Education, and Welfare,
U.S. Department of (HEW), 2; IG
reports on, 98–100; scandals in,
40
Health, Education, and Welfare IG
Act of 1976, 40, 50, 58–61
Health and Human Services, U.S.
Department of (HHS), 2, 141; coverage of activities by IG, 206,
207; deputy IGs, 182; evaluation
and analysis by IG, 195–96, 197,
198–99; expansion of IG office,
178–79, 181; IG appearances before Congress, 56; improvement
recommendations by IG, 220; independence of IG office, 181; investigators, emphasis on,
163–64; location of IG office,
185; Medicare/Medicaid bounty
episode, 151–55; qui tam investigations, 165; savings achieved by

IG, 101, 209–10; successful inves-
tigations by IG, 211; visibility of
IG results, 216–17
Heineman, Ben, Jr., 100
History of IG concept, 25, 27–35
Hodsoll, Frank, 135, 142
Holifield, Chet, 50
Houk, Robert, 132–33
House of Representatives, U.S.:
Agriculture Appropriations Subcommittee, 34; Commerce, Con-
sumers, and Monetary Affairs
Subcommittee, 58; Energy and
Commerce Committee, 212–13;
Energy and Commerce Subcommittee on Oversight and Investigations, 142; Government Operations Committee, 49–50, 58, 74,
75, 92, 106–07, 110–11, 129, 133,
167, 173, 186–87, 191; Government Operations Employment
and Housing Subcommittee, 70;
Health and Environment Subcommittee, 44; Intergovernmental Relations and Human Resources
Subcommittee, 31, 32, 58, 60–61,
64; Judiciary Committee, 165
Housing and Urban Development,
U.S. Department of (HUD): creation of IGship, 35; deputy IGs,
182; evaluation capacity of IG,
decline of, 200; savings achieved
by IG, 101; scandal of 1989, 1–2,
69–77, 168, 200; staffing of IG office, 163; visibility of IG results,
216
H.R. 12462, 49–50
Hyland, J. Brian, 86, 136, 137, 140,
173, 183

Iannone, John, 193
Improvement recommendations by
IGs, 220
Independent counsel legislation, 65
Ink, Dwight, 168, 200
Inspector General Act of 1978, 2,
11, 23; "access to executive

branch information" issue, 48–51; Amendments of *1988*, 128–31, 181; budgetary issue, 43–44; Carter administration and, 62–64, 67; compromise agreements in, 64–67; definitions of accountability, 14; drafters of, 58; GAO reports on, 41–42; goals of, 2; IGs' authority to conduct investigations and, 139–40; independence issue, 62–64; information imperative, 48–57; innovations included in, 225–29; job description, development of, 61–68; management issue, 47–48; on organization of IG offices, 175; origins of, 39; oversight issue, 45–46, 51; overview of, 23–25; passage of, 68; publicity issue, 44–45; Senate amendments, 67–68; staff trends in Congress and, 51–53; strategies of accountability, 11–12; on subpoena authority for IG investigators, 192–93; "trust in government" issue, 46–47

Inspectors general: accomplishments of, 101, 115, 121, 208, 209–10; assistant secretaries for management and, 91, 98; audience for reports, 95, 96, 124–26, 128, 150–55; audit as cornerstone of IG concept, 42; budgets for, 66–67; Bush administration and, 131–45; career profile, 84–87, 122; Carter administration and, 82–101; compliance accountability, focus on, 3–4, 22, 56–57, 224–25; confirmation process, 88–90; conflict of interest concerns, 86–87, 172–74, 233; congressional access to information and, 28–29, 30, 56; congressional-IG activity, patterns in, 53–56; crisis situations, reporting on, 24, 66, 228; deficit problem and, 114–15; demo-

graphic profile, 82–84, 150, 151, 152; departmental creation of IG post, 31–35; dual allegiance issue, 62–64, 69–77, 226; educational profile, 84, 122; expansion of IG concept, 25, 26; fallback rights, 105–06; "fire-alarm" oversight, 42–43; firing of (*1981*), 102–04, 105–06; first IGs, establishment of, 28–29; historical perspective on, 25, 27–35; HUD scandal and, 1–2, 69–77, 168, 200; improvement recommendations by, 220; "innovations" in search for accountability, 2–3; as institutional memory, 200, 234; integration of audit and investigation, 227; interference by departments and agencies, protection from, 67–68; investigations, emphasis on, 165–69; investigative authority, challenges to, 106, 135–43; job description, 61–68; job skills needed for IG position, 95–96, 97; legislation on, 27–28 (*See also* Inspector General Act of *1978*); "lone wolf" alternative, 59–61; mandate of, 23; monitoring function, 16–17; nature of IG job, evolution of, 126–28; opposition within departments and agencies, 62–64, 90; political appointees, relations with, 96–98; political influences, protection from, 23–25, 169–74; politicization of, 169, 186–87; problems with IGships, 118–20; program evaluation by, 145; Reagan administration and, 82–90, 102–20, 121–31; Reagan reform agenda, role in, 112; records of agencies, access to, 24, 30, 48–51, 229; recruitment of candidates, 23–24, 82–90, 171–72, 226, 233 (*See also* self-selection *below*); removal, president's power of, 63, 66, 226–27, 233; reporting requirements, 24, 66, 67, 69–77, 226, 228; reporting style, 130–31, 228; review of reports by department officials, 98–100; salary of, 65–66; self-selection by, 107–08, 116–18, 122, 134–35; small agency IGs, 131, 132–33; staffing issues, 92–95, 108–11, 124, 125, 158–59, 160, 162, 163–65, 168, 207, 209; strategies of accountability and, 16; title issue, 42; vague and tedious reports by, 74; wastefulness in government, view of, 124; whistleblowers, protection of, 67, 143–45. *See also* Auditors as IGs; Effectiveness of IGs; Investigators as IGs; OMB-IG alliance; Organization of IG offices; Reform of IG system; *specific agencies and departments*

Institutional memory, IGs' role as, 199–200, 234

Interior, U.S. Department of, 119–20, 192

International Cooperation Administration, 29

Investigators as IGs, 122–24, 149–50, 227; audience for reports, 150–55; auditors, relations with, 160–61, 168–69; civil service classification, 166; demographic profile, 150, 151, 152; external orientation, 156–57; go-for-broke nature, 158; job satisfaction, sources of, 157–58; law enforcement authority, 150, 189–92, 213; qui tam investigations, 165; reform of IG system, view of, 158, 159; staffing and, 158–59, 160, 162, 163–65, 168; subpoena authority, 192–94, 213–14

Justice, U.S. Department of: coordination of IG offices, 186; declination of IG cases, 212; IGs' authority to conduct investigations, challenges to, 106, 135–43; IGship created for, 129–30, 134; law enforcement authority for IG investigators, 150, 190, 192; objections to IG Act of 1978, 62–63; qui tam investigations, 165

Kaiser, Fred, 190–91, 192
Keating, Charles, 144
Kelman, Steven, 203
Kennedy, John F., 171
Kennedy, Robert F., 31
Kettl, Donald, 13, 51, 223
Kmiec, Douglas, 136, 138, 139, 183
Knowles, Marjorie Fine, 24–25, 83, 86, 100
Kusserow, Richard, 44, 56, 59, 181, 185, 209, 220; deputy IG and, 182; on evaluation by IGs, 189, 198; on FDA investigation, 141–42; on fixed term of office, 170–71; Medicare/Medicaid bounty episode, 151–55; on OMB-IG alliance, 116; on PCIE, 187; on qui tam investigations, 165; on recruitment of IGs, 86–87; staffing of IG office, 163–64; visibility of, 216–17

Labor, U.S. Department of, 94; IG investigation controversy, 136–40; IG staffing problem, 94; legal counsel for IG, 183–84; successful investigations by IG, 211, 213

Law enforcement authority for IG investigators, 150, 189–92, 213
Layton, John, 86, 120, 173
Lee, Darryl J., 193
Legal counsel for IGs, 182–84
Levin, Carl, 219
Levitas, Elliott, 43, 103
Lewis, Lorraine, 209
"Lone wolf" IG, 59–61

Loomis, Burdett, 44
Lynch, Marjorie, 59–60

McBride, Thomas, 86, 105
McCubbins, Mathew, 42
McGrain v. *Daugherty*, 48
McIntyre, James, 62
Mackenzie, G. Calvin, 105, 171–72
Madison, James, 63
Mangano, Michael, 198
Mann, Thomas, 74
Maria, Ray, 168, 183–84, 188
Martin, John, 86, 163, 173, 187
Maynard-Moody, Steven, 12–13
Media as audience for IG reports,
150–55
Medicare and Medicaid provider
fraud case, 151–55
Melchner, John, 187
Moe, Ronald C., 113, 114
Moe, Terry, 109
Monitoring, 16–21; reform of IG
system and, 230–31
Moore, Mark, 39–40, 204
Moran, William, 195, 196
Morris, Thomas, 64, 84, 86, 98–100
Morrison, Alexia, 65
Morrison v. *Olson*, 65
Mosher, Frederick, 13, 27
Moss, Frank, 40
Mulberry, Richard, 119–20
Mutual Security Act Amendments
of *1959*, 28

Naked Reverse (report), 142
National Academy of Public
Administration (NAPA), 22, 184
National Commission on the Pub-
lic Service (Volcker Commis-
sion), 109, 184
Naughton, James, 32, 63–64, 100,
140
Newcomer, Kathryn, 197
New Deal, 27
New York Times, 216
Nixon administration, 33–34

Novak, Michael, 116, 119
Novotny, Thomas W., 30

Occupational Safety and Health
Administration (OSHA), 136
Office of Community Services, 94
Office of General Counsel (OGC),
183
Office of Management and Budget
(OMB), 7; assistant secretaries
for management and, 112–14;
contracting-out initiative, 113;
coordination of IG offices, 186;
establishment of, 27; IG investigation controversy, 142; management initiatives, 47–48; management side of, 113–14; oversight
failure, 234; war on waste, 104.
See also OMB-IG alliance
OMB-IG alliance, 120, 224–25;
changes during Bush administration, 135; IGs' incentives,
115–18; IGs undermined by, 111;
OMB's incentives, 112–15;
origins of, 106–07; recruitment
of IG candidates, 107–08;
staffing of IG offices, 108–11
Office of Personnel Management
(OPM), 91–92
Office of Professional Responsibility (OPR), 129–30
Offices of inspector general (OIGs).
See Organization of IG offices
Okun, Arthur M., 165–66
Olson, Theodore, 65
Orange Book, 220
Organization of IG offices, 227–28;
coordinating mechanism for all
IG offices, 186–89; deputy IGs,
181–82; expansion of offices,
176, 177–79, 181; future prospects, 189–99; history of,
177–89; independence from par-
ent agencies, development of,
180, 181–86; law enforcement authority for investigators, 150,
189–92, 213; legal counsel,

182–84; legal requirements, 175; personnel system, 184–85; physical location of offices, 185–86; subpoena authority for IG investigators, 192–94, 213–14
Oversight, 15–16, 42–43, 45–46, 51

Palumbo, Dennis, 12–13
Pension Welfare Benefits Administration (PWBA), 136
Performance accountability, 3; comparison with other accountability methods, 14–16, 18–20; complexity of, 16; durability of, 16; management and oversight in, 15–16; mechanisms for achieving change, 15; monitoring and, 18–20; reform of IG system and, 230; sanctions, role of, 15
Personnel systems of IG offices, 184–85
Pierce, Samuel, 69, 75, 76
Politicization of bureaucracy, 109–10
Politicization of IGs, 169, 186–87
Porter, Elsa, 62
Post-bureaucratic paradigm for accountability, 21
Power River Basin coal lease sale, 119
President's Commission on CIA Activities within the United States (Rockefeller Commission), 35
President's Council on Integrity and Efficiency (PCIE), 104, 107, 112, 121, 134, 211, 212, 227 231, 233; coordinating function, 186–89
President's Council on Management and Efficiency (PCME), 112
Professionalism of IGs, 204–05
Program Fraud and Civil Remedies Act, 22, 141

Quality management, 17, 21, 76–77
Qui tam investigations, 165

Railroad Retirement Board (RRB), 206
Reagan, Ronald, 35, 102, 103, 104, 107, 231
Reagan administration: appointees, quality of, 112; compliance accountability, focus on, 102–03; coordination of IG offices, 186; firing of Carter-era IGs, 102–04; HUD scandal, 1–2, 69–77, 200; IGs' experiences during, 104–20, 121–31; recruitment of IG candidates, 82–90; Reform '88 program, 112–13, 114; trust in government and, 221; war on waste, 104. *See also* OMB-IG alliance
Recruitment of IG candidates, 23–24, 82–90; reform proposals, 171–72, 233; self-selection issue, 107–08, 116–18, 122, 134–35
Reform '88 program, 112–13, 114
Reform of IG system: bonus and awards system, 172–74, 233; enhancing objectivity, 231–33; existing proposals, 229; IG Act and, 225–29; IGs' opinions on, 158, 159, 231, 232; improving accountability, 229–30; improving monitoring, 230–31; *1988* reforms, 128–31, 181; recruitment mechanism, 171–72, 233; removal only for cause, 233; subpeona authority for IG investigators, 192–94, 213–14; term of office, 169–71, 233. *See also* Evaluation and analysis by IGs
Rehnquist, William H., 65
Reid, Inez, 103
Reingold, Beth, 221
Removal, president's power of, 63, 66, 226–27, 233
Research methods for this book, 4–5
Ribicoff, Abraham, 67
Richards, James, 120, 141, 149
Romney, George, 35

Rosenthal, Benjamin, 58, 59, 60–61, 68
Roth, William, 71, 143
Rourke, Francis, 12

Salem, George, 137
Sasser, Jim, 229
Sato, Frank, 82, 83, 86, 105, 122, 173
Savings achieved by IGs, 101, 115, 121, 208, 209–10
Schwartz, Thomas, 42
Scientific management, 21
Search commission recruiting process, 171–72, 233
Senate, U.S.: confirmation of IG nominees, 89–90; Finance Committee, 40; General Services, Federalism, and the District of Columbia Subcommittee, 144; Governmental Affairs Committee, 42, 68, 90, 129, 133, 134, 141, 142–43, 144, 161, 168, 188, 207; HUD investigating committee, 74, 75–76; IG Act amendments, 67–68; interest in IGs, 55; Oversight of Government Management Subcommittee, 219
Senior Executive Service (SES), 15, 92, 105–06
Seven-day letters, 24, 66, 228; visibility of IG activities and, 219
Shane, Peter, 48
Shays, Christopher, 1–2, 69, 75
Sherrick, Joseph, 163
Simmons, Rex, 25
Small agency IGs, 131, 132–33
Small Business Administration (SBA), 206, 207, 209
Smith, Sid, 90
Social Security Administration, 216
Staats, Elmer, 41
Staffing of IG offices, 92–95, 108–11, 124, 125, 158–59, 160, 162, 163–65, 168, 207, 209
Staggers, Harley O., Jr., 189

State, U.S. Department of, 110–11, 138, 163, 165; creation of IGship, 28–31; expansion of IG office, 177–78; problems with IGship, 118
Sterling, A. Mary, 169, 226
Stockman, David, 107
Subpoena authority for IG investigators, 192–94, 213–14
Success rates of IG investigations, 210–14
Superfund scandal, 118–19
Supreme Court, U.S., 65

Talmage, Herman, 99
Tanaka, Deidre, 212–13
Taylor, Frederick, 21
Term of office for IGs, 169–71, 233
Thomas, James, 86, 105, 173, 182, 183
Thurmond, Strom, 129
Time magazine, 1
Transportation, U.S. Department of, 92, 94, 192
Treasury, U.S. Department of, 48; expansion of IG office, 177–78; IGship created for, 129, 134
Trust in government, 46–47, 220–21

United States v. *Nixon*, 48
U.S. Information Agency (USIA), 209
U.S. v. *Iannone*, 193

"Value added" of government programs, 222–23
Vander Schaaf, Derek, 163, 173
Veterans Administration (VA): coverage of activities by IG, 207; location of IG office, 186; savings achieved by IG, 210
Veterans Affairs, U.S. Department of, 87
Visibility of IG results, 214–16; methods for achieving visibility, 217–20; quality and quantity concerns, 216–17
Vogel, Raymond, 87

Wallace, Chris, 151, 152–53
Walton, Mary, 17
Washington Post, 144, 216
Waste in government, 104, 203,
    221–22
Watt, James, 1, 76
Waxman, Henry, 44
Weber, Max, 20
Weiss, Janet, 16

When Americans Complain (Gell-
    horn), 33
Whistleblowers, IGs' protection of,
    67, 143–45
Whitten, Jamie L., 34
Williams, Walter, 231
Wright, Jim, 50
Wright, Joseph, 34–35, 107–08,
    113, 115, 116, 121, 135, 188